LITERARY IMPRESSIONISM
JAMES AND CHEKHOV

H. PETER STOWELL

Literary Impressionism, James and Chekhov

THE
UNIVERSITY OF GEORGIA PRESS
ATHENS

Library of Congress Cataloging in Publication Data

Stowell, H   Peter, 1939–
  Literary impressionism, James and Chekhov.
  Bibliography.
  Includes index.
  1. James, Henry, 1843–1916—Criticism and
interpretation. 2. Chekhov, Anton Pavlovich,
1860–1904—Criticism and interpretation.   3.
Impressionism.   I. Title.

PS127.I46S75   809.3   78-23737
              ISBN 0-8203-0468-9

Parts of this manuscript were previously published in *Russian Literature Triquarterly* (No.
11, Winter 1975), *Studies in Short Fiction* (Vol.
12, Spring 1975) and *Chekhov's Art of Writing:
A Collection of Critical Essays* (Columbus, Ohio:
Slavica Publishers, 1977). The permission of
the editors to reproduce this material is grate-
fully acknowledged.

To Sally and Johnny
who opened their home—
and much, much more.

Contents

ACKNOWLEDGMENTS

I would like to thank those who at one point or another read all or parts of the manuscript and offered very valuable advice: Richard Baldwin, Martha Banta, Robert Hudspeth, Karl Kramer, and Sally van Schaick. But it is to Karl Kramer that the hat must come off. He initiated the project and counseled me on the wonderful nuances of impressionism. He played that difficult double role: friend and teacher. Willis Konick was a source of encouragement throughout my graduate years. Movies were my respite and my wife, Anne, my strength.

In the quotations from Russian I have used the Library of Congress system of transliteration. But in the transliteration of characters' names I have chosen whatever spelling I felt would most easily convey the sound of the name to an English language reader. All translations are my own, unless otherwise indicated.

Introduction

*
Introduction

Only the impression, however trivial its material may seem to be, however faint its traces, is a criterion of truth and deserves for that reason to be apprehended by the mind, for the mind, if it succeeds in extracting this truth, can by the impression and by nothing else be brought to a state of greater perfection and given a pure joy.

Marcel Proust, *Le Temps retrouvé*

The usual imagery surrounding Anton Chekhov and Henry James suggests opposing impressions: a dying, consumptive, Russian peasant doctor distilling tightly compressed short stories and a few strangely elusive plays set against a well-fed and traveled American intellectual leisurely exploring the labyrinths of consciousness and society. They came from and lived in different worlds, and neither writer appears to have read the other, nor even been aware of the other's existence.[1] It is not that in the nineteenth century these two dark and distant countries produced no similar fiction nor felt the power of literary influence. For all the expanse between them, America and Russia seem to have had marked literary affinities.[2] In their own very individual ways Chekhov and James tried each other's most successful métiers, but have since become famous for the genre in which the other failed. For many years Chekhov had been drawn to the novel, but could not write one. He was essentially a taut dramatist. By the time he might have successfully launched a new attack on the impressionistically dramatic novel, he was too ill to experiment with the longer form. James tried and failed as a playwright, but had the time and stamina to exploit that experience in the creation of his great impressionist novels *The Ambassadors* and *The Golden Bowl*. Few impressionists remained comfortably situated in impressionism for their entire careers. And, in a strict sense, no "ism" could contain the vast imaginative and technical powers of Chekhov or James. Both broke from the transcendent subjectivity of romanticism and the omniscient objectivity of realism to forge the subjective objectivism of literary impressionism. Chekhov died without having been seduced by the Russian symbolists, while James's age and truculence prevented his developing in some new direction. Both essentially stopped writing in 1904.

Chekhov and James established themselves as literary impressionists and modernists when they realized their need to break with the discursive prose of the past and lose their omniscience in dramatic forms. Chekhov's tightly architectural structures and James's multiple impressions of consciousness led them to the architectonic prose of modernism.[3] Time becomes irrevocably tied to space through prose that compresses time into spatialized moments and space into blurred shards of frozen time. Each becomes the other, and this new way of seeing the world forces attention away from traditionally delineated character and narrative, shifting them toward patterns of simultaneity, juxtaposition, repetition, multiplicity, and phenomenal reality.

For years James has been uneasily linked with the realism of Zola, Turgenev, Howells, and Twain, and Chekhov has been too long associated with the "slice of life" school. Neither of these critical perspectives accounts for their impact on literary modernism, which with each passing decade owes less and less to realism. Chekhov and James actually have very little in common with Balzac, George Eliot, Tolstoy, and the other realists, and they have passed beyond the "new realism" of Flaubert, Maupassant, Vsevolod Garshin, and Ivan Bunin. Chekhov and James are impressionists, and it is literary impressionism that marks the beginning of literary modernism.[4] They are the supreme examples of this fleeting yet lingering phenomenon. Impressionism has always been a difficult concept to pin down. It was never really a movement, and no writer ever proclaimed with any sustained force that he was an impressionist.[5] It has seemed an ephemeral notion caught between the declarations of realism and the manifestos of expressionism, symbolism, and imagism. Impressionists were idiosyncratic and individualistic.

They saw themselves groping for a more credible vision of a changing world—the same world that Henry Adams saw as "a supersensual world, in which he [Adams] could measure nothing except by chance collisions of movements imperceptible to his senses, perhaps even imperceptible to instruments, but perceptible to each other, and so to some known ray at the end of the scale."[6]

Chekhov and James are the finest representatives of the impressionist phenomenon, because they guided their careers toward the achievement of quintessential impressionism. Yet scholars and critics of impressionism have generally overlooked James and have only recently begun to acknowledge Chekhov.[7] This criticism has concentrated on Stephen Crane, Marcel Proust, or stylistic innovations, and has generally avoided close analysis, fearful that the weight of its scrutiny might collapse the tenuous foundation of mere pictorialism. What passes for criticism of impressionism is often impressionistic criticism. It has been a literary phenomenon with a checkered critical history.

A good deal of attention was paid to impressionism in the thirties. Joseph Warren Beach in 1932 described its basic outlines in his chapter on modernism.[8] In 1935 Ford Madox Ford wrote an essay on "the Impressionist group" in which he included Henry James as a writer who "builds suggestions of happenings on suggestions of happenings" and who influenced Joseph Conrad, not literally but impressionistically. Crane was also a part of that "gang."[9] Herbert Muller in a 1938 article evocatively entitled "Impressionism in Fiction: Prism vs. Mirror," says that "impressionism, as I see it, is one of the key words in modern literature." He continues by listing Crane, Proust, Conrad, D. H. Lawrence, Dorothy Richardson, Virginia Woolf, Sherwood Anderson, Conrad Aiken, Katherine Mansfield, William Faulkner, and Thomas Wolfe as some writers who "have in various ways adopted to fiction the technique of the impressionist painters."[10]

Impressionism as a critical term lay dormant for the next twenty years until Arnold Hauser's influential chapter in his

final volume of *The Social History of Art.* Hauser notes that
James was an intellectual impressionist, but gives special emphasis to Chekhov: "The most curious phenomenon in the history of impressionism in Europe is its adoption by Russia and
the emergence of a writer like Chekhov, who can be described
as the purest representative of the whole movement."[11] For the
first time, Western critics began to recognize that literary impressionism could exist in a country that had taken little notice
of impressionist painting. Tolstoy, however, had noticed that
the "illusion of truth in Chekhov is complete, his pieces produce
the impression of a stereoscope. It seems as though he is flinging
words around in any fashion, but like an impressionist artist he
achieves wonderful results with the strokes of his brush."[12] But
it was Dmitri Chizhevsky who permanently implanted the importance of Chekhov's impressionism: "If, however, we want to
analyze the style of Chekhov's novelle, we should not be struck
by the sporadic use of the impressionistic device. . . . No! Chekhov's short stories, like his longer novelle and his plays, bear
throughout the traits of literary impressionism."[13]

Chekhov and James, living in such distant and dissimilar
geographical and social spheres, working in essentially different
forms, and writing about subjects quite foreign to the other,
only solidify the basic premise of their connection—that literary
impressionism was not a movement, but a far-reaching cultural
phenomenon that found its common foundation in the way it
presented the "new multiverse."[14] Chekhov and James were
perfectly situated, as was Henry Adams, both in time and by
intellectual inclination to see the special qualities of change
affecting the scientific and artistic turn-of-the-century world.
Adams believed that a "cataclysm" had occurred somewhere
between 1893 with the discovery of the Roentgen rays and 1904
with Arthur Balfour's announcement "that the human race
without exception had lived and died in a world of illusion until
the last year of the century."[15]

Claude Monet's painting, *Impression, soleil levant*, inspired
the appellation *impressionism* in 1874. Chekhov's impressionism
emerged from his comic sketches in 1883, and flowered in his

1899 story, "The Lady with the Dog." James's *The Portrait of a Lady* in 1881 became his first impressionist work, and in 1897 *What Maisie Knew* demonstrated a mature vision. Their active careers came to an end in 1904 with Chekhov's "The Cherry Orchard" and James's *The Golden Bowl*—both unsurpassed works of impressionistic modernism. Their masterpieces of impressionism were written during the eleven pivotal years Adams identified as the axis of the new world.

Beyond such propitious timing, the minds of Chekhov and James ranged over two very crucial spheres of common interest, science and the visual arts.[16] Literature for them was the canyon into which flowed the new science of multiplicity and indeterminacy and the visual spatialization of momentary time. Chekhov was a man of science who saw that "science and technology are now going through a period of greatness."[17] He was also a friend of the closest thing Russia had to an impressionist painter, Ilya Repin.[18] James was not a scientist, but having been raised in an intellectually expansive atmosphere he was cognizant of the kinds of scientism his brother William was involved in, including philosophical and scientific pragmatism.[19] James was also a good friend of Henry Adams's. More to the point, however, was James's intimate knowledge of painting and his late embrace of impressionist painting.[20] Chekhov and James both had synthetic minds, intellects that were not controlled by only a few powerful influences. Instead, like all literary impressionists, they found their métier in "the ambient air of nineteenth century speculation, whose main current was the preoccupation with the phenomenon of self-consciousness."[21]

Chekhov and James are an important and intriguing pair, because both their disparities and their affinities reinforce the argument that literary impressionism was a widely cast and loosely held net that bound together the most unlikely writers, all the while allowing them to swim freely.[22] That Chekhov and James seem not to have been aware of each other nor conscious of anything remotely resembling impressionism in literature makes it all the more interesting to frame them in a study of literary impressionism. For in this way it becomes possible to demonstrate their almost militant individuality, while establishing their common reactions to the pervasive undercurrent of cultural change.

In attempting to carve out the essential qualities of any "ism," one hopes that the movement, phenomenon, or set of elective affinities will transcend national and cultural characteristics, as well as those of any one literary genre. The argument that impressionism existed as a broad response to concrete scientific and intellectual realignments would be severely limited if one were to restrict one's analysis to, say, Chekhov and Bunin, two Russian short story writers with diverse cultural inclinations, or to James and Crane, two equally incongruous American novelists and short story writers. I believe the most effective method of presenting literary impressionism's breadth is to examine two writers of distant countries, disparate cultures, and distinct literary genres. Chekhov and James are literary brothers by virtue of their corresponding aesthetic concerns and their common vision of a newly emerging impressionistic world. Literary impressionism unites these two writers in a stunning arch that transcends many of the previously held notions of realism, the traditions of Russian and American literatures, and the distinctions between the novel, short story, and play. Chekhov and James felt their way toward impressionism. It is now possible to see that in their late works they had reached strikingly similar goals, producing some of the purest examples of literary impressionism.

Literary impressionism has always been a perplexing issue; it never seemed to catch on. And the fairly large body of criticism remains scattered, ill-defined, and elusive. There are no major critical works, and the entire concept seems to have suffered from neglect. With few exceptions, the point has not been driven home that impressionism was not simply a stylistic phenomenon that tried to capture the blurred and ephemeral images of the impressionist painters. It was not simply an attempt to communicate moments of literary pictorialism, but was rather a literary phenomenon of major proportions.[23] It rendered a furiously changing world precariously perched for the flight of modernism into the twentieth century. Its prismatic sensibilities absorbed the monochromatic rays of the nineteenth century and delicately, swiftly, emitted multiplicity. Literary impressionism is the incipient moment of modernism. It cannot be neglected.

The purpose of this study, then, is to define the multiform characteristics of impressionism, to describe the affinities between the painting and the literature, to chronicle the growth of impressionism in Chekhov and James, to offer an impressionistic reading of each work, and to project impressionism's impact on modernism. The argumentative thrust of this work has its basis in the divide-and-conquer approach. I am arguing against the omnivorousness of realism. Every literary form of the period remotely concerned with exterior reality of the here and now seems to have been gobbled up by realism or naturalism. And when the scholars of realism were confronted with a Henry James, for instance, they neatly invented "psychological realism." Impressionism is qualitatively different from realism. James and Chekhov, as two of the earliest impressionists, were torn by these two impulses: realism, with its initial attractiveness as a reaction against romanticism, soon paled and became dully retrogressive; impressionism, on the other hand, offered a more fluid and less didactic reality. Most realist fiction looks dated today, while impressionist literature is dynamically alive. My position is that James and Chekhov fought to rid themselves of their narrow realist tendencies, and that as their fiction matured it became progressively more impressionistic.

My method will attempt to fuse form and content. At the center of impressionism's aesthetic is the actual act of perception. Since someone must be doing the perceiving, and since the author has through sleight-of-hand maneuvering removed himself from the work, then what is perceived is largely determined by how it is perceived. The form of the world is inseparable from the emotional, attitudinal, and sensory patterns superimposed on that world by a perceiver. The themes of impressionist fiction emerge from this reciprocal relationship between apperception and the world, both of which are momentarily framed in the flux of continual movement through time and space. Form and content, like the impressionistically phenomenal subject and object, must be apprehended as one. Chekhov's and James's characters perceive a bewildering world, but learn to face its immense dimensions of change and uncertainty. Yet they too are changing in that world. Using Heisenberg's principle of indeterminacy as an apt analogy, there is no way these characters can determine both their position and rate of movement through the confusion. If they attempt to fix themselves in relation to the changing patterns, they will only succeed in further changing the phenomenal world. The question in each work, then, is how—but also whether—these characters can stay afloat in the impressionistic world. Will they discover a reservoir of existential faith—an absurd belief in their ability to survive and find a momentary sense of identity in the "supersensual multiverse"? This is a major theme in impressionist fiction, and it surfaces through characters' responding impressionistically to an impressionistic world. This theme will be developed chronologically throughout Chekhov's and James's impressionist works.

The design of this book will not adhere to a traditional comparison between James and Chekhov, a point-by-point merger, a carefully acknowledged fusion of themes, a side-by-side analysis of their methods. Four considerations compel me to try another pattern: (1) the apparent dissimilarities between James and Chekhov that would tend to call unwarranted attention to themselves in a point for point analysis, (2) the possible confusion caused by so many names and stories that are not often read by the same audience, (3) the desire to show a coherent progression in both James's and Chekhov's impressionism, (4) the belief that the themes and methods of impressionism can be shown more clearly through an analysis of individual works.

Part One
Literary Impressionism

> They said, 'you have a blue guitar,
> You do not play things as they are.'
>
> The man replied, 'Things as they are
> Are changed upon the blue guitar.'
>
> Wallace Stevens

* 1 *

Literary Impressionism
The Prismatic Sensibility

I * THE DEFINITION

As far as one ventured to interpret actual science, the mind had
thus far adjusted itself by an infinite series of infinitely delicate
adjustments forced on it by the infinite motion of an infinite chaos
of motion; dragged at one moment into the unknowable and unthinkable, then trying to scramble back within its senses and to
bar the chaos out, but always assimilating bits of it, until at last, in
1900, a new avalanche of unknown forces had fallen on it, which
required new mental powers to control. If this view was correct, the
mind could gain nothing by flight or by fight; it must merge in its
supersensual multiverse, or succumb to it.
                    Henry Adams, *The Education of Henry Adams*

Henry Adams saw and understood better than most men of
letters the special quality of change and upheaval that was taking place between the years 1870 and 1920. He faced squarely
the issues of a fragmented, relativistic, unknowable, accidental,
subjective, and accelerating world, while realizing how ill-
prepared he was to absorb and adapt to such a world. His
autobiography can in many ways be viewed as a historian's
analogue to literary impressionism.

Impressionists found themselves caught between the ferocious
revolt against the subjectivity of romanticism and the headlong
dash into the anarchy of modernism. Neither a literary movement nor a critical invention, literary impressionism was a
phenomenon that existed as a set of shared assumptions, elective
affinities, philosophic agreements, and common reactions to the
"supersensual multiverse." It has been difficult to define, because while there appears to be much agreement regarding its
salient characteristics, there is little agreement about who is

and is not an impressionist.[1] Many writers who exhibited impressionist tendencies did so on their way from one literary way-station to another (Joyce for instance), or demonstrated a predilection for, say, naturalism, impressionism, symbolism, and imagism all in one work, as Crane did in *The Red Badge of Courage.* Since impressionism was such a short-lived affair squeezed in among many competing yet compatible literary movements, and since no major impressionist ever consciously, or at least publicly, stated his intention to write an impressionist work, it should be no surprise that impressionism remains a most contrary phenomenon.

It has been argued that impressionism should be dropped from the critical lexicon, because "separate fleeting impressions can not be built up into an organic whole of sufficient size, nor can a single fleeting impression be maintained and developed long enough to produce a major work."[2] It is on this issue that much of the narrowly microscopic critical attention has been focused. Literary impressionism did not emerge full-blown from the collective brow of the French Impressionist painters. Literary impressionists were a disparate breed who composed the most important and influential set of shared literary assumptions in the fifty years surrounding the turn of the twentieth century. The major error in most studies of impressionism is the inclination to reduce its dynamic vision of a changing world into mere pictorialism. Literary impressionism could not have existed as simply a series of "separate fleeting impressions."

Calvin Brown suggests impressionism is, indeed, something more: "Its aim is to catch and reproduce the shifting, fleeting intangible impressions by which the outside world impinges on our senses—or as some more philosophically minded critics like to put it, to break down the distinction between the subject and the object. In this pursuit, the Impressionist abandons causality, formal logic, and any attempt or desire to fit his impressions into such predetermined forms as the sonnet and the sonata."[3] This statement implies that impressionism anticipated the most cherished qualities of modernism: the primacy of phenomenological perception, the atomization of a subjectively perceived reality, the acceptance of chance in a world so complex and unknowable as to render causality impotent, the necessity to come to terms with reality through the process of induction, and the realization that Henri Bergson's individualized flow of duration must merge with the quanta-like moments of phenomenological time.

While it is certain that some impressionist writers were stylistically influenced by *Les Impressionnistes*, it would be too facile to contend that the painters provided the essential experimental impetus. While there are common characteristics that help fuse the painters and writers into the shapers of modernism, it strains interdisciplinary enthusiasm to insist that the writers must have directly transposed the techniques of a visual medium into language. To demand that literary impressionism string out a continuous series of pointillistic impressions is to misinterpret an artistic process that searches for a technique to express a reality within the outer limits of its own medium. A writer cannot seize upon the mode of a spatial art and appropriate it wholesale into the temporal experience of literature. Literary impressionists stepped back from the painters and rendered human consciousnesses and acts of perception. Literary impressionism is a temporal process depicting both a spatial and a temporal act. Time durationally links the fragments of spatialized perception, and consciousness spatializes the flow of time into separate frozen instants. The impressions of perceiving consciousnesses in literature must be rendered uniquely. Literature is not painting.

Literary impressionism sprang from neither theoretical constructs nor rigid ideology, but from reactions to the shifting intellectual and social currents of the age. This sense of change was so rapid and comprehensive that the impressionists felt compelled to express their artistic responses in highly individualistic and experimental forms. Yet their stylistic qualities emerged from the realization that since they lived in a prismatically impressionistic world, they must recreate that world

of individualized sensory perception, epistemological indeterminacy, relativism, ambiguity, fragmentation, and surfaces.
They saw faith disintegrate into the confusion of chance, the
chaos of unknowability, and the crisis of change. They wrote of
a need to survive in this "supersensual multiverse" by having
enough faith in their expanding powers of inductive perception
to navigate the shoals of the unseen and unknowable.

The impressionists' first philosophical reaction was anti-
mechanistic. The realists and naturalists, while rejecting romantic mechanism, succumbed to the power of Darwin's
scientifically observable and morally justifiable unity. The impressionists saw the contradiction in this position. Retaining
empiricism, they rejected the thinly veiled moral didacticism
of the realist's aesthetic omniscience. Subjective and limited
sensory perception became the empirical truth for the impressionists, who believed, as William James did,[4] that while the
empiricist might attain truth, he cannot know when he has
grasped it: "We still pin our faith on its [the truth's] existence,
and still believe that we gain an even better position towards
it by systematically continuing to roll up experiences and
think."[5] The impressionists, then, created characters who floun-
der through an accelerating and ambiguous world of sensory
stimuli. They attempt to control, face, adapt to, and escape from
such a world—while discovering that all one can ultimately do
is "roll up experiences and think."

Against the background of an essentially Newtonian nineteenth century, the impressionists, braced by their scientific
training, or at least scientific curiosity, began to intuitively
anticipate the major scientific, philosophical, intellectual, and
cultural changes of the coming age. To the extent that their art
reflected these breakthroughs, they came to understand the new
concepts in optics and photography, the wave and particle
theories as applied to Bergson's *durée* and Husserl's phenomenological time, the empiricism and epistemological indeterminacy
of William James, the uncertainty principle of Heisenberg, the
relativity of Einstein's space and time, the phenomenologists'

recognition of a reciprocal perceptual reality between subject and object, and the Gestalt psychologists' model of an inexplicable synthesis based upon dynamic patterns of perceived fragments. Within this framework the impressionists discovered their aesthetic goal: the fusion of form and meaning through the portrayal of human consciousness compressed into a fluid network of brilliantly concentrated sensory impressions.

Impressionism's primary tenets emerge from this flux. Its basic stylistic impulse is the shift from a description of concrete and tangible reality to a *rendering* of apperception. This recreates the perceived mood and atmosphere surrounding concrete objects—or, to paraphrase Archibald McLeish's comment about poetry, "an impressionist piece of prose doesn't mean; it is."[6] This shift goes to the heart of impressionism's aesthetic: "The issue is of the sensation itself and, following this hypothesis, must we see in Proust and the impressionists . . . those for whom pure sensation are wholly important, or indeed, placed within the context of the views of Sartre or Merleau-Ponty, are we present at the spontaneous transformation of the sensation by perception, with the understanding that perception coincides with the progressive creation of the perceiver?"[7] For the impressionists, the answer to this question was clearly affirmative. They created characters who grow only as their ability to perceive the connections among fragments expands. The impressionists' belief in the primacy of perception forced the pose of the omniscient, didactic, and discursive author out of the work. He was replaced by an elusive presence who allowed all characters to perceive for themselves the ambiguous and ultimately unknowable surfaces of sensory reality.

Crucial to the impressionist vision is the relationship of subject to object, "inner ego to outer world,"[8] consciousness to external reality. Naturalists and realists believed the empirical method could only focus on objectified exterior reality; symbolists and expressionists concentrated on a solipsistically encapsuled inner world. The impressionists, however, sensed, along with the phenomenologists, that "consciousness must be consciousness of something" and that both subject and object are real. The philosopher Maurice Merleau-Ponty accurately describes the impressionists' method of reciprocating mediation:

If a friend and I are standing before a landscape, and if I attempt to show my friend something which I see and which he does not yet see, we cannot account for the situation by saying that I see something in my own world and that I attempt, by sending verbal messages, to give rise to an analogous perception in the world of my friend. There are not two numerically distinct worlds plus a mediating language which alone would bring us together. There is—and I know it very well if I become impatient with him—a kind of demand that what I see be seen by him also. And at the same time this communication is required by the very thing which I am looking at, by the reflections of sunlight upon it by its color, by its sensible evidence. The thing imposes itself not as true for every intellect, but as real for every subject who is standing where I am.[9]

The perceiving consciousness acquires existence and meaning only in relation to the objects and events of the external world. The relationship is one of subjective objectivity where both subject and object are immersed and juxtaposed in the spatio-temporal world of perception. This idea for realizing a new relation to reality was a major breakthrough for modern literature.

But it was in their approach to time and space that the impressionists made their greatest contribution. All the components of literary impressionism—the shift from description of objects to the rendering of atmosphere and mood, the importance of a perceiving consciousness, and the phenomenological relationship of subject and object—are, of course, inextricably woven into the impressionistic tapestry. Yet the dominant thread is the paradoxical union of Bergson's *durée* and phenomenological time and space. Hauser was really the first to notice the importance of time, believing that "impressionistic thinking finds its purest expression in the philosophy of Bergson, above all in his interpretation of time—the medium which is the vital element of impressionism."[10] But the impressionists intuitively felt that Bergson's subjective current of human time neglected the privileged moments of spatialized presentness. His notions contributed to the continuity of consciousness, the stream of

sensory impressions, the flow of human fulfillment: "Time
[impressionistic, Bergsonian, Proustian] is no longer the principle of dissolution and destruction, no longer the element in
which ideas and ideals lose their value, and life and mind their
substance, it is rather the form in which we obtain possession
and become aware of our spiritual life, our living nature, which
is the antithesis of dead matter and rigid mechanics. What we
are, we become not only in time but through time."[11] It is this
quality that distinguishes literary impressionism from painting.
Literature must create characters responding to events through
time. Most impressionists rejected concepts of time that would
render change definitive: the naturalists' belief that time was
solely the province of objective natural phenomena resulting
finally in death or the romantic conception of transcendental
moments resurrecting man from the crush of natural time. The
impressionists went a step further by fusing the subjective wave
of Bergsonian time with the subjectively objective quanta of
perceived phenomena. Phenomenological time stresses the "moments" of events, which, because they are imperceptibly framed
and spatially perceived, take on the literary impressionists'
hallmark: temporally extended frozen moments of spatialized
time that dissolve and return to the flow of durational time.
Bergson provided the humanizing force of continuity, where
"existence acquires actual life, movement, colour, an ideal trans-
parency and a spiritual content from the perspective of a present
that is the result of our past"[12] and the hope of our future.
Phenomenology suggested, however, "that one does not find a
continuous flow of the personal life, no instants, and no inter-
vals: but simply the consciousness of a changing world. No
'empty' moment of time between the vanished pulsation and
that which is about to be produced, but rather a particular object of consciousness made up of tremblings, tensions, relaxa-
tions, in which, with my body and by my body, I recover
space."[13]

Through their concern with time and space the impressionists
discovered their basic theme: change. All writers and thinkers
on the subject of time have recognized that time is change. The

impressionists felt driven to render the changing world in which they found themselves. Unlike historians, they translated their concerns over an accelerating, multiplying, and increasingly unknowable reality into characters who strive to hang on to the dizzying swirl of shifting consciousnesses, while responding to the changes in perceived events. The struggle, as Henry Adams so vividly saw it, was for survival, and the scales held sensitive perception of the known chaos against measured faith in one's "power to guess the unseen from the seen, to trace the implication of things, to judge the whole piece by the pattern."[14]

II * IMPRESSIONISM, CHEKHOV, AND JAMES

The impressionists have in the first place substituted the creation of atmosphere for inventory or set picture, subtle evocation for analysis or comment. They have discarded formal chronological narratives, with a definite beginning, middle, and end, in favor of retrospective, discontinuous, or unfinished actions, streams of associations canalized by emotion and the logic of the unconscious, or some kind of proliferous growth more nearly corresponding to the way in which we experience life—life, as Conrad insisted, does not *narrate*. They have broken up the relatively simple, trim patterns of characterization, presenting figures who have no shape to speak of and who defy simple summary or category. In general they have destroyed the solidity and rigidity of life as traditionally represented, blurred the contours and, like the painters, have sacrificed symmetry and neatness to intensity and expressiveness. Hence the mysteriousness in much impressionistic fiction, the shadows deepened by the very brilliance of its illuminations.

    Herbert Muller, "Impressionism in Fiction: Prism vs. Mirror"

The Shift to Rendered Atmosphere

The dissolution of plot, the broken cycle of causality, the unknowable ambiguity of perceived reality, the relativism of time and space, and the perceptual subjectivity of characters all forced a shift in literature away from directness and clarity of description—a sort of skirting of material reality. Objects and events lost their cleanly outlined shapes. The feel and tone of the literary impressionist's canvas became distinguished by fleeting impressions, vague gestalt images hurriedly glimpsed, arbitrary details selected almost to the point of triviality: splashes of color, blurred movement, and nuances of mood, gesture, and consciousness. Perceived particles of movement, attitude, and silence might signify meaning; just as often, however, that meaning could remain ambiguous and elusive. The heart of this impressionist complex was James's and Chekhov's commitment to the rendering of perceived reality, capturing the actual act of perception. The result was a stylistic interest in the limits of point of view and the epistemological effects of subjectivity.

Chekhov and James refused to force their own beliefs into their works through mouthpieces. They realized they could not didactically speak through characters who were meant to see the world for themselves. Nor did the impressionists wish to place themselves in relief against their fictional world, as Tolstoy, for instance, had done. They found it absolutely crucial to write themselves out of the narrative. While they controlled the linguistic and narrative elements of their work, they had to appear as though they knew no more than their characters. Both author and character would succeed or fail, then, according to the same criteria: whether they had the capacity to perceive keenly, to cultivate an expanding consciousness, and to act on what they saw and knew. They had to overcome the possible division between the *voir* and *savoir* of their experiences. They could not presume to know without seeing nor, because they saw, presume to know all. Perception and consciousness became woven into the fibre of knowability.

James and Chekhov have been often overlooked as impressionists because they took such care to create "centers of consciousness."[15] James warned of the dangers of first person narrations, and slices of life that aren't "done."[16] Centers of consciousness serve the dual impressionistic function of economy[17] and embrace,[18] which results in the "unity of impressionism."[19] While both Chekhov and James experimented with first person narrations, their most impressionistic works were written through third person central consciousnesses, or at times through dual or multiple reflectors. The fluidity of perceiving and knowing that is open to a third-person central consciousness provides greater freedom for that consciousness to glide through and fill in the void between outer world and inner ego. The impressionistic prism has consciousness at its center. Impressionism "is the technique by which one moment of reality is comprehended after the sensation has been modulated by consciousness and arrested by time."[20]

Although central consciousnesses allowed James and Chekhov the freedom to move beyond the restrictions of first person narration, their characters are essentially limited empiricists. Since they are able to perceive only the reality of the senses, they must learn to guess, intuit, and induct whatever "truths" lie scattered throughout the heaps of perceived fragments. Impressionists controlled what Dos Passos was later to call the "camera eye." Like the camera itself, it forces the reader/viewer into the role of subjective participant—we see only what the camera allows us to see through what the author/director selects. The usual tension exists between what is withheld from our view and what is withheld from the character's. The impressionist wishes to reduce that tension in favor of a common reader/character perspective. This in turn produces a tension between what the reader/character sees and knows through the camera eye and what it is possible to see and know—in other words, the mystery formula.[21] The impressionist, then, relies on the intensity produced by what lies outside the frame of reference, just as film exploits the conflict created by what may lie outside the frame. "Through an objective technique the impressionist seeks to create the illusion of participation in the reader. In order to achieve this effect certain elements in fiction may be repressed in favor of others. By eliminating the narrative the author avoids intruding on the reader's conscience through the persona of an explaining and describing narrator who stands between the reader and the world of the novel."[22]

The logical extension of this concept is the *nouveau roman et cinema* of Alain Robbe-Grillet. The reader/viewer becomes the coauthor;[23] participation based upon epistemological indeterminacy is total. Beginning with impressionism, unknowability rather than knowability became a major concern in literature. The progression of Chekhov's and James's impressionism can be measured by the extent of their characters' awareness of how little they know. Since perspective is always limited, the impressionist allowed his characters to make mistakes, rectify them as they see the reality change, and then even compound their earlier errors. They keep stumbling toward knowledge, vaguely realizing that as they come to know more, they must also know less about more.

As the modern world of science and technology became more chaotically threatening, so too did society and its individual members. Impressionism's goal was to render effects, understanding that causes and motives were too often unknowable. To posit a world of logically constructed causes and effects would only lead to further anarchy. It would compound the fragmentation in a desperately anachronistic search for the source of something that either did not exist or would be rendered meaningless by the accelerating atomization. Chance, accident, and coincidence have become the twentieth century's primary threads, reducing Melville's four elements in his "Loom of Time" by one. Necessity now has been lost to chance and free will struggles against the vagaries of existence. The characters of Chekhov and James search for reasons and attempt to plan their lives, only to have a chance encounter, a vague coincidence, or an accidental occurrence change their entire view of a person, their lives, or the world. This condition has the effect of breaking up both the traditional causal narrative structure and the concept of motivated characters whose outlines are clearly visible and whose movements are cleanly delineated.

The random listlessness of Chekhov's entropic characters, for instance, produces these effects on the narrative:

It leads to stress being laid on the episodical nature and irrelevance of all external happenings, it brings about a renunciation of all formal organization, all concentration and integration, and prefers to express itself in an eccentric form of composition in which the given framework is neglected and violated. Just as Degas moves important parts of the representation to the edge of the picture and makes the frame overlap them, Chekhov ends his short stories and plays with an anacrusis, in order to arouse the impression of the inconclusiveness, abruptness, and casual, arbitrary ending of the works. He follows a formal principle that is in every respect opposed to 'frontality,' one in which everything is aimed at giving the representation the character of something overheard by chance, intimated by chance, something that has occurred by chance.[24]

With certain clear differences in style and characterization, the basic thrust of this statement applies to James as well. Because the impressionist is rendering "the act of perception"[25] he can never give reality a symmetry, a posed frontality. Instead, the angle of vision is oblique, the object of perception is in movement or half hidden. Perception as a process of becoming inevitably leads to the arbitrary and inconclusive ambiguity that characterizes impressionism.

The Act of Perception

The starting point for the act of perception in impressionist literature is the perceiver. This pinpoints the shift from the eighteenth and nineteenth century's concept of "telling" to the twentieth century's belief in "showing." The impressionists believed that "everything rests upon the insurpassable richness, the miraculous multiplication of perceptible being."[26] They regarded the process of perceiving impressions as reality itself, not simply as a factor in the representation of it. "To the susceptible mind of the impressionist the surrounding world viewed at large is not simple and well ordered, but an indistinct and obscure picture made up of an irresistible flood of confused and ever changing sense impressions."[27] At any given point in time, one impression is as valid and real as any other.

The impressionist attempts to capture the feel, texture, and consciousness of the phenomenological *tabula rasa* or, in the impressionist lexicon, "the innocence of the eye."[28] For phenomenologists and impressionists alike everything is seen anew through fresh eyes. It is not surprising, then, that the most impressionistic early stories of Chekhov were of children experiencing a new world of sensory impressions. And James's first two impressionist novels, *The Portrait of a Lady* and *What Maisie Knew*, concerned young girls experiencing new worlds. While much impressionism filters reality through the innocent eyes of Crane's Henry Fleming or Proust's Marcel, it cannot be stressed too strongly that since perception is an act of becoming, all phenomenal perceivers view the world again, with each passing impression. Chekhov and James both understood this, so their mature impressionist works often have such older middle-aged men as Gurov in "The Lady with the Dog" or Strether in *The Ambassadors* as their central consciousnesses. After years of anesthetized perception these characters open themselves to the sensory world. The act of perception becomes more closely connected to the act of remembering. Memory for the now active perceiving consciousness has become Proustian, since the impressions of the past are held suspended in and given the texture of the present. The perceptive world is the world of the present. This concept anticipated the essence of existential phenomenology.

Tension in impressionist fiction pivots on the passive perceptual intake of sensory impressions set off against the gestalt synthesis of consciousness. Impressionism does not simply record the impact of pure, raw sensations on a passive receptor. If that were so, impressionist works would be little more than a compendium of impressions. Impressionism is the process by which impressions are absorbed by a perceiver and synthesized by consciousness into a gestalt that may lead to action or thought. Chekhov's and James's characters constantly fight the battle of Henry Adams—whether to succumb to the supersensual multiverse or actively merge with it. In their differing approaches to essentially the same world, James's characters too often attempt to control it, while Chekhov's appear to be content with an entropic merger with it. All tend to survive; all find some means of mediating their role as passive receptors with active consciousnesses.

The stylistic foundation of impressionism is the creation of linguistic and rhetorical effects that render sensory impressions on eyes, ears, and consciousness. Impressionist characters rarely think causally or conceptually. Instead, if they aren't directly involved in a sensory experience, their consciousnesses are sorting, resorting, and synthesizing perceptual fragments experienced over time, but reexperienced in each present moment.

One striking aspect of impressionism is the apparent disparity of subject matters, rhythms, sentence lengths, and word choices —to the extent that James, Chekhov, Crane, Woolf, Mansfield, Ford, and Proust would appear to have little in common. On this basis Chekhov and Crane might seem a more logical choice for comparison than Chekhov and James. Closer scrutiny reveals devices and effects that draw these latter two writers together. The most commonly acknowledged yet most inexplicable quality is the general vagueness of physical objects: outlines are blurred by distant perspective or are randomly incomplete because of narrowly focused glances; major features of an object become impalpably evanescent in the momentary mood and emotional selectivity of a perceiver; light takes on greater perceptual importance as objects are filtered back through allusive space; gestures and sounds are recorded through shifting space and time.

This entropic indistinctness harmonizes the total atmosphere. Chekhov's story, "Sleepy," is permeated by an ikon lamp's green light that mingles with the odor of cabbage. Together they seep into Varka's permanent state of half-sleep. These perceptions pervade the story's texture, so that the reader's sensibilities become wedded to Varka's as she comes under the control of these powerful sensory impressions. James, too, finds ubiquitous purpose in the gold imagery threaded throughout *The Golden Bowl*. This consonance is reinforced by the repetition of certain words and phrases that pull the fabric of the composition together into a sketchy, but evocatively precise prose.

James's most purely impressionistic scene is Strether's day in the country. Viola Hopkins Winner in *James and the Visual Arts* carefully analyzes some of the effects that most clearly characterize impressionist prose in this scene from *The Ambassadors*:

Color is presented through adjectives, and the light is represented as concentrated in the sky not diffused throughout. That the horizon is 'shady woody' suggests a traditional aerial perspective in which objects at a distance appear blurred. In contrast, the primary emphasis in the description of the village where he [Strether] stops for dinner is not on the thing modified by the adjective; instead, adjectives are converted into substantives, a grammatical shift which places the emphasis on the sensory quality of the visual experience rather than on the thing itself. . . . Color details are rendered with greater precision: the church is a 'dim slate-color' on the outside; the stream is 'grey-blue.' Distant objects are not described as in conventional perspective.[29]

There emerges from this scene and from impressionist prose in general an abundance of verbs of perception and a suppression of verbs of action. Only when rendering the perceived kinetic quality of an object can verbs of action be used. The density of nouns and adjectives steeps the prose in objects of perception and their textures. Nouns are often preceded by indefinite articles that accentuate the independence of the object, thereby fragmenting the vision. The dominance of adjectives over adverbs forces attention toward the sensory character of the object and away from action. This preserves the balance between subject (the perceiver) and object (the perceived). To further enhance both the fragmentation and the flow of impressions, Chekhov and Crane developed ellipses and discarded conjunctions, while James and Proust inserted conjunctions and relied on clauses.

Impressionists also practiced other rhetorical and linguistic strategems designed to increase the surface tension of sensory experience. James employed prolix syntactical arrangements to capture in language the direct perceptual contours of consciousness. His celebrated late style is the perfect impressionistic paradigm for reflecting the exact dimensions of complex perceivers with finely tuned consciousnesses. Chekhov's taut network of carefully worded rhythmic bursts illustrates the impulsive syntactical consciousnesses of less sophisticated but highly sensitive perceivers. Their fresh and continually naive approach to apperception with a concomitant transposition into language of surprise and wonder often results in bizarre imagery.[30] The passivity of Chekhov's languid characters increases the possibilities for startling configurations. Because they are so jaded by clichés, they become vulnerable to fresh perceptions. This leads to an oblique flow of energetic language.

There is also an important ontological shift from the verb "to be" to "seems," "appears," or "it was as if." These tropes underscore the tenuous nature of perceived reality, thrusting the textures of unknowable surfaces at the reader. The world of impressionism is the world of appearances.[31] It becomes necessary to accept a reality of surfaces because the burden of knowability has been placed firmly on perception. And since the accelerating pace of sensory stimuli continually assaults the perceiving consciousness, there is neither the time to reach out beyond appearances toward the heights of a romantically metaphysical universe nor the analytical means to probe beneath the surfaces of a rigorously neoclassical reality. One can neither penetrate nor transcend the multiple and ever-changing surfaces of the relative and ambiguous modern world—or as James put it, "Life is, immensely, a matter of surface."[32] The impressionist takes the world of appearances as reality, rather than struggling with the phantom issue of appearance versus reality. Each impression, then, is real. But not until the impression is tempered on the forge of experience and cooled in the vat of consciousness can it be authenticated by the gestalt. It can then be "known."

The subjective quality inherent in the impressionists' concern for rendering perception balances characters on a double-edged metaphysic that reshapes the romantic components of isolation and individualism. They are caught in an unknowable world where what they do know is perceived as floating adrift in spatio-temporal relativism. "Things and instants can link up with each other to form a world only through the medium of that ambiguous being known as subjectivity, and can become present to each other only from a certain point of view and in intention."[33] Characters in impressionist fiction find that they are often isolated from family, friends, and society because each sees his own limited world quite differently. Each realizes a vast, hidden world that is immediately inaccessible and each makes errors in perception. Militant isolationism often leads to self-righteous individuality, and yet the desire for human communication based upon multiple perspectives brings on confusion and loss of individuality. This becomes a major thematic tension in impressionist fiction.

In a relativistic world it becomes necessary to find measurable indices for one's position in relation to the surrounding reality. Isabel Archer and Maisie are besieged by alternate ways of seeing, often by those attempting to conceal themselves behind the multiple surfaces they present. Isabel and Maisie alternately absorb the immense profusion of sensory stimuli directed at them and close themselves off from all perspectives through reveries and leaps of faith that help them impose order on chaos.

Based on the emerging concepts of reader as coauthor and "zero degree writing,"[34] the reader is placed in the position of having to determine whether or not these characters are effective in negotiating their choices. The reader of James is offered as many perspectives as are the characters themselves. Only through the careful sifting of attitudes, values, and perceptions are we able to arrive at the judgment that Isabel has grown, that she now sees and knows more than Ralph Touchett, Madame Merle, and Gilbert Osmond, and that Maisie, too, perceives and is conscious of more than her parents, stepparents, and Mrs. Wix. James's characters strive to balance isolation and individuality with communication and compromise. Chekhov's characters also face a confusing and molten world, but they generally find themselves more isolated by their inability to articulate their frustrations and dreams.[35] James's characters talk and reflect endlessly; Chekhov's characters seem fixed in their dreary landscapes of consciousness and steppe. At best they make bumbling gestures of poetic revelation. Visual phantasmagoria often fills the space between outer world and inner ego. But these characters do not usually fall into solipsism because they accept a perceived world. The reader, then, becomes the vehicle

for communication with the outside world. The diary form of
Sartre's *Nausea* and Rilke's *The Notebooks of Malte Laurids
Brigge* evokes much of the same participatory pain and pathos
that seeps into Chekhov's characters. They struggle in isolation
for accessibility, often slipping into the void of their own
dreams, delusions, and death. Yet they tentatively, sometimes
willfully, but always humanely reach out in gestures of openness.

Their solitude and separation are measured by the numerous
silences that inundate the impressionist fiction of Chekhov and
James. They began what Beckett brought to completion:[36] a distrust of language as the dominant signifier, a realization that
expression and gesture can signify in a void, and a recognition
that much of one's life is spent waiting, waiting for silence in
silence. James's silences are the moments when characters either
perceive so much that language becomes incidental, or glimpse
how little they know, what isolatoes they have become. In *The
Portrait of a Lady* Isabel learns the extent of her lonely ignorance as she silently stumbles upon the silent colloquy of Madame Merle and Gilbert Osmond. In that instant she reads so
many signifiers that she comes to know more than those who
had previously shut her out of their world. She realizes how
closed she herself had been to the perceptual clues strewn about.
The Prince and Maggie of *The Golden Bowl* and Strether in
The Ambassadors also have silent epiphanies: the Prince entering upon the shattered golden bowl, Maggie stalking Charlotte,
and both of them on the terrace silently watching the game of
bridge, Strether inadvertently watching the distant boat glide
into view. Chekhov's characters, too, have their moments of
greatest awareness in silence, but only in the quietude of total
loneliness. Varka's stifling of the infant's screaming in "Sleepy"
paradoxically releases her from the silent suspension of sleeplessness; Riabovich's hushed kiss in the dark becomes so locked
into his consciousness in "The Kiss" that we must question its
very existence; Maria Vasilevna's soundless fusion of the past
and future in "In the Cart" blocks out the roar of the train;
Gurov and Anna Sergeevna mutely endure one another in "The

Lady with the Dog," yet find their greatest moments of happiness in the still dreams of their love. Silences in both James and Chekhov reveal to characters their relationship to the world. These moments reinforce the spatial, nonverbal qualities of impressionism, drawing it closer to painting.

Out of these silences and within the context of nonverbal communication, these characters hope to make sense out of the fragments of sensory reality by "rolling up experiences" and reaching inductive judgments. The logical foundation upon which impressionism rests, then, is induction. This process forces the issue of epistemological indeterminacy, since an inductive conclusion is never conclusive. It is based upon the idea that "psychology does not provide its explanations by identifying among a collection of facts, the invariable and unconditional antecedent. It conceives or comprehends facts in exactly the same way as physical induction, not content to rate empirical sequences, creates notions capable of co-ordinating facts . . . Since explanation is not discovered but created, it is never given with the fact, but is always simply a probable interpretation."[37] Induction is therefore open to the most hopeless of amateurs, those who can work at observing and thinking, believing that one day, for perhaps even a moment, the shards of their hitherto disordered existence will be outlined in the shape of a "truth."

But to experience and perceive first is crucial, whether for the writer or his characters: "The impression is for the writer what experiment is for the scientist, with the difference that in the scientist the work of intelligence precedes the experiment and in the writer it comes after the impression."[38] The failure of many characters in impressionist work to experience and perceive before they theorize provides the basic conflict, throwing into relief both the impressionists' aesthetic and their characters' psychological progression: "The gradual unfolding of meaning coincides with the slow process of perception. The total picture is the sum of infinite touches and sense impressions, and must be focused anew at each step or turn of the process: it is the characteristic manner of impressionistic rendering."[39] Isabel Archer arrives in England armed with theories and visions for her future happiness and freedom; the narrator of *The Sacred Fount* springs a vampire *donnée* on some unsuspecting guests, with only the barest and most subjectively thin evidence; Gurov enters into a relationship with Anna Sergeevna, preferring to forget everything he had learned in numerous earlier affairs; the peasant mother of "The Bishop" builds, perhaps, an entire reality on the wish that she had had a son who was a bishop.

The great temptation for these characters is to predict reality, to build an edifice based on deductive desires, and to turn smatterings of fleeting perceptions into facts. When they are confronted by a shattered and transitory world unraveling before their eyes they can no longer fall back upon their unsubstantiated generalizations and dreams. They must guess and intuit, rely on connotation and suggestion, pick up the pitch and tone of voices, and be content with distant perspectives and oblique angles of vision. They must realize that the best they can hope for is a partial view of an ambiguous picture. They will either adapt to the indeterminate multiverse by hanging on to the smallest shreds of secular belief and faith, or succumb.

Subject and Object

Adapting this heightened consciousness to the new reality of objects means fusing the inner ego with the outer world. This phenomenological relationship underlies the entire vision and aesthetic of impressionism.[40] It has been previously recognized as important,[41] but its position as the nucleus of impressionism has never been fully acknowledged. No longer is there a separation between subject and object, nor is one given precedence over the other. Reality is the synthesis of perceiver and perceived —each exists and each creates meaning for the other. The new aesthetic is based upon integrated juxtaposition, upon a gestalt: the perceiver superimposes on an object actual physical qualities based upon his own memory, mood, and perspective; the object takes on and reflects the physical properties of the surrounding environment; the object and its reflections—the entire *mise-en-scène*—simultaneously infuse the perceiver's own set of physical and psychological characteristics. This process continues ad infinitum, turning, spinning, reacting, blending—all in the moments of durational and phenomenological time.

There is one reality, the perceived consciousness of things continually changing. The literary impressionist would describe it this way:

The slightest word that we have said, the most insignificant action that we have performed at any one epoch of our life was surrounded by, and colored by the reflection of, things which logically had no connection with it and which later have been separated from it by our intellect which could make nothing of them for its own rational purposes, things, however, in the midst of which—here the pink reflection of the evening upon the flower-covered wall of a country restaurant, a feeling of hunger, the desire for women, the pleasure of luxury; there the blue volutes of the morning sea and, enveloped in them, phrases of music half emerging like the shoulders of water-nymphs—the simplest act or gesture remains immured as within a thousand sealed vessels, each one of them filled with things of a color, a scent, a temperature that are absolutely different one from another, vessels, moreover, which being disposed over the whole range of our years, during which we have never ceased to change if only in our dreams and our thoughts, are situated at the most various moral altitudes and give us the sensation of extraordinarily diverse atmospheres.[42]

Chekhov and James, like Proust, fill the subject-object relationship with the phenomena of consciousness and facticity, while sensory impressions act as the conduit: James with his seemingly endless and often silent momentary encounters between characters; Chekhov with his characters' continual search for sensory stimulation. Their canvases are immersed in the filled vessel of phenomenal sensations.

The stringent preoccupation with the subjective objectivity of objects that characterizes much of the *nouveau roman* was not so purely practiced by the impressionists. Instead, with the exception of Chekhov, they imbued their works with a plenitude of consciousness. Character is still a humanizing force for the impressionists; they have not wholly removed themselves from the ties of nineteenth-century literature. Chekhov's stripped style begins to move toward the empty entropy of Beckett's silences and objects, and the camera-eye coldness of Robbe-Grillet's obsessive, object-oriented perceiver. Impressionism, however, still basks in the warm light of humanism.

In Beckett and Robbe-Grillet objects emerge with crystalline clarity, whereas the impressionists find the contours indistinct. Fragmentation leads to decomposition. And this becomes as true for the impressionist characters as for the objects they perceive. Physical description seems lost in the welter of other objects, and metonymized through time. A character's physical characteristics are always subordinate to consciousness and scattered throughout the work. A character's psychological configuration is so protean that it becomes difficult to envision clearly outlined character traits. Both perceiver and perceived absorb and project the tones and features of the other.

In that prismatic reality between subject and object all outlines become hazy, while each element struggles for its own identity and existence. "All distinctions are eliminated, the physical and the psychological merge and sensations are one and the same, the ego dissolves and everything is an eternal flux which in some places seems to stop, in others to flow faster, everything is a movement of colors, sounds, temperatures, pressures, spaces and times, which on this side of the ego appears as moods, feelings, and desires."[43]

Time and Space

The movement of subject and of object and the relative movement between them, finds its most manifest expression in that figure of change, time, and its inextricable companion, space. It is often argued that time itself has become the actual subject of modern literature.[44] This is certainly true for Proust, Joyce, Woolf, Eliot, Faulkner, Robbe-Grillet, and Borges. While for centuries philosophers have been struggling with the major paradoxes of time, writers have generally accepted chronological or cosmic time—time in relation to a character's march through the hours, days, months, and years of existence or time in relation to a character's concern with death and/or eternity.

The impressionists and Bergson, however, were contemporaneously exploring the creative potential in the idea that, as Auden put it years later, "All our intuitions mock / The formal logic of the clock."[45] The impressionists were synthesizers who did not attack the concept of chronologically absolute time, but instead found that their sympathies lay more with fusing objective and subjective time, moment with duration, and space to time. These new conceptions formed the basic structure of the impressionistically architectonic fiction that has come to dominate modern literature.

If time is change, as most thinkers from Heraclitus to the present have recognized, then space is endurance. The impressionists experimented with moments of persistent, changeless time in the midst of constantly reforming space. Since they envisioned space and time together in a continually evolving relationship, it became possible for each to take on the characteristics of the other. The impressionist painters fought to capture the moment on their spatial canvases, a held instant in time, which through the vibrancy of color juxtaposition, the movement of objects, and the bursting of the frame transposed space into time. Literary impressionists, working in their temporal art, strove to spatialize time. They depended on simultaneity through the cross-cutting of scenes, the fragmentation of image complexes, and the sensory fusion of past and present. These elements formed the basis of the "privileged moment" or the mythos of "eternal repetition."[46] Proust was then able to proclaim that "time has assumed the form of space."[47]

This is not to argue that time is always spatialized, for as Roger Shattuck correctly reminds us, space and time are in a constant interchange.[48] The impressionists created moments of spatialized time in order to develop impressions, redirect the inherently temporal process of literature, alter the rhythms of prose and consciousness, and give their characters a respite from the flux of continual change. There is no immunity from change, however, because even space moves with the development of multiple perspectives: "If the observer sits in a boat and is carried by the current, we may say that he is moving downstream toward his future, but the future lies in the new landscapes which await him at the estuary, and the course of time is no longer the stream itself: it is the landscape as it rolls by for the moving observer. Time is, therefore, not a real process, not an actual succession that I am content to record. It arises from *my* relation to things."[49] Time is space and space is time, just as subject and object are each other in the revolutionary shift the impressionists made toward synthesis.

Their artistic impulses to spatialize time grew out of a more basic psychological framework: what later became known as gestalt. This led the impressionists to create instants of expanded consciousness, privileged moments, epiphanies. Embryonic gestalt thinking was not unknown to the impressionists. Not until Max Wertheimer's 1912 paper was there a founding statement for the Gestalt school, but Kant's doctrine of apperceptive synthesis partially anticipated gestalt thinking. For Kant, objects of experience formed integrated wholes, perceived in categories of time and space. Contemporaneous with the impressionists, Ernst Mach directly influenced the Gestalt school with what Hermann Bahr called the "philosophy of impressionism."[50] Finally, for Wolfgang Köhler, one of the founders of the Gestalt school, there is "one psychological fact that plays a central role in productive thinking. This fact is a subject's awareness of *relations*."[51]

Gestalt thinking is at the heart of the way impressionist characters learn to deal with their world. With their intuitive and inductive grasp of perceived fragments, they work, not to analyze those parts, but to comprehend the entire structure from above down. In this context the golden bowl of James's novel becomes the perfect impressionistic metaphor. It and what it signifies cannot be understood by Maggie or the Prince until it is shattered. The fragments of their lives then become synthesized through reactions to the broken bowl. And the process of refitting the pieces together into new relations continues ad infinitum. James was fully aware that this concentric infinitude posed the same difficulty for the artist as it did for his characters: "Really, universally, relations stop nowhere, and the exquisite problem of the artist is eternally but to draw, by a geometry of his own, the circle within which they shall happily *appear* to do so."[52] The characters of James and Chekhov, then, find themselves in the relative flux of changing relations. They eventually realize that only through a geometric redefinition of their relationship with the kaleidoscopic environment can they begin to reshape their own identity.

Often this takes place in moments of heightened awareness when the character reacts to an object, an action, or another character in such a way that he achieves a gestalt synthesis. This kind of moment has been given many names in literature and is not solely the property of impressionism, but these privileged moments, epiphanies, visionary instants, timeless moments, impressions, *instantanés*, or *moments bienheureux* do form a crucial basis for the impressionistic vision. These moments are not always transcendent, as they must be for the romantics. They are, however, the product of a change in perceptual perspective and occur at moments of heightened perceptual awareness. They may not "mean" anything beyond what they are, but they do result in a new grouping of fragmented experience. This often leads to a new way of seeing, a change in direction for the character, or an expanded consciousness. James saw these moments as the experience of a "suddenly-determined *absolute* of perception. The whole cluster of items forming the image is on these occasions born at once; the parts are not pieced together, they conspire and interdepend; but what it comes to, no doubt, is that at a simple touch an old latent and dormant impression, a buried germ, implanted by experience and then forgotten flashes to the surface as a fish, with a single 'squirm,' rises to the baited hook, and there meets instantly the vivifying ray."[53]

This is the fusion of time and space, for "the whole cluster of items" is taken from impressions scattered through time, but not until they adhere to and congeal around an extended present moment. Time becomes spatialized, frozen, in what seems to be an eternal moment, a hoped for reprieve from the continually multiplying prism of relations. The moment seems to detach itself from the background of normal awareness. "Consciousness then passes through progressive stages of intensification and unification, culminating in the ecstatic identification of the self and the world. . . . In this state of participation the nature of knowledge undergoes a profound change. There is no longer a subject which knows and an object which is known. Knowledge now becomes an intuitive, unitive act which . . . appears to reveal the 'essence' of things, or the essence of life itself contained in things."[54]

This ephemerally crystalline instant evaporates as easily and mysteriously as it appeared; it returns to the flux and flow of durational time. What was realized can become lost, forgotten, or confused. On the other hand these moments may lead to action, increased consciousness, or changed perceptions. But it must be recognized that none of these qualities have inherent positive or negative values. Action may result in the murder of an infant in Chekhov's "Sleepy" or in the ambiguous reunion of Maggie and the Prince. Changed perceptions can lead to the impression that the world is now smiling on Riabovich in "The Kiss," but when the kiss fades into the past, his life settles back into the entropic tedium that so distinguishes the Chekhovian character. Increased consciousness drives Isabel Archer to believe she knows more than she does and gives Strether the confidence to return home.

These privileged moments in James and Chekhov offer only instants of synthesis and stability in an entire life of change. In Chekhov they take the form of daydreams and in James they are moments of silently complex intensity between two people, sometimes even a kind of inadvertent voyeurism. The space of that privileged moment is between the dreamer and the dream, the voyeur and the object of vision, and the confrontees. It is the space of signs, allusive and connotative. Such a moment could mean nothing. But through a coincidental confluence of fragments at an inexplicably propitious instant the perceiving consciousness can reach for the intuitive leap, and meaning simply appears. These moments combine both intuitive "knowledge, which establishes itself in the moving reality and adopts the life itself of things,"[55] and intelligence, which "starts ordinarily from the immobile, and reconstructs movement as best it can with immobilities in juxtaposition."[56] An instant that emerges from the *durée* seems to hypostatize time—but, of course, the moment itself has its own duration—then it returns to the flow of time. It is like the freeze-frame that holds the image on the screen, suspended in time. However, that image remains caught in the inexorable clawing of twenty-four frames per second, while the viewer imposes his consciousness on that image over the span of those moving yet frozen seconds. Time is immobilized within movement. In Bergson's terms, intuition and intelligence become one.

The basic aesthetic of the impressionists grew out of these moments, juxtaposed for simultaneity. Privileged moments were those rare instances of composed impressions. The impressionists' method depended upon the absence of temporal transitions, and this contributed to the effect of spatial montage. Anticipating the cinema, impressionistic time had the feel of presentness, even if narrated in the past. Images, though created in the linear progression of language, were affecting stasis. Their kinetic fragmentation offered both a seamless persistence of vision and a simultaneous immediacy of controlled juxtaposition.

Impressionistic pointillism was achieved through metonymy and spatial fusion through metaphor. And yet it is the interdependence of metaphor and metonymy, first developed by Flaubert, that is the staple of film and modernism. The impressionist (the realist, for Roman Jakobson) "metonymically digresses from the plot to the atmosphere and from the characters to the setting in space and time."[57] Metaphor in impressionism brings stasis, unity, and those lyrical qualities that place it within the tradition of the lyrical novel;[58] metonymy gives the prose and fictive world mobility, contiguity, and those qualities that place impressionism within the sphere of realism.

In semiotic terms, impressionism finds its function in the dissolving of syntagmatic units with paradigmatic indices. In privileged moments, the instant in time is detached from the flux

of time. The lyrical stasis endows the randomly trivial with significance, while it is simultaneously returned to the contiguity
of moving reality. The narrative in general is constantly interrupted by linguistic discontinuities, rhythmic overtones, allusive images, and multiple points of view. Superimposed on this
metaphoric set of tropes is the elliptical foreshortening of time
and the ambiguous juxtaposition of constantly shifting metonymic images.

These essentially spatial qualities reinforce the temporal force
of impressionism, immersing the reader in the fictive life as
though we were present at the very instant of the very instant
of presentness. Impressionism is the world of the transitory, the
immediate, and the fresh perception—it is the world of becoming. The impressionist painters' aesthetic vision grew out of the
need to paint *plein-air*, to catch the vibrancy or lassitude of the
moment, to seize and hold an instant of light and movement,
and to transfer the mood and feel of that instant onto the canvas
with a sense of immediacy and simultaneity. The literary impressionists saw their task in basically the same terms, only they
had to deal with a more complex temporal structure. They could
neither simply string impressions together nor maintain a continuous flow of eternal presents. The impressionists had to discover a way of moving beyond Bergson's *durée*, while retaining
his sense that "becoming no longer signifies *being changed* but
changing; the act, that is to say, by which in transforming himself man incessantly reinvents his own being: 'To exist is to
change, to change is to mature, to mature is to create oneself
endlessly.' " [59]

Duration accounts for the privileged moments and the imperceptible flow of tenses. Time—past, present, and future—seems
immobilized in a conjoined present, while it also slips through
the divisions. But Bergson's duration could not account for the
impressionists' need to create successive moments, to break up
the uninterrupted *élan vital*. They sensed that the moment was
a transitory fragment of presentness, not part of "one indivisible
present." [60] Bergson's *durée* led to stream of consciousness, yet

for all its affinities with this mode (which the impressionists influenced), impressionism's distinct quality rested on the fusion of duration and succession.

The impressionists allowed their characters to experience both the unifying flow of privileged moments and the phenomenological succession of presentness. Phenomenological moments are contingent, so that those elements of the past and future that do exist are not only contained completely within the present, but in fact *are* the present. The durational moment, on the other hand, embodies within its flowing presentness the actual entities of past, present, and future. Impressionism offers an interchange between Bergsonian duration and phenomenological succession as the only way of rendering the creative and destructive, suspended and moving, enduring and transitory, fluid and fragmented, subjective and objective qualities of truly lived time. Time for the impressionist is a subjectively experienced sense of objective events. It continues through the dynamic relationship between the quanta-like fragments of successive instants that change constantly and the enduring wave of "times" that flows uninterruptedly through human consciousness.

Impressionist prose is suffused with "instants," "moments," "seconds," and "minutes" that fill the narrative canvas with a thousand strokes of immediacy. In Chekhov's fiction the past might be recalled in a gratuitous flash of time or the future may race toward images of inconclusiveness. Each image settles in a character's mind for an instant before dissolving into the vacancy of the present. His characters do not realize that those annihilated moments once palpably existed in the present. Living in the despair of washed out images, they hang on to time as though it were their only salvation. But they seem unable to maintain a faith in their present identity long enough to sustain a present/past or a present/future.

Chekhov stands somewhere between Proust, who was able to realize the *durée*, and Beckett, whose world irrevocably slid into the entropic silence of total nowness. Chekhov's characters struggle for respite from the present by immersing themselves in either the past or the future. It becomes a way of forcing out the bewildering changes that invade their consciousnesses. Theirs is a world of succession, because they can never embrace more than one moment or one time.

James approaches time from quite another angle: "Far from being, as with Proust, a past that was rarely and fortuitously recaptured by the operation of the involuntary memory, the past for James is always present, always spreading out like a drop of oil upon consciousness; so much so that, in the final analysis, the great problem for James is not remembering but, on the contrary, disencumbering his thought by forgetting."[61] This sense of presentness is so strong that it might seem as though James is not really concerned with time. He is, of course, for he has said "above all, of that most difficult of all things for the novelist to render, the duration of time . . ."[62] James, in fact, provides almost none of the conventional transitions from one time to another, preferring instead a "discriminated occasion" or a present episode treated without any other temporal reference.[63]

He renders the impressions of movement through juxtaposed space rather than time. "Ordinarily the Jamesian character has little duration; or rather his duration is not composed, like that of the Flaubertian or Tolstoian character, of a temporal density; between his immediate existence and the depths of his mind stretch no thick layers of memories . . . it consists in the successive localization of a selfsame entity in different points of space. . . . Its nature does not change; what changes is the relationship all the other points of space have with it."[64] Both Chekhov's and James's surface structure suggests the protean impressionism of successive time. But the other more textured structures, the repetitive imagery and sensory associations that trigger streams of images, produce a pointillistic harmony of durationally experienced time. So their characters are not only immersed in the vast quantity of fragments, but in their geometric progression as well. The prospects for making sense out of such a labyrinth are staggering, yet they often hold out for some new combination that could mean renewal. These are clutched at in the hope that a new component might appear and contribute to the human and aesthetic need for balance.

Impressionist works and their characters are always slightly and suspensefully out of balance. Neither temporal nor spatial formations are ever complete. Time seems to fade into the background as the rush of objects and images, captured almost simultaneously, takes precedence. After the dazzling fusion of images and the overpowering bombardment of fragments, time returns to smother the spatial experiences. The relationship between time and space is dynamic and relativistic. In this respect impressionism placed itself firmly in the forefront of modern literature, anticipating the innovations of Proust, Joyce, Faulkner, and the *nouveau roman*. Space is no longer geometric; time is no longer measurable. Both are apprehensive.

Conclusion

Impressionism is the synthesis of a number of paradoxes that control the basic tension between stasis and movement. Some scholars, while acknowledging these polarities, force a resolution.[65] For instance, passivity is often thought to be a prime human and aesthetic element in impressionist fiction. It has been correctly argued that characters are the passive receptors of sensory stimuli and that the "reduction of the artistic representation to the mood of the moment is, at the same time, the expression of a fundamentally passive outlook on life, an acquiescence in the role of the spectator."[66] And that "impressions of the surrounding world are to a large extent determined by circumstances; color, for instance, is no exact quality, but the result of a certain intensity of light or shade. Our condition of mind at any given moment must also be taken into consideration. These factors are beyond our power to influence; therefore the impressionist's passive recording of an illusory reality. . . . This passive attitude is basic not only to the impressionist's art but to his entire *Weltanschauung*."[67] But it is too much to claim that "impressionist protagonists are all passive."[68] Most, in fact, have active, restless consciousnesses. While they passively absorb a bewildering flood of moving externality, apperception continually casts itself over sensory fragments, searching for relations, patterns, and meanings. Impressionist characters often find creative syntheses in passive perception and active conception.

This dualism is often expressed in the alternation of waiting and action. Chekhov's characters believe they are trapped in sensory monotony, so they are always poised for a sudden flight into daydreams or love. The complex consciousness of the Jamesian character must wait long enough to accumulate the necessary fragments for the pursuit of its objective. Chekhov's characters, however, tend to be too passive for too long, while James's are too active too quickly. Each strives for a balanced synthesis, but in the "supersensual multiverse" the impressionists cannot allow their characters final, unequivocal resolutions. They must forever be condemned to live waiting for the other shoe to drop.

Chekhov, James, and other impressionists blended arrested motion with movement. This became embedded in their approach to time, which is both durational and successive, and space, which is both subjectively temporal and objectively inert. Their rendering of events and objects is a combination of carefully random partial details and blurred contours of vaguely suggestive movement. The result is a vision of fragmented reality. At the same time these perceiving consciousnesses grope for some unifying configuration. But only through the merger of subject and object can this occur. Perceiver and perceived become one in the phenomenal, sensory world. By synthesizing the subjective and the objective, impressionists were able to yoke the romanticism of the nineteenth century with the realism of the twentieth.

In fusing themselves to the phenomenal world, James's and Chekhov's characters increase the danger of becoming alienated from the social world. Yet they are also immersed in the flow of exterior reality, which can itself be considered a social sphere. They often become isolated from the human community because they see the hopelessness of penetrating the depths of another's consciousness. Life is so much a matter of surface that these perceivers seem left with only the external signifiers of consciousness. They are caught in the transitional moment between their romantic desire for a transcendental glimpse into the "Truth" of human consciousness and their realization that there is no "Truth," only perceived fragments of ambiguous sensory stimuli. A truth may be suggestively and momentarily perceived, but it will always be returned to the temporal flow of the other bits and pieces of reality.

In order to actualize these paradoxes the impressionist had to suspend the contradiction between experience and language; they needed to translate nonverbal experience into a verbal medium. In their shift from conception to perception the impressionists were forced to render sensory experience through a delimiting range of words. James and Proust flooded the space between subject and object with every conceivable mode of expression. Because they circled around the instant and found five ways to express a gesture, the object of perception loses its linguistic specificity and becomes one with its alluvial context. Chekhov, however, obtained the same effect through a sparsity of language that allowed gestures to be only metonymically hinted at. The holes are then filled by the reader's nonverbal imagination.

The impressionists gleaned their major theme from the irresolution of these paradoxes: the struggle for identity in a constantly shifting balance of perception and knowledge. One can never perceive enough to obtain definitive knowledge, and knowledge can never be acquired without perception. One must carefully perceive, then guess and intuit enough to believe that one knows—knows not all, just enough. Identity in impressionist fiction consists of perceiving and knowing one's fluid relationship to the ever-changing world. It is not surprising, then, that a great deal of impressionist literature takes jealousy as its subject: Proust's Odette and Swann, James's *The Portrait of a Lady* and *The Golden Bowl*, Ford's *The Good Soldier*. The final epistemological representation of this issue is Robbe-Grillet's *Jealousy*. If not jealousy, then love becomes the major subject. Both turn on unseen relationships that show themselves, if they do at all, in the hurried gestures, hidden glances, and half-heard whispers of vague but sharply felt emotions. Jealousy, love, desires, daydreams, and initiation into the "supersensual multiverse" become the subjects of impressionism, because they all center on a character's need to define himself in relation to the ambiguous sensory impressions of a protean reality.

III * PAINTERS AND WRITERS

Look for the kind of nature that suits your temperament. The motif should be observed more for shape and color than for drawing. There is no need to tighten the form which can be obtained without that. Precise drawing is dry and hampers the impression of the whole; it destroys all sensations. Do not define too closely the outlines of things; it is the brush stroke of the right value and color which should produce the drawing. In a mass, the greatest difficulty is not to give the contour in detail, but to paint what is within. Paint the essential character of things, try to convey it by any means whatsoever, without bothering about technique. When painting, make a choice of subject, see what is lying at the right and at the left, then work on everything simultaneously. Don't work bit by bit, but paint everything at once by placing tones everywhere, with brush strokes of the right color and value, while noticing what is alongside. Use small brush strokes and try to put down your perceptions immediately. The eye should not be fixed on one point, but should take in everything, while observing the reflections which the colors produce on their surroundings. Work at the same time upon sky, water, branches, ground, keeping everything going on an equal basis and unceasingly rework until you have got it. Cover the canvas at the first go, then work at it until you can see nothing more to add. Observe the aerial perspective well, from the foreground to the horizon, the reflections of sky, of foliage. Don't be afraid of putting on color, refine the work little by little. Don't proceed according to rules and principles, but paint what you observe and feel. Paint generously and unhesitatingly for it is best not to lose the first impression. Don't be timid in front of nature: one must be bold, at the risk of being deceived and making mistakes. One must have only one master—nature; she is the one always to be consulted.   Camille Pissarro

Were the literary impressionists consciously attempting to re-create in literature the goals of the painters? There is no doc-umented evidence to support such a thesis, but the collective direction of these eclectic writers suggests the inevitability of impressionism as a cultural phenomenon. René Huyghe, in at-tempting to locate the common ties that held the impressionist painters together, establishes a more far-reaching cohesion: "Thus, it is plausible to conceive of the group as a generalized entity; in bypassing petty historical details, one can define the motivating forces that they held in common; in transcending the limits of the painting itself, one is able to see a dominant thrust, a drift characteristic of their period as a whole and span-ning the various aspects of its art, literature, philosophy, and science. One could not hope for a more expansive point of view in order to define the deepest points of an underlying sense of homogeneity."[69] In his introduction to a centenary exhibition catalogue of impressionist painting, Huyghe describes the paint-ers' relationship to the impressionist era. The components of this era link the painters and writers. They all had a vision of a new universe that included rational sensualism, instinct and intui-tion, intellectual relativism, anti-materialism, consciousness of immediate sensory data, and *la durée*.[70] It is rare to find an art critic willing to place painting in so wide a cultural and scien-tific context.

There is no evidence that the French Impressionists had any direct impact on Chekhov, although he made three trips to Paris in 1891, 1894, and 1898. He neither stayed long nor enjoyed his trips. He often travelled with Alexander Suvorin, his publisher, who made some contacts for him with the artistic world of Paris. It would have been difficult for him not to have known of impressionism, for in those years it had become quite widely accepted, though not scandalously newsworthy. Chekhov never commented on impressionism. He was probably aware of the movement, but not consciously struck by an affinity. He was not blind to painting, however. Two of his friends were Russia's foremost artists of the time, Repin, a realist, and Levitan, a sort of unconsciously primitive impressionist. Of all the literary impressionists, Chekhov stands furthest from direct influence.

James, on the other hand, an avid viewer and reviewer of painting, was constantly in the center of artistic circles and fully cognizant of the aesthetic implications of each movement. However, he was not an early admirer of impressionism. In the 1870's he wrote that Whistler's "manner is very much that of the French 'Impressionists,' and like them, he suggests the rejoinder that a picture is not an impression, but an expression —just as a poem or piece of music is."[71] Gradually the term impression came to be used more often and with increasing urgency in his critical lexicon. In his 1884 essay, "The Art of Fiction," James had retreated from his earlier position on impressions in art: "A novel is in its broadest definition a personal, a direct impression of life: that, to begin with, constitutes its value, which is greater or less according to the intensity of the impression."[72] By 1894 he was beginning to embrace impressionism quite consciously and directly in his own fiction: "Further evidence that he had assimilated the impressionist method is found in an 1894 notebook entry: the 'formula' that would enable him to contain the idea of 'The Coxon Fund' in a story of only 20,000 words 'is to make an *Impression*—as one of Sargent's pictures is an impression.' "[73] And finally by 1905 he had virtually swallowed the Impressionists whole. In *The American Scene* he writes sensuously of a great new house, "in which an array of modern 'impressionistic' pictures, mainly French, wonderous examples of Manet, of Degas, of Claude Monet, of Whistler, of other rare hands, treated us to the effect of a large slippery sweet inserted, without a warning, between the compressed lips of half-conscious inanition. One hadn't known one was starved, but the morsel went down by the mere authority of the thing consummately prepared."[74] The other literary impressionists, culminating in Proust, all paid some kind of homage to *Les Im-pressionnistes*.

The Destruction of Matter

Literary impressionists did not consciously imitate the aims of the painters: "to capture, in the painting, the very way in which objects strike our eyes and attack our senses,"[75] and to depict, "that most impalpable of essences, the resonant light whose function it is to transmit all appearance, everything visible in the world."[76] When these ideas are translated into literature the purely visual emphasis is diminished, but the essence remains. Literary impressionists were interested in the impalpable surfaces of sensory data that attack consciousnesses. This transliteration meant that their subjects were not the water, snow, blossoms, clouds, sailboats, crowds, steam, speed, and mist of the painters.[77] Instead, the writers found equally ephemeral subjects: love, jealousy, growing up and growing old, daydreams, sleeplessness, modern warfare, and the myriad emotions and intrigues of changing human relationships.

The writers discovered that interior consciousness could be accurately and realistically portrayed only through the manifestations of sensory perception: the stolen glimpse of an oblique glance, the feel of a room filled with subtle tension, the partial gesture viewed from a distance. Both painters and writers were searching for a way to describe the same phenomenon—the death of matter. "In all areas of thought, the late nineteenth century substituted the moving for the fixed—the unstable and indefinable for the immobile and the precise. Within this fabric, the Impressionist thread is quite strong: it is the visual manifestation, the imagery of a new conception of the world—a world remaking itself in all its aspects."[78] The literary impressionists broke matter down by shifting from the description of an object to the rendering of atmosphere. The fragmentary wisps of reality that so envelop both subject and object cause each to lose its clearly defined outlines.

Examples abound in both Chekhov and James. A description of Chekhov's process should prove supremely effective, since each story is in itself a compressed gestalt. However, for this very reason it is difficult to extract a "pictorially" impressionistic example. In his early stories there are those passages that break down the posed image, that convey the fluid, ineffable fragmentation of objects. Later, however, he came to realize that the story itself must be an impressionistic image. In "The Lady with the Dog," "The Bishop," and "The Betrothed," for instance, there are few impressionistically pictorial passages. Each sentence contributes to the effect of the whole story, not to the impressionistic coherence of a passage. This network relies on the obliquely repeated objects, sensory associations, words, and relationships. Both Chekhov's and James's prose alludes to buried nuances in the text. Without intratextual references we are lost. Traditional prose did not build elliptically. Its line had a continuous horizontality, which assumed that one sentence, one paragraph, one scene all led directly into the next. All the information necessary for comprehension was contained within the even flow of its narrative transitions. Impressionist art cannot be apprehended through a separate analysis of its parts; it must emerge out of the gestalt.

It becomes impossible, therefore, to determine whether Gurov loves Anna, the bishop was a bishop, or Nadia really changes her life. We are left with only impressions. Yet they linger and deepen so that we remember the sense of frustration in the Chekhovian character long after we have forgotten what the story was about or who did what to whom. Chekhov's mature stories are suffused with carefully controlled nuances, the play of perceived sensory data, the vibrant juxtaposition of feelings, images, and impressions, and the checkered reflections of daydreams. They are essentially the same qualities of Monet, as Théodore Duret described them.

It is possible, however, to identify in some of Chekhov's stories the framed pictorial passages that fragment and dissolve matter: "Maria Vasilevna stood at the crossing waiting for the train to pass, her whole body shivering with cold. From there could be seen Vyozovye, the green roof over the school and the church with its blazing crosses that reflected the setting sun; and the station windows were aflame, too, and a pink smoke rose from the engine . . . And it seemed to her that everything was shivering with cold" (9:251). In this scene from "In the Cart," the colors range from the isolated green of a distant roof to the impressionistically formless and pinkish foreground smoke of, say, Monet's "La Gare Saint-Lazare, Paris," or the mixtures of Turner's "Rain, Steam and Speed." There are also the undefined colors of the "blazing" crosses and the windows "aflame." The composition contrasts the static background with a moving foreground. The entire scene is then washed over with the sense that both Maria and the world are shivering from the cold. She phenomenologically projects this coldness onto the objects of her perception, even though much of the imagery is of heat and warmth. The elements of impressionism are here: visual perspective, motion and stasis, harmony of feeling, formlessness of colors and shapes, random and isolated detail, and the pervading source and reflection of light at a particular time of day.

One does not immediately associate impressionist paintings with scenes from Chekhov. His bleak spaces do not reflect the warm, rich fullness of the painters' scenes. Instead, they project that quality captured in Emily Dickinson's lines: "There's a certain Slant of light, / Winter Afternoons / That oppresses, like the Heft / Of Cathedral Tunes—." And yet there are such paintings: Monet's "Le Père Lathuile Restaurant" captures the languorous and distant intimacy of Anna and Gurov in "The Lady with the Dog," and Pissarro's "The Wash-House" seems to look out through the small, spare trees over the near-winter landscape of the steppes and into one of Chekhov's small, dull, and slightly grubby towns.

James's impressionism develops through the different demands of the novel, where more fully revealed characters move through the vast maze of seemingly meaningless and disconnected detail. His characters register the "trivial touches of tone and brush,"[79] as moods, glimpses, and sounds flow together. They look into the distance and see "someone" or "something" that for a brief moment, through the formless blue of space, becomes a recognizable reality. That instant might carry great significance (Maisie seeing her mother with another man, Strether aimlessly watching the boat come into view, or Maggie seeing Charlotte on the terrace) or it might simply be a new perceptual fragment that contributes to the process of a character's growth. In either case, the moment is a fresh experience for innocent eyes, and both writer and painter render the moment impressionistically.

In *The Golden Bowl* when Maggie unconsciously stalks Charlotte on the terrace at Fawns the encounter is one of pursuit and flight, confrontation and evasion, and impressionistic recognition:

> When she [Maggie] stood there she hung over, over the gardens and the woods—all of which drowsed below her at this hour in the immensity of light. The miles of shade looked hot, the banks of flowers looked dim; the peacocks on the balustrades let their tails hang limp and the smaller birds lurked among the leaves. Nothing therefore would have appeared to stir in the brilliant void if Maggie, at the moment she was about to turn away, hadn't caught sight of a moving spot, a clear green sunshade in the act of descending a flight of steps. It passed down from the terrace, receding, at a distance, from sight and carried, naturally, so as to conceal the head and back of its bearer; but Maggie had quickly recognized the white dress and the particular motion of this adventurer—.[80]

The high angle perspective is clear and the motion complex. Maggie is in a languid state, ready to turn away, to effect a change in scene and perspective. At that very moment the scene itself changes, captured in the glimpse of her turning head. It is formless and still, yet, paradoxically, sharp and intense: "all of which drowsed below her at this hour in the immensity of light" and "the brilliant void." James's "the shade looked hot" seems borrowed from Renoir's "Nude in the Sun," where with "a tender, almost caressing, brush Renoir proceeded, through warm shadows."[81] Charlotte remains an anonymous and disembodied object—"a moving spot, a clear green sunshade in the act of descending a flight of steps. It passed down the terrace, receding at the distance, from sight." Despite the distance, movement, fragmentation, and seemingly listless mood, Maggie "quickly

recognized the white dress and the particular motion" of Charlotte. This impressionistic scene forces impressionistic seeing
that leads to impressionistic knowing. The perspective might
have been that of Gustave Caillebotte's "Boulevard Seen from
Above" or Monet's "Terrace at Sainte-Adresse." The coloring
and light are reminiscent of Monet's "Parisians Enjoying the
Parc Monceau" or "Women in the Garden."

James created the restless sketchy surface through particles
of light and shade, detached primary colors, and almost arbitrary detail. Details are vague even in their concreteness and
neither facial features nor expressions are described. In the distance a blaze of white could suggest for Sisley and Manet the
vague forms of houses offering respite from the reflections of a
hot day or orange-white masses might seem for Cézanne to prof-
fer the cool warmth of stability. A white dress or a pink parasol
could strike through the summer haze of green and white light,
projecting an attitude of familiarity, as in Monet's "Terrace at
Sainte-Adresse," or the unruffled social pleasures of both Renoir's and Monet's "La Grenouillère."

The Primitive Eye

James and Chekhov experimented in the early stages of their
impressionism with the natural eye of children and adolescents.
Isabel Archer, Maisie, Grisha, Varka, and Egorushka are inno-
cents who perceive in a fresh, untutored way. They make mistakes of perception; they see distant shapes decompose and close
ones fragment; they cannot grasp the relationships developed
outside their purview; they hear partial sentences and words
they don't understand. Since they have not yet learned how to
perceive, they have no idea what their perceptions mean. And
while their bewilderment may be greater than that of those who
believe in distinct forms, they are far more able to perceive the
phenomenal realities of becoming. Thus, the natural eye of the
artist—sophisticated, but having made itself "primitive again
by ridding itself of tactile illusions and their convenient dead
language"[82]—submerges itself with his characters' perspective.

Line exists neither for impressionist painters nor for children. Their primitive perceptions usually record the shattered bits of tone and pitch. Both impressionists and children refuse to acknowledge illusions, finding instead new configurations of language to express the fresh sights and sounds in a continually changing world. Phenomenologically "the world is always 'already there' before reflection begins—as an inalienable presence; and all its efforts are concentrated upon re-achieving a direct and primitive contact with the world."[83] So it is not surprising that many impressionists were fascinated, for a while at least, with the perceptions of children, until they began to ask a more provocative question: could an adult encumbered with a worldly and sensitive consciousness perceive as a child? The painter found that he first had to be accused of painting like a child before he could express the spontaneous immediacy of the phenomenal world. Both literature and painting "were making parallel attempts to reject the codification imposed by the intellect on the abstract and indefinable truth of life, and to reestablish a natural dialogue with it."[84]

The literary impressionists discovered that with mature characters they were able to deepen time. The instant of pure presentness became a moment of past/present or future/present. The model the impressionist painters had provided could no longer be sustained. Children can function in a world of limited memory. But like Proust's Marcel, the narrator of *The Sacred Fount*, Strether, Gurov, and Nikolai Stepanovich of "A Dreary Story" are caught between the *élan vital* of present sensations and the grip of past sensory associations. As Strether walks through the countryside a confluence of visual fragments recalls the moment he missed his opportunity to buy the Lambinet painting he had loved. Strether now becomes surrounded by and exists in his own living Lambinet—but it has been transformed into a Jamesian impressionist painting. This contrast between his impressionistically fluid existence and his conventionally Lambinet past helps force him toward his epiphany, the sight of Chad and Mme de Vionnet in the boat. Memory is based upon series of impressions, so the writer, unlike the painter, must create a multiplicity of moments. Monet, however, painted his equivalent of the literary continuum, series of haystacks, cathedral facades, and poplars: "In the facade of the Rouen Cathedral, which seems to have gone through centuries with almost no change, Monet discovered a vital fluency, a fluid presence, changing from second to second. He watched the facade as the hours passed with a rhythm of their own; it ʼwas as if he could feel the pulse of the cathedral facade in the midst of timelessness [*la durée*]."[85] This countered the literary impressionists' painterly spatialized moments. But whether it was three months in *The Ambassadors* or an instant in a Renoir, each period of time became charged with the feel of fragmented presentness.

The writer always seemed positioned behind the painter, rendering the expression of the painter's impression. An impressionist character sees with the eyes of an impressionist painter. The literary impressionist worked slowly and meticulously to affect *plein-air* spontaneity. He would write as though he were attentively watching an impressionist painter at work, as Renoir did in "Monet Painting in his Garden" or Manet did in "Monet Painting on his Boat." Meanwhile the writer's "painting" seems to slowly dolly in on the optical sensibility of the painter's consciousness, which "has changed time and time again, has been upset in its appreciation of the constant and relative values of the landscape tone—imponderable fusions of tone, opposing perceptions, imperceptible distractions, subordinations and dominations, variations in the force of reaction of the three optical fibrils one upon the other and on the external world, infinite and infinitesimal struggles."[86] Literary impressionism is the transformation of the painter's painting and the painter's consciousness in the act of painting.

Part Two
Anton Chekhov

You write that you find everything bewildering, in confusion. . . .
It is good for things to be confused, my sweet little actress, very
good! It indicates that you are a philosopher, a woman of parts.

Anton Pavlovich Chekhov to Olga Knipper, September 8, 1900

∗ 2 ∗

The Emerging Impressionist
1883–1887

I ∗ INTRODUCTION: SUBJECTIVE OBJECTIVISM

One of the most perplexing issues in Chekhov studies centers on
the nature of his presumed objectivity. His adherence to scientism has always been an attractive factor: "It has become almost
a truism, in the critical literature about Čechov to speak of him
as dedicated to the scientific view and the scientific method."[1]
Was it Chekhov's medical training and practice,[2] his early association with Dmitri Grigorovich,[3] his reading of Emile Zola and
the influence of Claude Bernard's *Introduction à la médicine
générale*,[4] or the powerful wave of naturalism flowing out from
the cultural and scientific centers of Europe? Chekhov's remarkably adept synthetic imagination and precise perceptual intellect absorbed all these *fin de siècle* currents, adapting them to
fit his own vision. He was repelled by determinism's limitations
on subjective consciousness, but drawn towards its meticulously
veracious examination of the external world. While Tolstoy rev-
eled in determinism's dualism, Chekhov needed synthesis. So he
embraced the subjective objectivism of phenomenology, thereby
projecting his impressionism into the vanguard of literary modernism. He found his different drummer in the harmonies of
impressionism, the melodic structure of perceiving consciousnesses, and the rhythms of phenomenological time.

As Chekhov's impressionism gains wider acceptance, it is important to show how he moved it toward the labyrinths of phenomenological literature (neo- or post-impressionism?). The
French literary historian R. M. Albérès makes vivid the connection between impressionism and phenomenology:

In this indecisive universe where subjectivism mingles with objectivity, the novel is no longer a story, but a confused colliding of sensations, impressions and experiences. It is not "ready-made," shown in advance, shaped and packaged by a trained writer-narrator. It is suggested to the reader like a fluid, poetic and enigmatic substance, and instead of following the plot line, we wander around as if in a daydream or as if in life . . . with Proust, Musil, Kafka, possibly Joyce, and Virginia Woolf (later with Michel Butor and Alain Robbe-Grillet), everything is inverted: the novel's hero is no longer placed in the world where he lives; rather, the vision of the "real" world is subject to the relationship between the hero and the world . . . the consciousness of the novel's hero dominates, the "real world" exists only so far as it is reflected by this consciousness. In 1890 we would have given this vision of the novel the qualification of "impressionist" or "subjectivist." Today we say "phenomenological."[5]

This incipient phenomenology in Chekhov's impressionism may have been suggested to him by Bernard's writings. Henri Bergson's influence on Proust, Woolf, and other modernists forged the link between Chekhov and phenomenology. Bergson's conduit was the chapter in *The Creative Mind* devoted to Bernard's method of showing "how fact and idea collaborate in experimental research. . . . Scientific research is therefore a dialogue between mind and nature."[6] If scientific inquiry must acknowledge the subjectivity of the perceiving consciousness, then certainly a literary character's investigations into the life that surrounds him can also not remain wholly objective. Chekhov's most impressionistic stories have a detached quality of scrupulous observation that seems comparable to the phenomenologists' method of reduction. Experiences appear momentarily suspended from the continuity of time. Each phenomenon is seen as though for the first time, and so must be continually recreated by the perceiving consciousness. Phenomena in this bracketed, external world take on an almost self-contained objectivity. Chekhov's impressionism consists of a profusion of objects captured in moments of objectified timelessness, flashes of frozen time. The result is the Chekhovian dreamlike mood of silent waiting.

Chekhov's world, which is always refracted through the prismatic sensibility of a perceiving consciousness, has both the

blurred suggestiveness of Proust and the hard-edged concreteness of Kafka. This seemingly contradictory style is possible
through Chekhov's preference for third-person narrations that
focus on subjective consciousnesses, while blocking the possibility of solipsism.[7] Chekhov's ambivalent retreat from his perceivers creates an objectivity far different from the realists'
illusion of omniscient objectivity. The product is phenomenological objectivity. Characters subjectively perceive what objectively exists. Subject and object coexist.

Robbe-Grillet's theoretical *donnée* is that all "writers believe
they are realists."[8] The impressionists were not exceptions.
Robbe-Grillet goes on to say that verisimilitude does not characterize the "new realism," but instead it is "the little detail that
rings false."[9] Chekhov's best fiction contains elements of the
bizarre.[10] When viewed from Robbe-Grillet's phenomenological
perspective, the bizarre rings false because it is so uniquely true
for a perceiving consciousness. "The bizarre is not necessarily
absurd; it is, as it were, a statement, or a situation, which has
no logical place in the context or in the sequence of events."[11]
In Chekhov this is a random manifestation; in the *nouveau
roman* it has become a totality: "The world is neither meaningful nor absurd. It simply is. That, in any case, is the most remarkable thing about it. Things *are there.*"[12] It is important to
Chekhov's impressionistically heightened sense of objectivity
that the eccentric detail has no symbolic or even intrinsic meaning. It remains an experimental fragment, nothing more. In a
letter to Olga Knipper just before his death, when he might have
indulged in a final flourish of metaphysical musing, he answered
her in terms that would have appealed to the writers of the
nouveau roman: "You ask: what is life? It is the same as asking
what is a carrot. A carrot is a carrot, and that's all that's known"
(20:277).

John Hagan's article "Chekhov's Fiction and the Ideal of Objectivity" lists Chekhov's attitudes toward objectivity: his desire
not to judge his characters, his feeling that he should leave the
evaluation of characters' speeches up to the "jury" (i.e., the
readers), and his belief that it was "high time for writing folk,

especially artists, to admit you can't appraise anything in this world."[13] These correspond to Merleau-Ponty's views that "the novelist's task is not to expound ideas or even analyse characters, but to depict an inter-human event ripening, and bursting it upon us with no ideological commentary, to such an extent that any change in the order of the narrative or in choice of viewpoint would alter the literary meaning of the event."[14] It is the subjectivity of Chekhov's objectivity that has been missing in Chekhov criticism. Scholarship tends to separate humanism from objectivity. Robbe-Grillet, however, understands Chekhov's method. He says that when we are able to participate in a character's perceptions, the objects of perception become humanized.[15] Phenomenological literature makes us aware of perception. The key to Chekhov's humanistic objectivity is his use of perceiving consciousnesses and phenomenological time. These connections between Chekhov and the *nouveau roman* should in no way be construed as a description of the same literary phenomenon. With an awareness of Proust, Kafka, Beckett, and Faulkner, the authors of *nouveaux romans*, like Borges's Pierre Menard, write with the rich echoes of ambiguity not available to Chekhov.

Both Chekhov and Robbe-Grillet are drawn to the restraint, precision, and laconic flatness of what Roland Barthes has termed "zero degree writing."[16] This is the neutral, colorless prose that Sartre has called *l'écriture blanche*. It indulges in neither metaphor nor other figurative tropes, but relies on the concreteness of nouns and verbs of perception. It has the initial effect of a recording machine. But configurations begin to reveal the consciousness of the perceiver. Robbe-Grillet's characters are often judged by readers to be obsessive psychopaths, but only because *we* make connections that seem to fit psychopathic patterns, not because they do. Chekhov's and Robbe-Grillet's characters see objects that are equally real, whether perceived in the outer world or in their imaginations.[17] Varka's dream-like images in "Sleepy" are as real as Egorushka's natural perceptions of the steppe. Zero degree writing enhances subjective objectivism because it shows no distinctions between the "real" and the imagined. Since this prose style concentrates on *what* is seen and heard, the interface between subject and object becomes more equally balanced. Psychological "meaning" seems diminished by the profusion of sensory stimuli.

Perceiving consciousnesses are always present, however. Chekhov's stories usually open with a flat, data-like rendering of the external world. But he moves quickly and unobtrusively into the third person consciousness of a character.[18] In "Grisha," for instance, a three-year-old child takes his first trip outside the house. The enormity of this experience on his consciousness is rendered not through his thoughts, but through the confusing swirl of huge, unidentifiable objects. He is so overwhelmed by the "burst of new impressions he has just experienced" (5:10) that upon his return his mother thinks he is ill. These "new impressions" not only signify a bewilderment of the unknown, but the expansion of consciousness. Grisha knows more after the excursion than before, yet he also knows less about more. The reader of impressionist literature also becomes entangled in that same uncertainty. Grisha is taken to a small, dingy flat where his nursemaid meets a friend, drinks some wine, and gives Grisha a taste. It is tempting to read into this matter-of-fact description a secret and romantic assignation.[19] Chekhov does not indicate an interpretation, but his zero degree writing allows for the reader's participation in a pattern of unknowability. So one may read, if one wishes, this scene as a meeting of lovers, provided the reader is willing to accept the ultimate indeterminacy of the scene.

In "The Fat and the Thin" a penumbra of objects surrounding Fat changes Thin's vision of himself: the lips as buttery and glossy as ripe cherries, the perfume of sherry and orange, the decorations of a privy councilor, the fat, well-fed expression of self-satisfaction. While this description seems to be rendered with objectivity, the phenomenological implication is that it is Thin for whom these sensations exist. The juxtaposition of odors forces him to realize his own less florid essence. "Oysters" and "Typhus" gain their perceptual reality from characters whose illnesses intensify the vast accumulation of sensations invading their consciousnesses. They have become both so dissociated and sensitized that all perceptual stimuli have become painfully distorted.

This effect is more striking in a more complex story, "Sleepy." In her desperation for sleep, Varka finally perceives that death is connected to everything surrounding her—the green ikon lamp, the black trousers, the baby's diapers, the lullaby, the father's death rattle—and that all these are connected to the infant who won't let her sleep. Varka rivets her attention on the infant. In killing it she transforms the baby into an object, an obstacle to sleep. She smothers it with no awareness of its humanness. In "The Steppe," Egorushka's entire education, which remains immeasurable, consists of the steppe. Egorushka becomes the phenomenological embodiment of the naive perceiver. In the later stories—particularly "A Dreary Story," "The Student," "In the Cart," "The Lady with the Dog," "The Bishop," and "The Betrothed"—Chekhov created more mature consciousnesses.

As his impressionism ripened, his characters became more cognizant of time. They began to structure their lives around and through time. They often looked forward to a future that would never materialize or back on a past that no longer had meaning for them. They didn't realize or they forgot that they could only find meaning in an existential present, the present of the past or future. The reality of presentness drove Chekhov to depict characters who set themselves adrift in a timeless void. He wrote under the spirit of Bergsonian time, the time of subjective consciousness. Yet he also had much in common with the phenomenologists who felt that time was objectified when it was perceived, not through the durational continuum of past-present-future. "The objectivity of time can only be seized in time, that is, in shifts, in the succession of phases of consciousness."[20] In other words, time is objectified only when captured moment by moment without, the imperceptible Bergsonian *durée*. Chekhov's prose has the feel of time *now* and the quality of an enduring present. The brush strokes of "instants" and "moments" permeating the narrative canvas form an urgent sense of immediacy. Time takes on the paradoxical feel of changeless change. The "moment denies continuity"[21] and the instant dissolves the past. Chekhov's only flow of time is beneath the surface, on the surface it is a series of hypostatized moments. Change exists in temporal movement. Yet at the same time the freeze-frames of presentness can become the void of waiting, the timelessness of silence. Chekhov's impressionism demonstrated the immobilizing effect of silent dreamlike states, the elusive and disintegrating past, the inability of characters to understand themselves in relation to change, and the seasonal cycle of the eternal return.

The passage of time in Chekhov is basically destructive. Those characters who are incapable of living in the present have nothing to remember and nothing to look forward to, those who live in the past are out of touch with the present, and those who live for the future only exist for a hopelessly ephemeral dream. Lopakhin in *The Cherry Orchard* deals with the present by continually asking what time it is, as if knowing the time will confirm his existence. Firs, who has become atrophied in the past, mumbles at the end of the play: "They've forgotten me" and then: "Life has gone by as if I had never lived" (11:359–60). As the three sisters huddle together bleating out their eternal "*V Moskvu! V Moskvu! V Moskvu*," they find themselves, paradoxically, in the same situation as Firs. At the end of *The Three Sisters*, Olga mourns because "time will pass and we shall be gone forever, they will forget us, they will forget our faces, voices and how many of us there were" (11:303). These characters do not exist, for they refuse to live in time, in the presentness of their own consciousnesses. They are unable to believe in the presentness of either the past or the future. And so Chebutykin's song, "It's all the same, it's all the same," is superimposed on the sisters' questions about the meaning of life. It does seem to be the same in Chekhov, except that we have watched these characters move through moods and attitudes, we have seen them struggle through present after present, change after change.

Chekhov has fused this paradox of time into a vision of endlessly recurring cycles, the eternal return, best exemplified by

Nadia in "The Betrothed." In the spring, before she is to marry
—that ritual of new beginnings—Nadia comes to feel the stir-
rings of oppression, the need to feel free and begin life with
oneself. When she decides to leave and not marry, her mother
lectures her on the cycles of transformation from daughter to
mother, and so on. Nadia rejects her mother's explanation in
favor of what she believes to be an entirely new beginning.
When she leaves and summer comes (she would have been a
June bride) she hears only the restless sounds of time passing,
as the nightwatchman strikes the familiar, "Tic-Toc . . . Tic-
Toc." She begins to feel homesick already. Fall and winter pass.
When she returns home her perceptions have already become
suspect; she sees her mother as older and plainer, but nothing
has changed. And once home she wishes to revolutionize herself
again, "and it seemed to her that everything in the town had
been growing old for a long time, and the town itself had out-
lived its day and was not waiting either for the end or for the
beginning of something fresh and young. Oh, if only this new
pure life would come more quickly" (9:626). The children of
the town mock her with the shrill taunts of her past/future,
"the bride, the bride." They remember only the loss of her conventional dream of marriage to Andrei. What they don't understand is that Nadia envisions a life based on a marriage with the
future. She denies herself the prospect of living in the present
by always looking for change in the future and the past. Just as
she saw the townspeople waiting for either the end or the beginning of something, so Nadia lives out a cycle of timeless nothingness.

Nadia centers her life on an ever-present hope in future
change, not realizing that she is in its midst, that each moment
is itself change. These instants are not merely momentary alterations, as George Poulet points out:

The human being . . . is a being who tries to find justification for his existence. Not knowing who he is, either he is like someone stricken with
amnesia who goes from door to door asking people to tell him his name,
or he feels himself to be what things indifferently become in him: a bun-
dle of anonymous images that obliterate themselves and reform, like the

iridescent spray from fountains of water. He is nothing or anything by turns, anything which is still nothing. Now this being who is nothing finds himself thrown into a moment which resembles nothing and rests on nothing. And since this instant is inevitably going to be annihilated by another, he sees in this instant his own death, and he does not know whether he will be born again, or into what sort of being he will be reborn.[22]

For Chekhov, as well as Proust, identity is linked to time and time to death and death to only a possible rebirth. Each moment is the instant of both life and death, where each second signals the death of the past and thus the death of each human being.

As early as "The Fat and the Thin" Chekhov understood this principle. In the beginning of the story Thin is in harmony with an identity that suits his sense of modest well-being. But when he discovers that his old friend and peer, Fat, has over the years attained the stupendous rank of privy councilor, the thin chameleon freezes. He "shrivelled and shrank and stooped and his suitcases shrivelled and grew wrinkled" (2:11). In this freeze frame we have witnessed the death of Thin. He seems to dissolve into a Dickensian grease spot, only to reemerge as a new man—an obsequious, mawkish *chinovnik*. The chameleonism in Chekhov's stories is not really the ability to adapt to a new situation, but is instead the reaction that the force of space has upon time. One's identity will be destroyed with each given moment and with each new requirement of environmental juxtaposition. One's faith in one's station in life will become tenuous. When Riabovich in "The Kiss" ceases to believe in the kiss he received in that dark room one night, it signals the death of his new life and his fresh way of looking at the world. In "The Story of Miss N. N." images of death follow Natalia's attempt to understand whether or not she loves Petr Sergeich. She does not seize the moment; instead she falls into a sleep that resembles Varka's in "Sleepy"—the sleep of death.

Chekhov's characters seem to have the power to seize chance moments, the Proustian *moments bienheureux:* a kiss, a bit of love, or a touch of happiness may emerge from the blur and mist of time to give an ordinary life a privileged moment, an instant of changed perceptions. Time passes, though, forcing those rare moments of vitality back into the death of the past. Everything fades away in Chekhov. The Chekhovian character's life slips into dreary nothingness, because he has so little faith in the inherent vitality of the present moment.

II * EXPERIMENTS, 1883–1887

Chekhov found his earliest impressionistic métier in the "chameleon stories."[23] During this phase Chekhov's protagonist, like his namesake, the chameleon, changes his appearance to suit surrounding conditions. In this world of perceived surfaces change is determined by relationships to an environment. An inexplicable shift in mood will produce a change in sight, sound, odor, or texture. It makes no difference that it seems capricious; the identity of the chameleon is altered. If the chameleon adapts himself to avoid the danger of isolation in a potentially hostile environment, he also faces the possibility of losing his identity in the merger of self and habitat.

The chameleon always changes in relation to something— and it is usually space rather than time. He turns green in the spring and brown in the autumn because he must fit the visual pattern of the space around him. The same would be true of a geographical or topographical change. His shifting identity is affected by spatial juxtaposition, but it is a reality in flux through both time and space. The changes time engenders on space, whether through the cycle of seasons or the physical transformations of human and vegetable growth, all result in the phenomenological relativism of chameleonic metamorphosis.

The impressionist painters were also interested in chameleonic juxtaposition. Their paintings showed how something appeared when a certain quality of light struck it at a particular moment. Sometimes in a series of paintings they rendered the changes that different light made when shed on the same object. Their experiments demonstrated that a color changed when juxtaposed with colors of different hues, values, and tones. The literary impressionists positioned their subjects in conflicting settings. This contiguity dramatized the changes that affected the atmosphere of an entire environment. Chekhov's early impressionism was an experiment in spatial chameleonism and its effects on the identity of his characters.

Chekhov's most important chameleon story, "The Fat and the Thin" (*Tolstyi i tonkii*), 1883, concerns two old school mates, one thin and the other fat, who meet by chance at a train station after many years. The thin man, who initially feels proud of his family and confident of his position in life, is transformed into an obsequious nonentity when he realizes his old friend's higher rank. During the story Thin will remain thin, continue to smell of ham and coffee grounds, and keep smiling; Fat will remain fat, exude sherry and *fleurs d'oranger* cologne, and project the deportment of a privy councilor. But Thin, the chameleon, will change identity: once satisfied with himself, his family, and his life, he is reduced to a state of cringing, fawning servility. The chameleon is neither inherently self-satisfied nor essentially docile. His identity is shaped by his limited perspective of a seemingly limitless world of relations. In this sphere of relativistic surfaces, the chameleon, forever unsure of his reality, finds that only in abrupt transformations of appearance can he feel momentarily at one with his milieu. Chekhov explores only the manifestations of change, not the causes of transformation. One of the touchstones of Chekhov's impressionism is changeless change. Thin's outward appearances remain; there is the odor of ham and coffee grounds and the smile. Yet the new perspective transforms his inner surface. When the two men leave, neither will appear to have changed. In later stories the cycles of change cloaked in changelessness will become more complexly important.

In the beginning of the story, Fat spots Thin and is delighted, exclaiming that "it's been ages since we met!" (2:10). Recognition is instantaneous. Presumably, both appear quite as they did many years ago—time has not physically recast them. Thin responds with "Where did you come from?," as though he must

search out the origin of this vision from the past. That question
is left unanswered, Chekhov objectively noting that "both were
pleasantly surprised." This joy can hold only so long as the void
of the past does not become the confrontation of the present. The
past makes no demands upon them; they only remember they
had been friends. Thin begins to ask questions that will inevitably lead to comparisons. So long as the chameleon remains
within a stable environment his color will not change. He will
not change unless he finds himself confronted with a new relational configuration, one that could threaten his present identity. This thin, unaware chameleon blithely launches into a
self-satisfied introduction of his family and a modest but pleased
account of his achievements. Unable to allow the relationship to
exist in this unjuxtaposed emptiness, Thin asks about his friend's
accomplishments, even suggesting in the generosity of his own
satisfaction a rank slightly higher than his own. Fat, also pleased
with his success, asks Thin to guess higher. It is finally revealed
that Fat has attained the breath-taking rank of privy councilor.
The chameleon freezes.

Time stops, and for an instant we witness a grotesque spatial
metamorphosis: "Thin suddenly paled, became petrified, but his
whole face was immediately distorted by smiles; yet it seemed
as though the sparkle in his face and eyes completely disap-
peared. He shrivelled, shrank, and stooped. . . . His cheap suit-
case shrivelled and grew wrinkled. . . . His wife's long chin grew
longer" (2:11). In this process, hypostasis precedes metastasis;
Thin essentially fossilizes (okamenel) before he returns to the
living in a changed form. The smile which had earlier been
simply an expression of pleasure becomes a distorted gesture of
pain. He and his environment "seem" physically transfigured.
Chekhov situates the verb "to seem" (kazat'sia) precisely before
the almost surreal transformation, so that the perceived changes
remain indeterminate. And he does not enter Thin's consciousness, preferring instead the impressionist's technique of rendering psychological turmoil through physical change. The smell
of ham and coffee grounds now completely personifies him. He
reintroduces his wife and son, because he feels that not only does

he have a new identity but that everything connected with him must also have changed. The repeated introduction dramatizes this—the same words bathed in a new light become completely different, the tone and ring of the words create a new man. In the first introduction they conveyed a sense of pride, now they fall flat with apology.[24] The earlier friendly assurance, "my dear friend," is replaced by, "your excellency," and, as a finishing touch, Thin loses all his dignity with the traditionally silly *chinovnik*'s giggle, "he, he."

The rest of the story plays out the resulting instability of reality. Fat immediately notices the transformation: "Why use this tone?" (2:64). His desire for permanence in the face of a changed reality both angers and puzzles him: "We are childhood friends—what is this respect for ranks!" (2:11). Fat is determined to resist the tenuous transience of past/present. The past, however, no longer exists; it has vanished with the present juxtaposition of ranks and stations in life. Fat succumbs to the changing environment when a feeling of nausea sweeps over him at the sight of the mawkish grovelling written all over Thin. Fat also turns away, presumably changed by the experience.

The final line of the story, "All three were pleasantly surprised" (2:12), highlights the impressionist's irony and method. It is a repeated variation, like Thin's introduction and reintroduction of his family, of the initial joyful surprise expressed by both men on meeting one another, which when repeated after the metamorphosis turns sour. Thin has been completely recast, and in his eyes so has his family, but yet nothing seems to have changed; he is "pleasantly surprised" both before and after his transformation. The ironies and implications of this final line are complex and elusive. It demonstrates the openended ambiguity, the repetitive brush strokes of changed effects, and the harmonic tinting of impressionist stories. "The Fat and the Thin" has no plot and remains simply a momentary impression of a small piece of time.

The chameleon stories are important to Chekhov's impressionism, because they form the seed for so many later structures that will find more complex human and aesthetic forms: the simple change of color will become a fluid network of human alterations constantly seeking to find an identity among the nuances of a shifting reality. Ambiguity, changeless change, fragmentation, and isolation will all reappear in Chekhov's highly compressed impressionistic vision. Chekhov continued his apprenticeship by writing stories about children as innocent perceivers and delirium as a cause for perceptual distortion. These stories became vehicles for testing the limits of subjective perception. It is as though he felt he must learn to see the fresh, chaotic, and expanding world of a child through the child's primitive eyes and that he must also discover the point at which perceptions can become realistically distorted before passing into the illusions of fantasy.

In the story "Oysters" (*Ustritsy*), 1884, Chekhov combines a child's point of view (first person narration) with a delirious state, filtered through a perceived remembrance of a perceived incident. The immediacy of present sensations becomes superimposed on the distant past. This effect evokes both the tenuous ambiguity of memory and the concrete credibility of instantaneity. This will become an important technique in Chekhov's impressionism. The narrator of "Oysters" recalls an incident that took place when he was eight years old. He has come with his father to beg for food and it is his first publicly humiliating experience. His hunger has grown to the point that he is delirious. So when he sees a sign with the word *restaurant* on it, his mind becomes a mass of swirling projections, random perceptions, and intensified sensations. These are not rendered expressionistically, but through the subtle play of intensified perceptions Chekhov creates an externalized object that shifts, moves, and swirls in the same manner as the perceiving mind:

> Before us was a large three story house with a blue sign: "Restaurant." My head drooped weakly backwards and to one side, and I could not help looking up at the lighted windows of the restaurant. In the windows flashed human figures. I saw on the right side of the orchestration, two oleographs, hanging lamps. . . . Staring into one of the windows, I perceived a white patch. The patch was motionless, and its rectangular outlines stood out

sharply against the dark, brown background. I looked intently and made out of the patch a white sign on the wall. Something was written on it, but that name—I couldn't see. . . .

For half an hour I kept my eyes on that sign. Its white magnetized my eyes as if it had hypnotized my brain. I tried to read it but my efforts were futile.

Finally the strange disease took over.

The sound of the carriages began to seem to me like thunder, in the stench of the street I was able to distinguish a thousand smells, the restaurant and street lights blinded my eyes like lightning. My five senses were strained and seized beyond the limits of normalcy. I began to see what I had never seen before. (2:84)

The most imposing element in this passage is the passivity of the boy's perceptions: "I could not help looking. . . . Its white magnetized my eyes." A perceiver without consciousness, as Henry James made abundantly clear, becomes a passive agent through whom sensations pass. This narrator, like Henry Fleming in *The Red Badge of Courage*, simply stands in confused and inert awe as the elements of a broken world flash by him. His eyes seem to wander, then come to rest on the sign in a futile effort to exert control over his perceptions and his world. This fails because the "something" that was written seems hidden from his view. Later, it seems he did not understand the word "oysters." Perceptual ambiguity takes on many forms. To control these forms is the active quest of the impressionistic sensibility. Until the boy can find a way to momentarily check the chaotic world, to stay the flood of imbalance, as many of James's characters do, he will be forever dominated by the external world. The equilibrium of subject and object occurs when the perceiver understands that limited perception can only be translated into limited knowledge. The narrator of this story becomes lost in the sign, not because it will not reveal itself to him, but because he is unable to conceptualize the entire configuration of a word that has no empirical referent for him. Lack of knowledge and hunger conspire to transform a simple sign into a fragmented and impressionistically distorted experience.

What the boy sees, then, are raw perceptions directly expressed with the speed of their movement and the uncontrolled randomness of his growing delirium. The story's structure is based upon the boy's growing ability to make associations out of the uncontrolled passivity of arbitrary perceptions. His experiences begin in the incoherence of disconnected objects: "lighted windows," "human figures," "two oleographs, hanging lamps," "white patch," "something written," "sound of carriages," "thousand smells," "restaurant and street lights." These objects direct him to the incomprehensible word *oysters*, which is nothing more than another random object, but he asks his father what the word means. This gesture of curiosity initiates him into the more orderly world of human consciousness. His father does not at first hear the boy's question; he too, in a very Chekhovian way, is isolated in his own perceptual world: "He was watching the movements of the crowd and following every passer-by with his eyes." The boy asks again and the father responds that an oyster is an animal that lives in the sea. The boy's perceptual imagination locates the only images associated with his world: "I instantly pictured to myself this unknown sea animal. . . . I felt that his smell was tickling my palate and nostrils, that it was gradually taking possession of my whole body. . . . I moved my jaws and swallowed as if I really had a piece of this sea animal in my mouth." This imaginary picture exists as a perceptual reality for him. But when his father tells him that oysters are eaten alive and have shells like tortoises, the flavor immediately changes and he now pictures an animal that looks like a frog staring at him as he is about to eat it. This image triggers a new and disgusting perceptual reality.

The hunger-induced delirium has sensitized his perceptions; he has grown: "My five senses were strained and seized beyond the limits of normalcy. I began to see what I had never seen before." The pain of hunger and exposed perceptual nerve endings is a concomitant part of his expanded perceptual awareness. Finally, in desperation and recognition he shouts out the word "oysters." He is taken into the restaurant and forced to eat so many oysters that he passes out as a wave of laughter from the spectators washes over his consciousness. Too much hunger and excessive satisfaction strain the senses. He dreams of "a frog

sitting in a shell moving its eyes," and when he awakens he sees
his father, all arms, "walking up and down gesticulating" (2:
86). The dream is like his waking imagination and his waking
vision of his father gesticulating is dreamlike. For the impressionists all levels of reality have sensory validity and all surfaces
are real.

"Grisha" (1886) returns to the simple spontaneity of the
naive perceiver, the child, whose perceptual world will expand
in the crucible of new experiences. "Grisha" represents the best
of Chekhov's "children's stories" (disallowing "Sleepy" and
"The Steppe," which transcend such a narrow genre). These
stories allowed him to experiment with pure, raw, and seemingly unintellectualized perceptual impressions. While Grisha absorbs what exists, he also explores and tests what he sees, hears,
and smells against what he knows.

Grisha is almost three years old and off on his first trip outside the house. The progression of this story (actually no more
than a series of impressions determined by his physical movements) moves from Grisha's room, where he feels the familiarity
of known objects, to the less recognizable rooms of the house,
and finally outside into complete confusion. His movements
through space correspond to the expansion of his consciousness.
He will attempt to make the connective links of the less familiar
sensory world with those of the more familiar. What he knows
consists of toys, a bed, a mother who looks like a doll (when he
has two known objects he attempts to order his world through
visual associations), a nurse, a cat that feels like his father's fur
coat (tactile juxtaposition). In the outer reaches of his home he
focuses on those objects that have some immediate relationship
to him: color (red chairs), the anger of adults (seen as a stain
on the carpet "for which fingers are still shaken at Grisha" [5:
7]), doors through which he is not allowed to enter (the study
of that strange, enigmatic person who is his father), and a drum
given to him (by a lady who continually appears and disappears
—his aunt). Grisha's world is limited, so Chekhov must define its
limits; his world is largely inexplicable, so Chekhov must demonstrate its lack of causality and knowability; his world is ego-

centric, so Chekhov must convey only those impressions directly and immediately perceived by Grisha.

When Grisha confronts the outside world, he continues to perceive everything in terms of what he knows, but the multiplication of those relationships thrusts him into the terrifying morass of uncertainty: "there are so many papas, mamas and aunts that there is no knowing who to run to" (5:8). The huge horses have nothing to do with either pictures or play horses: "Grisha gazes at their moving legs, and can make nothing of it. He looks at his nurse for her to solve the mystery, but she does not speak." This kaleidoscopic world thrusts Grisha into new and mystifying perspectives.

"Typhus" (*Tif*), 1887, is a less significant but intensely concentrated rendering of a man's delirious perceptions as he realizes that he has contracted typhus. A train speeds him through the transient countryside, yet he remains enclosed in the train's rush through time, creating an imperceptible void. Time becomes so compressed that he feels only the sensations of space. The typhus intensifies all perceptions, as hunger did for the boy in "Oysters," so his entire delirium consists of a vast barrage of fragmented sensory stimuli that breaks down the distinctions between dream and reality:

His thoughts seemed to be straying not only within but also outside his head, among the seats and people wrapped in the nightly mist. Through the chimera, as though through sleep, he heard the murmur of voices, the clattering of wheels, the slamming of doors. The clanging of bells, the guards' whistles, people running up and down the platform were heard more often than usual. Time flew quickly by, imperceptibly, and then it seemed that the train stopped at the station every minute, at each stop could be heard metallic voices. . . . The noise, the whistle, the Finn, the tobacco smoke . . . all this mingled with the menacing, flickering, and misty images, forms whose character healthy men are not able to remember. (6:105)

The delirium allows Klimov to perceive new combinations of elements: the concrete sounds and smells "mingle" with the vague forms of "people wrapped in the nightly mist" and "metallic voices." This passage effectively demonstrates the early

pictorial quality of Chekhov's impressionism: the fusion of subject and object, and the use of "seems" ("his thoughts seemed to
be straying . . . among the seats"), the strong emphasis on disconnected and disembodied sensory objects, and the quality of
imperceptibly transient moments. The story ends on a note of
ambiguous irony. When Klimov awakens after his long bout
with typhus he discovers that his sister had contracted his disease
and died. His guilt, pain, and loss commingle with his own joy
at being alive. The typhus has opened the possibilities of a bewildering world of joined polarities and disparities. His sense of
loss finally gives way to the joy of life. Klimov's consciousness
has grown through his impressions of a delirious journey.

   With "Typhus" Chekhov ended a highly rewarding but purely experimental phase of impressionism. He had explored the
figurative chameleons who find that they must radically change
to fit the shift in their newly perceived environment ("The Fat
and the Thin," "The Chameleon," "This and That," "Two in
One"); children who exemplify the phenomenological *tabula
rasa* ("Grisha," "The Boys," "A Common Trifle," "At Home,"
"Vanka"); and characters who because of hunger, sickness, or
other excessive physical demands find their perceptions distorted
("Oysters," "Typhus," "Dreams"). These stories are suffused
with objects of perception rendered so as to correspond to a character's perceptual consciousness.

III * THE LOST PAST, 1887

In 1887 Chekhov wrote three stories which launched him into a
more mature, controlled, and complex period of impressionism:
"Verochka," "The Kiss" (*Potselui*), and "The Story of Miss
N. N." (*Rasskaz Gospozhi N. N.*). These stories form a triumvirate of characters who remember an incident that might have
made life richer had an opportunity not been missed or a privileged moment not faded into the confusion of the present. These
stories explore an ephemeral reality through perceived time and
memory. They evoke, simultaneously, a sense of loss rendered

through the passage of time and a sense of renewal achieved through the recapture of the past in the immediacy of relived presentness. The past becomes the present, as Chekhov moves into a character's "central consciousness."

In the opening of "Verochka," Chekhov brings the past into sharp focus through an associational object: a straw hat. Ognov, the narrator, "remembers how on that August evening he noisily opened the glazed hall door and went out onto the terrace. He wore a light cloak and a wide-brimmed straw hat—the very hat which now, beside his boots, lies in the dust beneath his bed. He remembers that he carried a heavy package of books and manuscripts, and that in his free hand was a heavy walking stick" (6:60). It is not clear whether the straw hat triggers the remembrance or simply represents the indiscriminate and involuntary emergence of the past. The cause of the reminiscence remains undetermined. But an ambiguous relationship between the past and the present breaks into open conflict: the present clarity of his past is at odds with his earlier belief that the past "would recur only in memory as the shapeless impressions of a dream" (6:71). Remembering the past with such vividness suggests a permanence that Ognov does not recognize. He believed that the immediacy and importance of any moment would be lost in the flickering image of passing time. Experience filtered through the prism of time would have no more reality than a dream. Yet his detailed sensory recollection of Proustian "pure time" belies his beliefs. The life of the past has been reperceived and fused into a present moment of living past/present.

Unlike the chameleon stories, time rather than space provides the basis for perceived change. Whether change is perceived through space or time, it remains ambiguous and elusive. Ognov tells Vera that "now we feel the present, it absorbs and agitates us, but in the future we will not remember the date, the month, even the year, when we sat on this bridge together for the last time. You, of course, will be changed. You will change" (6:67). The irony of time is that he now remembers with great accuracy the fact that he said they would not remember. But as he sat there in the past with Vera, immersed in the immediate concerns of the moment, Ognov failed to notice the links between those fragments of his existence that constitute change. Seeing only the grand view of change, Ognov neglects the alterations taking place before his very eyes. Only when he becomes aware that Vera has not been listening to his pompous oratory, but has been preoccupied instead with her love for him, does he begin to perceive instantaneous change: "only now did Ognov notice the change that had come over Vera."

Chekhov's characters enter a story giving the impression of having led a life of unqualified boredom and triviality. During the course of the story something happens to momentarily unsettle their lives, then it passes back into the stream of time. They seem to return to their stagnant lives. Have they been changed? Something has happened to these people! Faulkner's Quentin Compson in *Absalom, Absalom* best describes Chekhovian change: "Maybe happen is never once but like ripples maybe on the water after the pebble sinks, the ripples moving on, spreading, the pool attached by a narrow umbilical water-cord to the next pool which the first pool feeds, has fed, did feed, let this second pool contain a different temperature of water, a different molecularity of having seen, felt, remembered, reflect in a different tone the infinite unchanging sky, it doesn't matter."[25] Perhaps only their temperature or molecular structure has been altered, but that *is* change, however hidden and inexplicable. Chekhov's characters, however, seem incapable of perceiving in themselves the necessary indices of change. Even when they peer into the past, the ironies of time are lost on them.

From the mid-eighties Chekhov focused on the evanescent quality of love and the resulting precariousness of shifting relationships to convey the tenuous nature of impressionistic reality. Ognov's sense of indeterminacy permeates the central issue of "Verochka": "I am now twenty nine years old, yet have never had a single romance! In all my life so far, not one! So of trysts, paths of sighs, and kisses, I know only by hearsay. It is abnormal. Sitting in my own room in town, I never notice the void. But here in the open air I somehow feel it . . . strongly . . . it is almost annoying." "But what is the cause?" asks Verochka.

"I don't know" (6:64). Ognov understands that he cannot identify a cause for his emptiness, yet it is just as impossible to find
an explanation for those things that do happen to him. Could
Vera perceive the cause of her love for Ognov? Could he understand the cause of his lack of love for her? Can they, in fact,
understand the nature of love itself? The sensation of having to
confront something for which he is not prepared, does not understand, and cannot feel, drives him to emotional extremes, forcing him to perceive his situation from different perspectives.

Vera's declaration of love challenges the fixed stability of his
statistical world. Nothing in his prior experiences has prepared
him for the vicissitudes of love, guilt, confusion, fright, and uncertainty. His rapid shifts in perception and feeling reveal the
fluctuating qualities of impressionistic reality:

The atmosphere of mournfulness, warmth, and sentiment inspired by the
liqueurs and leavetakings, suddenly made way for a sharp, unpleasant
feeling of awkwardness. Feeling that his whole soul had been turned inside out, he looked shyly at Vera. . . . "What does it all mean?" he asked
himself in terror. "And then . . . do I love her . . . or not?—that is the
problem." . . . The wood, the patches of mist, even the black roadside
ditches were charmed, it seemed, as they listened. But Ognov's heart felt
only estrangement and pain. . . . But Ognov felt not the pleasure or vital
joy which he himself yearned for, but only sympathy with Vera, and pain
that a fellow creature should suffer so for his sake. Heaven only knows
why it was so! All that Ognov had said, even his last words, seemed to him
flat and hateful. The feeling increased with each step. . . . It seemed to
Ognov that she had suddenly grown slighter and that her shoulders were
narrower. . . . His movements expressed doubt about himself. . . . For the
first time in his life he realized how little one's actions depend on mere
goodwill. . . . With Vera, it seemed to him a part of his youth had passed
away, and he knew that the precious moments he had let slip away without profit would never return. (6:68–69)

Ognov's sudden transformations of feeling and attitude, while
they appear to take place in the flow of time, are so abrupt that
the impact is felt in discrete units, one against another—spatially. There is no causal sequence. The changes simply occur.
Chekhov's story appears to be about impressions experienced in
instants of evanescent love (Proust's themes). But since these
momentary flashes are isolated from one another in Ognov's

consciousness, hypostatized in almost plastic images, they are not apprehended in sequence. They are felt as separate moments in time—almost timeless, now—lost and trying to be recaptured. Ognov's attempt to recover the past cannot be read as his effort to understand the present, but simply as a random bid to seize something that might have been. "Verochka" stands as a breakthrough for Chekhov. It is one of his pivotal stories, which, like "The Steppe" and "Sleepy," leads him to new and more complex ground.

"The Kiss" continued many of the same impressionistic motifs found in "Verochka." The shifts in perceived reality are more pervasive and the ambiguity more controlled. This story has not one passage in present tense, but, as in "Verochka," the texture of immediacy is intense. This past presentness is important to Chekhov's impressionism, for it allows the freedom and credibility of distance and the energy and immanence of immediacy. The impressionist must continually balance these polarities so as to maintain an equilibrium between the inner and outer world.

The first indication that Riabovich's perceptions will become the subject of this story occurs when he goes to a neighbor's party: "On first entering the room, and later, when he sat down to tea, he was unable to fix his attention on any one face or object. The faces, dresses, cut glass decanters of cognac, the steaming glasses, the molded cornices—all merged into a single, overwhelming impression which inspired in him a feeling of alarm and a desire to hide his head. Like a lecturer appearing before the public for the first time, he saw everything that was before his eyes, but seemed to have only a vague conception of it (physiologists call such a condition, in which the subject sees but does not understand, 'psychic blindness'). After a little while Riabovich grew accustomed to his surroundings, recovered his sight, and began to observe" (6:341). Chekhov not only renders this scene with scientific precision and psychological accuracy, but he also works a new variation on the chameleon theme.

Riabovich's subjectively perceived encounter with an event or believed event (the kiss) will create for him a new identity.

Viewing his surroundings through new eyes will produce a reciprocal reaction, so that those at the party will regard him differently as well. This, of course, can only lead to a new self-image. In the beginning he is struck by the insincerity of the guests, by the stale odor of the flowers and trees, and by his own sense of timidity and inadequacy. But on returning to the drawing room, "he met with a little adventure. . . . At that moment he was surprised by the sound of hasty footsteps and the rustle of a dress; a breathless, feminine voice whispered, 'At last!' and two soft, perfumed, unmistakably feminine arms were thrown around his neck, a warm cheek was pressed to his, and at the same time there was the sound of a kiss [*i odnovremenno razdalsia zvuk potselui*]. Immediately the bestower of the kiss uttered a faint scream and sprang away, as it seemed to Riabovich, in disgust" (6:344). What is remarkable about this scene is the number of passive constructions, the sense of sheer accident, the planting of the "kiss" ("there was the sound of a kiss"), the number of sensory perceptions operative here in the dark, and finally Riabovich's feeling that she was revulsed by the mistake. He did not create the event, being instead the passive receptor of a chance occurrence. Yet this "kiss" will alter his perceptions and create a new reality.

Chekhov is moving even further toward the evocation of a totally ephemeral reality. In "Verochka," Vera said that she loved Ognov (it is entirely possible that Chekhov, on the outer reaches of epistemological indeterminacy, wishes to throw that, too, into question, since it is only through Ognov's memory that she declares her love for him). In "The Kiss" we are held more completely in the sway of Riabovich's unconfirmed belief in a quite ambiguous "kiss." Was he or was he not kissed? It ultimately makes no difference, because when Riabovich reenters the party he has become a chameleon:

He shrank into himself and looked about uneasily, but after convincing himself that everyone in the room was dancing and chatting quite as calmly as before, he gave himself up to his new and never-before-experienced sensation. Something strange was happening to him. . . . His neck, round which the soft, perfumed arms had so lately been clasped, felt as though it had been anointed with oil; on his left cheek near his mustache, where the unknown lady had kissed him, there was a slight tingling, a delightful chill, as from peppermint drops, and the more he rubbed it the stronger the sensation became; from head to foot he was filled with a strange new feeling which continued to grow and grow. . . . He wanted to dance, to talk, to run into the garden, to laugh aloud. . . . He completely forgot that he was round-shouldered and colorless, that he had lynx-like whiskers and a "nondescript appearance" (as he had once been described by some ladies whose conversation he had accidentally overheard). (6: 344)

The transformation is complete. The problem now facing Riabovich is how to maintain this pleasing color he now possesses. The kiss permeates his entire vision. So long as he is able to retain that memory, his fresh, exciting life will exist. Yet he feels he must find a rational explanation for it: he "tried to understand what had just happened to him. . . . This was how Riabovich explained to himself the kiss he had received. . . . And who is she?" (6:345). He forces himself to reconstruct the woman from a composite of the women at the party. Impressionist characters, however, cannot control their falsely unified world: he "tried to gather together the flashing images in his mind and to combine them into a whole. But nothing came of it. . . . All this he pictured to himself clearly and distinctly, but the features of the face, the sweet sleepy smile, just what was characteristic and important, slipped through his imagination like quicksilver through the fingers" (6: 348, 349).

Later, as he begins to lose his grip on even these images, he resorts to fantasy: "but how he bade farewell to logic and gave himself up to dreams" (6:350). Failing in this, he desperately forces *his* reality out into the external world to be tested. He tells the story of the "kiss" to his comrades. There is nothing to tell, however, because the kiss was not an event but the perception of a sensation. Not only is the existence of the kiss questionable, but the highly individualized quality of his sensations defies translation into language. Scrutiny by the other officers begins to destroy his image: "She must have been some sort of lunatic," "a similar thing once happened to me," "how could you see the lips if it was dark?" (6: 352, 353). Riabovich sought out these officers not only to keep alive the reality of his "kiss" but also to break the loneliness of his isolation, an isolation created by the knowledge that his "kiss" might not have occurred. Riabovich vows never to tell a confidence again. This way he can preserve the romantic flavor of his existence, while he retains his romantic isolation from the human community. So he acts as though he were in love: "The days flowed by, one very much like another. All those days Riabovich felt, thought, and behaved as though he were in love" (6:353).

His thoughts become more fragmented as he obsessively clings to an image that begins to disappear. He calls up random bits of detail from his past and listens to pieces of conversation from his comrades. He makes no attempt to order his experiences. Believing it necessary for him to actually reexperience the "kiss," he returns to the town where the party had been held and waits for an invitation. But this chameleon senses that his now vibrant coloring will revert to its original flat, dull tone. He prepares himself for this eventuality (actually of his own self-perceived making), by viewing the kiss as a mundane moment in a humdrum life:

Now that he expected nothing, the incident of the kiss, his impatience, his vague hopes and disappointment, presented themselves to him in a clear light. It no longer seemed to him strange that the General's messenger never came and that he would never see the girl who had accidentally kissed him instead of someone else; on the contrary, it would have been strange if he had seen her. . . . And the whole world, the whole of life, seemed to Riabovich an unintelligible, aimless jest. . . . And turning his eyes from the water and looking at the sky, he remembered again how Fate in the person of an unknown woman had by chance caressed him, he recalled his summer dreams and fancies, and his life struck him as extraordinarily meager, poverty-stricken, and drab. (6:355)

Riabovich, the chameleon and lost dreamer, realizes that he can no longer preserve the "kiss" and that it can never be actually reexperienced. So he changes his perspective, thus changing his identity: if the past pervades the present they become one, but when the beautiful past returns to its isolated distance, the present then seems "meager, poverty-stricken, and drab" by comparison. But for that moment of the "kiss," and only in its afterglow, Riabovich experienced the splendor, romance, and sensory impressions of pure love through pure time. It had been a changeless frozen moment, but as it became subjected to the vicissitudes of transitory time Riabovich's perceptions of it changed. He does not have the power to believe in something he can no longer see, feel, hear, and smell. So he loses faith in the past. The cycle becomes complete—change within changelessness.

In "The Story of Miss N. N.," Chekhov again places in relief the enduring fluidity of time that produces ecstasy and loss. Natalia Vladimirovna remembers a summer afternoon some nine years ago, when everything she felt, saw, and smelled was imbued with her love for an impoverished assistant magistrate, Petr Sergeich. Natalia was in love with Petr, the smell of the hay, the sound of the rain beating on the grass and roofs, the thunder, and the "slanting rain." She was also in love with herself. It was a moment in which love pervaded her whole being, a moment reminiscent of Tolstoy's natural pantheism. As storm clouds suddenly break, her sensory perceptions become heightened to impressionistic imagery: the dark clouds become juxtaposed against the "house and the church [that] looked white, and the tall poplars seemed turned to silver" (6:383). The thunderous storm produces in Natalia and Petr a concomitant turbulence of emotional and perceptual exuberance. They laugh together at the prospect of entering a medieval castle at the moment it is struck by lightning. For the first time in a Chekhov story joy and death become fused through the union of subject-object, changing weather and the cycle of seasons. Nature, as the impressionist painters knew, can act as the perfect index for projecting the changing perceptions of man onto the constant transformations of his environment. Chekhov began to explore this relationship most fully in "The Story of Miss N. N." Later it will become the very heart of his impressionism.

The story opens with the past set against the present. The past is the summer of the year and of Natalia's life; the present is the end of the story, the winter with "red coals changed into ashes and going out" (6:387), the frost knocking fiercely on the windows, and her life ruined by a sense of irretrievable loss. She seems to be asleep by the end of the story, slipping into what appears to be hibernation and death. Death, then, is just as natural a process as laughter, and both are a part of man and nature. Laughter, joy, and love are the things man wishes to hold on to, while he attempts to retreat from the inevitability of death. Both require stopping time. Natalia and Petr cling to their moment of joy. He says to her, "I would give everything I possess if I could only remain thus and look at you forever" (6:384). She sees him with the raindrops in his beard and mustache glistening, "and they too seemed to look at me with love." She personifies the raindrops, so that, like the poets, she can objectify and thus grasp the evanescence of love. Nature and man become one and she sees the three of them, Petr, nature, and herself, conjoined in a phenomenal relationship. He asks her to "continue to be silent," as though he can stop time through the void of silence. She too feels the desire to live like this forever: "I wished to look at his brilliant eyes and listen to him without end." But the storm clouds pass away and the thunder becomes silent, signalling the end of their interlude of tumultuous passion and love-filled silences. Nature reflects the change before Natalia can see it, because the raindrops still glisten in Petr's beard after both the storm and passion have passed away.

That evening Petr tells her that "when you ate fresh cucumbers in the winter you had the taste of spring in your mouth" (6:385). This folk saying acts as the controlling sensory metaphor for both the entire story and Natalia's experience. It is like the Indian summer of Emily Dickinson's poem, "these are the days when birds come back." Natalia's reverie of lost love is her fresh cucumber. The intense immediacy of the taste momentarily overcomes the rush toward the future and the loss of the past. Chekhov's characters, like Proust's, relive their pasts again and again, hoping they might encounter a momentary respite from continual change. This only exacerbates the oscillation between life and death, joy and sadness, realization and loss, stasis and change.

Later that same evening Natalia lay awake in bed giving herself up to the "indeterminate feelings that possessed my soul" (6:385). She tries to understand, as Ognov had done, the incomprehensibility of love. She thinks of herself as loved, but even more so as rich and distinguished—she objectifies herself. Finally, "not being able to understand anything I fell asleep." Natalia cannot decide whether to yield to the indeterminate or strive for complete understanding. This equivocation sends a shiver of cold through her, driving the warmth of love and joy from her. She simply cannot accept the enigmas of love. She wakes up the next morning with the vestiges of yesterday's joys, but they are no longer the life of the moment and so must disappear like Riabovich's kiss: "And what then? And then—nothing. Winter . . ." The incisiveness of the prose is staggering; with these few strokes Chekhov destroys the future with the past and offers nothing but the winter. Miss N. N. must live out a dreary present without moments. Winter, imperceptible time, walls of separation, voids of silence, and images of death await those who can no longer believe in the presentness of the past.

Chekhov, the impressionist, changes the tone, images, and mental state of Natalia when she moves to the city for the winter. Petr still speaks of their love, "but how different it sounded when spoken in the village." Natalia muses on the slothful degeneracy of society. Yet the feeling that her moment has passed traps her in the indolence of enclosed time and space. Memory fades as the walls of human isolation become thicker and the cold freezes the happiness of her soul: "And all this so charming and wonderful in recollection passed quickly by me unvalued, as with everybody, leaving no trace and vanished like a mist. . . . Where is it all? . . . My father died. I have grown old" (6:386). This is, of course, the natural cycle. But her desire for stasis and the realization of its impossibility isolates her from the natural feelings love had once so freely bestowed upon her. She begins to see the world as "a flat empty plain." This entropic image will give "Sleepy" and "The Steppe" a Beckett-like backdrop against which change is played out. Life becomes a journey where movement seems negligible in relation to the vast plain of time and space. There are no beginnings and endings, no highs and lows.

Winter ends and spring approaches, but Natalia cannot recapture the past, even though she "whispers the same words." Petr is always near, but this only increases her distance from him as they sit in long silences or attempt the incantations that brought them to life that one summer. Nothing works. He leaves with a gesture of impotence, which only heightens her feeling of pity for him. She returns to her bedroom where once again the frost is on the windows, the coals have turned to ashes, and the wind sings a song about "something." Her final sleep/wake suggests an escape from life, a drift into the past of lost love, and a movement toward death.

In these five years of serious beginnings, Chekhov produced some truly impressionistic stories. Many of the elements in these stories would find their way, with more controlled ambiguity and more subtly fragmented brushstrokes, into his most important stories. The early stories often seemed to verge on caricature, parody, or sketch, reflecting the journalistic commercialism of his apprenticeship. But Chekhov's early style was also restlessly searching for an impressionist aesthetic. Change, even then, was at the heart of his stories. He explored the possibilities of change in relation to space and time. He demanded that his characters respond only to perceived reality, while he worked on the problems of central consciousness. He soon discovered that by examining a subject such as love in relation to time he could render the ephemeral nature of impressionistic reality.

His chameleon stories demonstrated a concern for the fusion of subject and object. Appearances become reality in the relativistic shifts of space and time. The chameleon finds himself caught between the green leaves of the tree and the brown of its bark. To change is to be protected, but there will always be that transitional instant when he is left isolated and exposed against an inharmonious background. How does he perceive his world and himself? Children, too, find their existences just as precarious, because they perceive more than they can know. As their

perceptual frame of reference grows—through physical movement in relation to changing objects—their consciousnesses
expand. But since they can never complete the connections between objects, or between themselves and objects, a sense of
vertigo characterizes their perceptions. The stories of physical
stress leading to perceptual distortion are simply variations on
this pattern.

The stories of the lost past break more complex ground. Chekhov deepens his central consciousnesses by having them tell a
story of lost love, but with no present realization that that moment of love is forever lost. These stories are narrated in a third
person past tense, but with a highly intense sense of subjective
presentness. Chekhovian irony emerges from a past that is so
distant from the narrator that it comes closer to the reader. The
past is more real than the protagonist ever realizes. This contributes to the impressionistic shift from objects to atmosphere.
The details of the past are seen through the receding mist of
forgetfulness, and the objects of the present cannot exist when
one clings to the past. These characters remember only the sensations of past love, but sensations quickly disappear in their
own impalpability. The fundamental ambiguity of sensations,
their power to create and their brief duration, paved the way
for Chekhov to step up to a higher level of impressionist prose.

* 3 *

Achievement and Hesitation
1888–1897

I * MUSICAL IMPRESSIONISM

From 1888 to 1897, an interval we may broadly describe as his middle period, Chekhov pursued many interests and often found himself adrift in multidirectional phases. In 1888 he thrust himself into national prominence with two impressionistically musical pieces, "Sleepy" (*Spat' khochetsia*) and "The Steppe" (*Step'*). These stories marked an important transition from the the one-dimensionality of his chameleon and perception stories and the emerging impressionism of his lost past stories to a rich and varied impressionistic texture. The next year, 1889, brought on another long and quite important impressionistic piece, "A Dreary Story" (*Skuchnaia istoriia*).

These three stories provided Chekhov with a deep enough lode of impressionism to carry him through the next eight years as he worked other influences out of his system. In 1890 he made his now famous and perhaps fatal trek to Sakhalin. When he returned, his prose, with a few exceptions, became the battleground for two strong influences in his personal and artistic life: objective Darwinian realism against didactic Tolstoyan realism. Each lay in tatters by 1897 when with "In the Cart" (*Na podvode*) Chekhov returned to the impressionism that would dominate his final years.

In 1888 Chekhov wrote to his friend the writer, Korolenko, that his story, "The Man from Sokol," is, "it seems to me, the outstanding work of recent times. It is written like a musical composition, according to all the rules dictated by the artistic instinct" (14:12). That same year Chekhov created two musical compositions of his own that blend the aural and visual sensations of "The Steppe" with the fugue form of "Sleepy." "The Steppe" is a long, undulating, linear piece. As Egorushka journeys across that vast plain he is allowed only the briefest transience of sight and sound. Each perception is different and none doubles back on his experience or imagination to repeat itself. His trip is the rhythmic skimming of the melodies of wind, birds, and night sounds. There are no echoes to create the resonances of harmonic simultaneity. The movement of the piece is forward. In "Sleepy," however, Chekhov composed an impressionistic fugue that is tight in its thematic unity, polyphonic in its juxtaposition of contrapuntal levels of reality, time, and space, and dense in its overlapping fragments of perceptual experience. Varka, the thirteen-year-old nursemaid, caught in the oppression of forced sleeplessness, must break the static pain of her life by fusing the fragments of past and present, sleep and sleeplessness, lullaby and death rattle, laughter and death, sleep and death into one final epiphany—infant/death. She must escape her sleepless oppression. Unlike most of Chekhov's characters, however, she succeeds—that is the tragedy.

The story is deceptive in its drive toward a conclusion so inexorable that it seems not to have the ambiguous drift that characterizes so much of Chekhov's impressionistic work.[1] Varka, because she has a goal—to sleep (*spat' khochetsia*)—is able to unite and reduce all the seemingly disparate fragments of her perceptions into such a powerfully lucid image that it will precipitate a terrifyingly definitive murder. We are forced forward by the staccato rhythms of her mental shifts and the sharp commands of her master and mistress, and yet held in suspension through the encircling labyrinths of her four levels of reality. Underlying this rapid, suspenseful surface movement is a highly complex network of verbal, aural, and visual associations that link and later force a gestalt synthesis of these planes into the triggering of her final act.[2] Not only must Varka intuitively cohere the decomposed images that beset her unconscious mind, but she must also find some means of piecing together the four distinct realities that constantly shatter her consciousness. Only when she unites these strata into a stretto-like crescendo will the suppressed fragments of her unconscious manifest themselves in a conscious act.[3]

Her first level is a partially lived-in world of external reality consisting of abruptly rhythmic commands that must be immediately obeyed. They have no connection to her own consciousness and they tend to isolate her from herself, although each order is prefaced with her name. That which should be hers alone becomes an object of increasing abstraction. In her world of half-sleep (*poluson*) these orders take on the unconscious sensation of a drum beating against her head, which resembles the physical beatings her master regularly serves up to her. This drumming drives a growing hostility ever deeper into her consciousness.

The next level of Varka's reality is represented by the distorted images of the diapers, the huge black trousers, and the shadow of these objects that the green ikon-lamp throws upon the ceiling. Initially, they are simply neutral objects, but as she becomes more desperate they "begin to move in the half-opened, lifeless eyes of Varka" (7:13). As she is drained of self, they begin to fill the void, finally, possessing her brain as they wink at her in some strange sort of personified complicity. Varka also absorbs the stifling odors of the cabbage and leather goods. These are intensified by the suffocating heat that saturates both the house of the master in the present and the hut where her father is dying in the past. These unverbalized sensations—stifling and suffocating (*dushno*)—serve as one of the associational devices that trigger her act of stifling or suffocating (*zadushit'*) the baby to death. It is as though Varka comes to feel, perhaps even understand, what she must do through the linkages of these seemingly demonic images and sensations. Since her desires are too horrifying for conscious thought, she projects murderous animation into these lifeless sensory objects.

The third level of Varka's reality consists of a surreal vision of men and women dragging themselves along that same barren and endless road that emerges in so many Chekhov stories ("Dreams," "The Steppe," "In the Cart"). Shadows follow them, just as the shadow from the diapers and trousers fell on

Varka as she rocked the cradle. Now they suggest shadows of death. These people, trapped on a metaphoric road leading nowhere and enshrouded in a mist through which a dark forest is barely visible, fall in the wet, slimy mud. Varka asks why. But she is also questioning the nature of her existence. The answer— "To sleep, to sleep!" (*Spat', spat'*;)—is, of course, the wish-fulfilling answer to Varka's own condition. The sleep of these exhausted people resembles death. Varka is progressing toward a completed composition.

It is at the fourth level that Varka is able to find the images needed to free herself from her oppressed condition. The lullaby, "*baiu, baiushki, baiu*," that she sings to the infant, releases the remembrance of her father's dying sounds, "*bu, bu, bu, bu*," and thrusts her, almost physically but detachedly, into the past: "and now she sees herself in a dark, suffocating hut." The memory of her father's death and the subsequent humiliation of poverty and oppression finish the piece. To free herself from sleeplessness she must fuse these four planes of existence into one strikingly definitive image—the shattering stretto.

The fugue form would then be complete. "Sleepy" consists of a six part fugue structure: subject, answer, countersubject, exposition, episode, and stretto. The command, "Varka," states the subject of the fugue. Her identity, her sleeplessness, and her desperate act are all tied to these tortuously rhythmic orders. The fugue's answer is the image of the winking, complicitous shadows of diapers and trousers, a reminder of her oppression. These objects take an active part in resolving her dilemma. The screeching shadows of death that follow the falling, sleeping people on the road counter the commands. This countersubject follows the subject through "Sleepy" like a shadow, initiating the associations with death. The fugue's episode is connected to the subject and countersubject by the lullaby Varka must sing to the infant and the death rattle of her father. The episode brings the past into the present and the baby into juxtaposition with death. It releases the themes of the story into a climax of simultaneity, the stretto: that moment when all the threads of Varka's existence become galvanized both into amplification, an operatic fusion of life, and reduction, an analytically definitive invitation to the final letting go—infant/death and sleep.

This union occurs through the increasing frequency with which Varka jumps mentally from one level to another. Finally, the visual, aural, and olfactory sensations from each level seem to coalesce into one image. That image—infant/death—offers only one solution to Varka's predicament: bring death to the child. The common denominators of Varka's sensory levels have been death and the infant. The crescendo of Varka's fugue is the reduction of all themes, harmonies, and images. Externally, the mistress, the baby, and a cricket all screech (*krichat'*).[4] Internally, Varka "sees dark clouds chasing each other across the sky screeching like babies." In this image she has combined the visual and the aural into a fairly early example of Chekhov's strange images (*ostranenie*). Surreally, she envisions crows and magpies perched on telegraph wires, "screeching like babies, trying to wake up the sleeping people." For Varka the screeches are the sounds of pain and oppression, the sounds that hover over her, never permitting sleep. They reinforce the desperation of her sleepless distortions. She does not actively participate in the screeches; she is only the observer. Her lack of involvement explains why the screeches do not connect the fourth level of death with the other three levels of sleeplessness. In order for her to act out her unconscious aggression, she must directly participate in a perceptual activity. Thus, the lullaby's *"Baiu, baiushki, baiu,"* which she herself sings, flows into the *"bu, bu, bu, bu"* of her father's death.

The story builds toward the final four-dimensional stretto. Just before it strikes the final notes, all the perceptual fragments and levels of reality overlap, uniting Varka's unconscious and conscious selves:

"Varka, rock the baby!" rings out the final order.

In the stove the cricket screeches; the green stain on the ceiling and the shadows from the trousers and diapers again penetrate Varka's half-opened eyes, wink at her, and obscure her brain.

"Baiu, baiushki, baiu," she hums. "I'll sing a song for you." But the baby screeches and is exhausted from screaming. Varka again sees the

muddy road, the people with bundles, Pelageia, and her father. She remembers them all, recognizes them all, but through her half-sleep she is
unable, in any way, to understand what force binds her hand and foot,
crushes her, and stifles her life. She looks around her seeking that force in
order to get rid of it, but she cannot find it. Finally, tortured, she strains
all her strength and sight, looks up at the winking green stain and hearing the scream, finds the enemy who is stifling her life.

   This enemy—the baby.

   She laughs. (7:17)

   All the elements that have permeated the story and her brain,
but which had eluded her until now, strike her in what is certainly the shock of recognition. The staccato harmonies of the
piece have been: the command, "Varka," the screeches associated
with the child ("screeches like babies"), the linked lullaby and
rattle, the suffocation of Varka's life commingled with the stifling odors of cabbage and leather, the closeness of the hut, the
final release through the infant's death, the sleeplessness that
pervades the entire story, and the feel of death that seeps
through all levels of Varka's being. It is the infant's scream that
finally assembles the components of the composition into a
fugue. All images cohere around that sight and that sound.

   The dominant downbeat note is the command, "Varka." It
focuses the oppression that does not allow her to sleep. The baby
must be rocked all night and work must be performed all day.
That vicious cycle of exploitation needs to be broken—she must
sleep to avoid going mad or she must go mad in order to sleep.
As she "strains all her strength and sight," she sees the animated
stain that combines the forces of her oppression: the green
ikon-lamp of religion, the diapers of the child, and the huge
black trousers of the master. She feels that her life is being
"stifled." This is the prevalent sensation in the hut of her father's
death and in the master's house permeated with the stink of
cabbage and leather. The baby's screams personify all these
images and seem to say to her, "stifle the life of this baby, the
one who has caused this sleepless oppression, and escape into a
deathlike sleep that will free you from your visions and your
exploitation."

   By reducing the shards of Varka's existence into a concept she feels she could control, Chekhov has anticipated a number of modern literature's most cherished psychopoetic dualities: the fusion of sleep with death, death with laughter, and past with present. The lullaby reminds Varka of her father's death rattle and her desire for sleep is so great that she associates sleep with her father's death. Her vision of the men and women dragging themselves down that surrealistically endless road only to collapse in the mud suggests both sleep and death. Sleep can only come to Varka if the screaming of the baby ends. She may either go passively mad with sleeplessness awaiting the child's sleep or control her life by "stifling" the life out of it. When Varka finally achieves her sleep, she "falls asleep, as though she were dead" (*kak mertvaia*) (7:17). Sleep and death are as irreconcilably wedded as joy is to death: "She suffocates him, then collapses on the floor, laughing with joy, now that she can sleep." Her joy could be the result of her freedom from oppression, and yet that freedom is itself death.

In "The Story of Miss N. N.," written the year before "Sleepy," Natalia's supreme moment of happiness coincided with her fear of being killed by lightning. Joy and death, like love and death, are virtually identical in their unconscious expression of the ultimate letting go. This release transcends the boundaries of time. As in Proust's *"moment bienheureux,"* Varka's points of contact, those sensory associations that joined sleep with death and joy with death, also weld the present to the past in a drive toward the future. Varka transports herself into the past, discovers herself in a timeless juncture where people stumble down an endless road, and then finds herself thrust back into the present with a crack on the head or an order from her mistress. The presentness of both the past and the present is striking. Her projections into the past are narrated in the present tense. The only reason for these journeys into the past is to find a way out of her present and into a future of sleep. In her state of half-sleep Varka seems, on the one hand, suspended in a time void, and on the other, desperate to annihilate this half-state of nothingness by creating a definitive act of presentness. Proust's "pure time" and Faulkner's suspended past-present mythos seem direct legacies of Chekhov's vision.

Varka's spatial world must be as fluid as her temporal. She imaginatively projects herself into her spatial past: "She sees herself in a dark suffocating hut . . . Varka sees a wide road covered with slimy mud" (7:13). As her levels of reality build toward a crescendo they gain meaning and power through their impressionistic juxtaposition with one another. Chekhov's rapid, montage-like spatial cutting forces a merger of images. They begin to commingle, because if Varka is to perceive them as a single epiphany, they must be spatially apprehended, together in one instant of time.[5] Chekhov transcends sequential language by uniting past and present, image and sound, smell and mental state into a moment of what Joseph Frank has termed "space-logic."[6] Varka's seizure of the infant/death image occurs through her fusion of mentally juxtaposed fragments. It is a memorable and horrifying picture. It is a resounding fugue-like composition.

"The Steppe," written in the same year as "Sleepy," became the pivotal point of Chekhov's transition: it was his first lengthy piece of prose, it gained him critical acclaim, and it included themes, motifs, and passages he felt "neither critics nor readers would understand" (14:19). Chekhov saw himself moving in a new direction, but, as always, he viewed that change with the wry self-deprecation that characterized both his public statements and his paradoxical attitude toward change. In a letter to M. V. Kiselev he commented that, "I strike out on original lines, but my originality will bring me no more than I got for my 'Ivanov.' So much talk, and no more" (14:28). In this remark Chekhov uncovered in his own life what would become a major theme in his work: life is a journey through endless change; it is a continuous cycle of beginnings and endings, of imperceptible shifts in the nature of things, of fleeting glances at moving objects and snatches of incomprehensible sounds. Egorushka travels across the steppe in what appears to be the age-old voyage of youth toward manhood. But while he encoun-

ters new experiences and perceives changes in nature, he seems
not to have been transformed. Each moment on the steppe
brings change, but there seems to be no noticeable accumulation. Stasis within movement and movement within stasis, the
journey through changeless change becomes a central motif in
Chekhov's impressionism.

Egorushka finds himself in shifting positions of subordination
and domination where he must encounter the external world of
what Henry Adams saw as the "infinite and infinitesimal struggles."[7] Perceivers watch the alternations in nature and people,
while they themselves are in the process of changing. The literary impressionist expresses that mutual flow through a narrative
prose that constantly reinforces the internal changes of characters and the external changes of the world: "Subject and object
are then irretrievably in motion, inapprehensible and unappre-
hending. In the flashes of identity between subject and object
lies the nature of the impressionist painter's genius."[8] Egorushka believes that a windmill is moving toward him when he is in
fact moving toward it. Seen from a more objective perspective,
both the windmill and Egorushka are moving in space and time
toward each other. The impressionist forces the reader to acknowledge varying perspectives. Time and space press people
and objects together only to force them apart. What they experience in one moment of time and in one particular place can
never again be empirically experienced.

The impressionists' interest in transience throws characters
into a fluid reality that increases their sense of chaos while allowing them to adapt to the changing environment. In order
for Chekhov's characters to find congruence in the spatial and
temporal transformations that accost them they must define
themselves by neither overreacting nor succumbing to the
changes. The motif of the barren, endless road becomes a vehicle
by which characters move through time and space in an effort
to settle on an identity. Yet their chameleonism prevents them
from achieving a unified sense of self. Because the shifting environment acts with such force upon their shallow or narrowly
formed personalities, they tend to adapt so completely to their

impressionistic world that they often become indistinguishable from it. They find themselves spinning through voids of timelessness and ever-returning cycles of time.

Egorushka sets out upon an impressionistic journey. Chekhov, aware of the kind of fiction he was reaching for, wrote to Korolenko in his sprightly self-effacing manner that "each page turns out compact like a short story, the pictures accumulate, crowd together and, obstructing each other, spoil the general impression. As a result one gets, not a picture in which all the details merge into a whole, like stars in the sky, but a summary, a dry record of impressions" (14:11). Chekhov understood the paradoxical nature of impressionism: a general impression of the steppe and Egorushka becomes unified by tone, while the fragmented impressions remain as individually bright as the "stars in the sky."

Egorushka sees, hears, and feels what a nine-year-old child is capable of perceiving but not understanding, and what a child of his age could never express. The fluidity of the subjectively objective third person narration allows for both the psychologically accurate limitations and the authorial release of a child's inexpressible feelings. Both are necessary if the impressionist is to create a character, particularly a child, who can demonstrate his sensitivity while exposing the epistemological limitations of youth. Twain was interested in showing how much children could learn of the world; Chekhov and James were concerned with rendering how little they know when they know so much. Egorushka and James's Maisie dramatize the strengths of central consciousnesses. Egorushka travels the vast steppe and experiences new people, new landscapes, new sounds, and new images. At the end of the journey when Father Khristofor delivers a sermon to Egorushka on the need for learning, the areas of knowledge he describes are no more vast than the steppe itself. Egorushka does not know the steppe. But he has absorbed some of its textures and has been exposed to some of its surfaces.

Chekhov has taken great care to structure Egorushka's experiences so they are neither understood nor understandable. The vindication of the method of central consciousness is demonstrated in the story's dual design of unknowability. Egorushka, in his childish innocence, knows neither the sources nor the results of his experiences: "the boy, not understanding where nor why he was going, sits on the boxseat" (7:19). His restricted perspective makes it impossible to identify many of the objects of his perception: the narrative is imbued with "somewhere," "someone," "for some reason." At the same time Chekhov himself seems to speak poetically of man's epistemological limitations: "You go on and on, and never can see where this horizon begins or where it ends. . . . And now, behind a hill, a solitary poplar appears, who put it here, and why is it there, God alone knows" (7:22). This is not a statement of religious belief, but it underlines both Egorushka's and man's inability to explain and understand phenomena of nature. As Chekhov's impressionism matures, the problem of unknowability will become wedded to the secular crises of faith. Neither Egorushka nor man can know all because they cannot perceive all; they cannot believe because they cannot know. Either they lose their sight through lost faith or they increase their powers of perception through their struggle to know more. Egorushka has his feet planted in both the phenomenological children's stories, where faith is not an issue because those children have no identity, and the existentially phenomenological stories, where identity seems to get lost in the chameleonic flux between subject and object. "Steppe" has the components of a mythic initiatory journey. But Chekhov's leveling impulses and impressionistic commitment led him to question the certain knowledge and definitive change that characterize the initiated of this genre.

This is not, however, the tale of a young boy who has no capacity for growth and knowledge. Egorushka is a fairly passive observer. He makes no grand synthesis of what he has perceived nor does he seem pressed to make decisions that would require him to acknowledge a major change in his life. Because Egorushka is taken care of throughout the trip, he may allow the bits and pieces of inexplicable perceptual experiences to wash over him in all their spontaneous immediacy. Each fragment becomes real, and in its own way definitive: it may at any moment render Egorushka's state of mind or it may contain a glimpse of his elusive and dynamic relationship with the steppe. His world becomes filled with the broken impressions of movement, relativism, fear, life, death, and change. Yet he resists change: "The boy observed all the well-known spots, but that hateful brichka fled past them, leaving them all behind" (7:19). The idea that he should have to leave all that he has known for a venture into the unknown drives him into the protection of perceptual egocentricity. He sees himself remaining stable, while the carriage abducts him from the world of his familiar and comfortable past. There is in Egorushka and in the impressionistic sensibility both the perceptual relativism of movement in relation to fixed objects and the primitive Ptolemaism which needs to see all other objects move. A child must first find himself at the center of his universe; he may then develop a sense of identity in a larger, more complex world.

Space and time become measured by neither the distance between two objects nor the strokes of a clock. While Egorushka feels that he can resist change by seeing fixed objects move, he finds that he must still respond to the relative distances and time shifts of an impressionistic journey across the steppe:

At first, a long way ahead, where the sky is divided from the earth near the tumuli and the windmill—which from a distance looks like a little dwarf waving his arms—a broad bright yellow streak of light crept across the earth; in a few moments the light of that streak had come a little nearer. . . . But after a short lapse of time the dew evaporated, the air lost its freshness and the misguided steppe reassumed its languishing July appearance. . . . Egorushka involuntarily looked ahead into the lilac distance, he began to think that the windmill with its waving fans was getting nearer. It was growing larger and larger and he could get quite a precise idea of its fans. . . . The brichka went to the right and the windmill began to move somewhat to the left; they went on and on, and it moved always to the left without disappearing from sight. . . . and still the windmill was not left behind, but continued to watch Egorushka, waving its polished fan. What a wizard! (7:21–25)

Time and space have conspired to take on an animated life of their own, while Egorushka remains passive and immobile in the face of change: the windmill moves and watches; the light and atmospheric conditions alter dramatically; Egorushka loses control over his perceptions as he "involuntarily" looks into the distance; the "misguided steppe" returns to its former state. Change abounds, but not within Egorushka—his subjective perceptions have isolated him. The uniform vastness of the steppe exhibits a paradoxical monotony: "for in the steppe, where there are neither forests nor high mountains, the sky seems fearfully deep and transparent—at this moment it appeared limitless and torpid with grief" (7:22). The sky not only reflects the quality of the landscape, but also becomes charged with human emotion. While Chekhov personifies the sky for Egorushka, the image carries with it the pervasive quality of a momentary fragment of perceptual objectivity. "Seems" (*kazhetsia*) and "appears" (*predstavlialis'*) force the image back on the perceiver and question his ability to record objective truth at the same time that the instantaneous nature of the perception denies the need for such truth.

The steppe reveals to Egorushka the paradox of space and time that is a major element of the impressionists' fluid world. The steppe seems limitless, vast, open. It seems to Egorushka that he will never reach the windmill, that the journey will last forever, that the steppe will continue on into the infinite, and that it will remain unchanging and uniform. Yet the steppe is filled with momentary sounds; objects flash past and disappear. Even the hills and windmill move toward him and eventually vanish. Space seems endless and time suspended. The windmill in the distance seems to hang in the air connected to nothing, even appearing to be something other than what it is. The repeated image of "the lilac distance" (*lilovaia dal'*) suggests an atmosphere of extreme subjectivity, while detached through distant space and time: "The lilac distance, which had remained motionless till now, began to rock, and together with the sky move somewhere farther away; some noiseless power was drawing it, and the heat and that wearisome song started in pursuit of them. Egorushka's head dropped forward and his eyes closed" (7:31). Spatialized time changes the unchangeable. Egorushka finds that the heat of the steppe and the unchanging boredom of the distance oppress him: "How was he to kill that long time (*ubit' eto dlinnoe vremia*) and where was he to go to escape the heat? A difficult problem" (7:29). Egorushka and Varka set the pattern for the many characters in Chekhov who will live through time while trying to kill it. Space—the lilac distance, the heat, the boredom—can remain motionless through the filter of time or move for some unknown reason to some indeterminate destination. In his weariness Egorushka perceives floating ambiguity. This makes it possible for him to passively absorb an outside world that resembles his state of mind. It is the perfect impressionistic image for a merger between subject and object.

When Egorushka awakens it is almost dusk and the camp is ready to move. The languid timelessness and lilac distance commingle with the more immediate perspectives of movement: "The next minute the brichka had started on its way. It seemed as if the travellers were going back instead of forward. The landscape was the same as it had been at noon. The hills faded into the lilac distance—one saw not the end of them; the steppe-grass, the pebblestones flashed by, the bands of reaped corn rushed past, and there were all those same rooks and the kite sedately flapping their wings flying over the steppe" (7:34). Finally "the daylight crept away" (7:33) and the visual experiences of day recede.

The transition between the visual perceptions of day and the auditory perceptions of night takes place in a tavern. Dusk obliterates Egorushka's visual sense, so that when the wagon approaches the tavern "there was a sound of glad voices" (7:35). Inside the tavern there is a balance between sight, sound, and smell. Egorushka is introduced to strange looking figures and a house such as he had never before seen. He hears snatches of incomprehensible adult conversation and smells the odors of a tavern, which seem so much stronger and more loathsome than those at home. When he falls asleep his dreams are rendered no differently from his waking perceptions. The impressionistic cycle of juxtaposed waking/half-sleep/dream images is completed when Egorushka suddenly wakes up to see a startlingly dreamlike image: "Suddenly, quite unexpectedly, half a yard away from his face, Egorushka saw a pair of dark velvety brows, large brown eyes, soft dimpled cheeks, and a smile, which like the rays of the sun, was diffused over the whole face—someone who smelled quite delicious" (7:48).

With nightfall Egorushka is transferred to another wagon. Night on the steppe introduces a completely new atmosphere. As the light disappears so does the familiar and kindly Father Khristofor who is replaced by the strange teller of death tales, Pantelei. Deniski, the playful coachman, has now been replaced by his dark double, Dymov. The uniform music of night sounds displaces the monotonous distance of the day. Egorushka will have to kill the rhythmic timelessness of night as he did the day, through sleep. As he is lulled to sleep, he experiences the richness of fleeting sounds: "You drove along aware that you are dozing, when suddenly, from somewhere comes the short alarmed cry of some unsleeping bird, or there echoes an undefinable sound resembling some human voice saying an astonished 'a-ah,' then slumber again closes your eyes" (7:51). The sounds that invade his sleep are as indeterminate and fleeting as the sunset and the shadows he saw earlier: "Who it calls to, and who listens to it in this plain, God alone knows, but its cry has something sad and plaintive." Egorushka cannot always discern the sound, its origin, nor to whom it is directed. He cannot even describe the tone of the noise.

The journey continues with the same cycle of days and nights, sights and sounds, monotony and change. He becomes aware of tone and begins to interpret language that he doesn't understand, sounds that have no origin, and sights that cannot be clearly made out. He keeps shifting his perspective to keep some distance from Pantelei's tales of death and the suggested sadism of Dymov. As he searches for a means to endure the endless time and space of the steppe, he flattens out the continuously fleeting perceptual fragments and constantly reevaluates what he sees and hears. At the journey's end he is reunited with Father Khristofor, who delivers an ironic lecture on the necessity to learn and know all. If Egorushka has learned anything it should be that he can never know everything. Egorushka travels the steppe, comes in contact with life, death, time, space, change, and boredom, and by the journey's end seems to know no more than when he began.

By the end of the story nothing seems to have changed. The same motifs recur and Egorushka feels and reacts as he did when he left home. Life is an endless cycle with the momentary details of change resisting uniformity. Egorushka runs, "not knowing why," (7:111) from the window and into his room. He feels that when his uncle and Father Khristofor left, "all that phase of life which he had known up to now was gone forever like smoke." Both the death of the past and the beginning of the future elicit the sadness of an ephemeral present. He resists the change in his life now, just as he had in the beginning of the journey. He feels exhaustion and "impotency" in the face of his new and unknown life: "What will that life be?" The details of life are paradoxical, needing the balance of fluid perspective. Egorushka seems to be able to cope with life, though he does not understand it. One phase of his many cycles is completed; he is now ready to embark on another.

"Sleepy" and "The Steppe" exhausted the impressionistic potential of the child-dreamer for Chekhov. In these two stories he successfully incorporated his earlier experiments with perceptual juxtaposition, expanding apperception, and lost time into an incredible array of rhythmic impressions that forced one character to murder and the other to enter a world of dazzlingly brief sensations and timeless monotony. Varka's all-consuming sleeplessness drives her toward a necessary synthesis of impressions. These images and sensations from both her past and present become fused into a horribly immutable epiphany. This instant provided Chekhov with his first undeniably impressionistic privileged moment, his least characteristic. For it is not often in Chekhov that perceptual associations and knowledge are framed together in definitive action. Chekhov is the artist of the mistimed moment. His impressionism feeds on the partial conjunction of inchoate sensations impinging on an unwary consciousness.

Varka and Egorushka, then, form two extreme examples of

the basic Chekhovian duality: the search for synthesis and the impossibility that it should be complete and everlasting. So, in late 1888 and 1889 Chekhov turned away from children as subjects, just as James did after *What Maisie Knew*, as though they forced him into simplistic patterns through their undeveloped consciousnesses. He became interested in more mature, complex, and self-conscious protagonists who, not unlike their younger counterparts, search for an identity in the elusive maze of impressionistically relativistic reality.[9] Chekhov became fascinated by the inverse issue of impressionistic consciousness (which to an extent he had explored in the stories of the lost past) : can a character with a fully developed, intellectualized consciousness reverse the process of enclosure from the spontaneity of immediate impressions (*futliarnost'*)? Can he expose himself to the external world of transient, ephemeral sensations—a return to the state of the innocent eye—without stripping his consciousness of its complexity? "A Dreary Story" is the most interesting and impressionistic of these pieces.

Nikolai Stepanovich wears the many hats of an actor searching for a true identity, but Chekhov, the impressionist, can paint only a few of the many surfaces of his existence. As Nikolai vainly searches for his unattainable essence, he is actually experiencing the minute mutability of each day. One surface is as real as any other. Chekhov understands this, but his characters rarely do. The greater the character's consciousness, the more he actively fragments life and feels the wrenching of the individual parts.

This story, subtitled "From the Notebook of an Old Man," is an autobiographical confession that captures, as Rilke, Gide, Proust, and Sartre would later do, the bold yet subtle strokes of immediate pain and anguish. The presentness of committing to paper the experiences of moments simply lived through, forces time upon the narrative. Again, the impressionist creates a fluid temporal center for the axis of his story. Whether recalling moments of his past or fearfully awaiting his approaching death, Nikolai recreates the continuum of his life through a presentness of waste and *poshlost'*. It is a subjective, fluid, and fragmented history based upon the dissipation of the past, the despair of the present, and the fear of the future. The past and the future are seen as present moments lost. Since Nikolai sees himself and his life as a boring, dreary stretch of years that have little meaning to anyone, he does not quite know how to approach either himself or his narrative. So he begins in the dry, detached manner that would satisfy his academic sense of objectivity and irony.

His narrative follows the structure of a maelstrom. It begins with a calm exterior surface and slowly moves inward toward the depth and heart of turmoil. Nikolai launches into himself from the outside as he examines his name, the name of a famous person, from many perspectives. This immediately creates the effect of a man dissociated from himself. At the heart of the narrative is a curiously ironic tone which throws an ambiguous light on his moments of self-praise and a sense of protesting too much when he abuses himself. We are never on stable ground with this highly intelligent and elusive narrator-protagonist (shades of the Underground Man, Prufrock, and Herzog). Nikolai then moves quickly to the surfaces of physical description and mental capacities. But since each is simply an attempt to describe himself from an objective, uncommitted point of view, the surface remains stable; he has not let himself go. Every early chapter begins with the same pattern: opening with an objective description of his present life, then revealing fragments of his past existence, moving to a more subjective analysis of himself, past and present, and ending with a scrutinizing, free-associative *durée*. With each almost psychoanalytic session Nikolai finds he is able to break in at a deeper level, yet each session must begin with some manner of foreplay designed to loosen the psyche.

In the earliest chapters Nikolai opens at a safe distance from himself. But with each subsequent entry he becomes less comfortable, plunging rapidly to deeper surfaces and becoming more fragmented, desperate, and associative. This progression gives the narrative an impressionistic unity and psychic credibility that belies Nikolai's statement that "there is a lack of sequence in my thoughts, and when I set them down on paper it always seems to me that I have lost the knack of integrating them" (7:225). This comment, flung out so casually, throws into relief the paradox of impressionism. What Nikolai hopes for is a coalescence of images and thoughts before he dies, the existential epiphany of Tolstoy's Ivan Ilyich. What he believes is that he will leave this world with nothing more than the seemingly random order of his notebook. The unity he searches for, however, lies in the unapprehended paradigmatic structure of those entries, there for the reader alone to glean. Nikolai is so enclosed in each individual entry and thought, so wrapped up in self-awareness that he fails to perceive, until they are past, not thoughts but sensory impressions: "My rank and fame have deprived me forever of cabbage soup and tasty little pies. . . . Gone is the gaiety of the old days. . . . Gone forever the feeling of exhilaration from one glass of wine, gone is Agasha, buckwheat and bream" (7:249). What Nikolai does not realize is what Marcel comes to know in *Le Temps retrouvé*, that one can transcend the lost past and return it to the present only if one is open to the sensory impression that defines it.

Drifting toward sleep and death, "a half-conscious state in which you know you are not asleep, but dreaming" (7:264), he becomes even more detached from himself and others. His narrative becomes more fragmentary. The pain of his impotence drives him to remember a night of great anguish, a "sparrow night" (*vorob'inaia noch'*). This scene remains one of Chekhov's most perfectly rendered impressionistic pieces and brings Nikolai to the verge of a privileged moment. This night races forward into the present through a haze of felt impressions, discontinuous sensations, and suspended time. He begins a rage to live, to perceive all the details of existence, and to make contact with that part of indeterminate life he had rejected for over sixty years. All this is set off against the power of impending death. Everything that had touched the narrative is now given a new range of feelings. His past is no longer part of another world that is "gone"; it is simply life. Where before his mental processes had been attuned to the nuances and ambiguities of consciousness, his perceptions now focus on felt life: "There is the scent of new-mown hay, and something else that smells sweet. I see the tips of the fence palings, the gaunt drowsy trees by the window, the road, and the dark strip of woodland; the moon shines serene and bright in the cloudless sky. It is still; not a leaf stirring. It seems to me that everything is looking at me, holding its breath, as though it is waiting for me to die" (7: 273). Identifiable smells, unknown parts of objects, silences, and personified nature are now rendered through the sensations of present tense and cluster around the sense of dissolving life— death. The moment he becomes aware of the transience of sensations is the moment he condemns them to the past. He begins to intellectualize the causes of natural phenomena that an instant before he had accepted as randomly experienced impressions. Time begins to return to the dull hopelessness of a dreary life. Dawn breaks and he rationalizes that he must have been dreaming. Nikolai finishes out the rest of the narrative, his life, counting the strokes of the clock, as these "last months of waiting for death to come have seemed longer to me than all the rest of my life. And never before have I been so reconciled to the slow passage of time. . . . The clock in the corridor strikes five, six. . . . It grows dark" (7:277).

II * TRANSITION

"A Dreary Story" marks the end of one phase of Chekhov's career. What immediately followed has been the subject of much biographical speculation. His journey to Sakhalin in April of 1890 became either an interruption in or an escape from his writing.[10] When he returned his fiction took on a stable, even conservative form, in what Karl Kramer has accurately termed his "dialogue with melodrama."[11] These stories of "melodrama" constitute a distinct movement away from impressionism, demonstrating quite lucidly, I believe, that impressionim was Chekhov's métier.

In 1892 he wrote a two-page story entitled "A Fragment" (Otryvok), which indicates, however briefly, a continuing inter-

est in the impressionistic forms of multiple perspective and fragmentation. "A Fragment" is simply a random entry from the
diary of a deceased state councilor. His house had been torn
down and a tavern erected in its place. The tavernkeeper left the
entries on a table for those guests who were in need of extra
writing paper. This "fragment" is one of those sheets of paper.
One night the narrator arbitrarily picks up one of the sheets and
proceeds to impose an equally arbitrary meaning on the fragment: "It evidently refers to the very beginning of the deceased's
agricultural activities and it contains the following entries" (7:
477). There is no way of knowing the chronological progression
of these entries, since only the days and months have been recorded and there is nothing in them to suggest that they were
written in the state councilor's youth. Even more disconcerting
is the fact that the entries seem to have nothing to do with "agricultural activities." We have been led into this story by what
turns out to be an unreliable narrator. The unreliable narrator
has since become a mainstay of modern literature.[12] Chekhov
had touched on this device in his early stories of perceptual distortion. We didn't feel that we had been duped then, however,
since there had always been some physical or psychological
source for the distortion. This story becomes a pure exercise in
impressionistic multiplicity.

For the next five years Chekhov experimented with a number
of styles, forms, and subjects. During this period he wrote many
of his most famous—and most conventionally realistic—stories,
as well as some others that explore the impressionistic world
view from varying and sometimes specialized angles. There are
the stories of time and ambiguity, dreamers, identity, and those
that attempt to bind subjectivity to social change.[13] The most
illustrative attempt to hang on to his impressionism is a return
to the spatial juxtaposition of "Sleepy." The same fugue-like
"space-logic" exists in "The Student" (Student), written in
1894. Ivan Velikopolskii sees an unchanging world of oppression, by acknowledging only the negative aspect of Good Friday
—the day of the horrifying crucifixion of Christ. To support this
image he calls upon Russia's violent eras: "Oppressed by the

cold, he fell to thinking that just such a wind as this had blown in the times of Riurik, Ivan the Terrible, and Petr and in those days men suffered from the same terrible poverty and hunger; they had the same thatched roofs filled with holes; there was the same wretchedness, ignorance, and desolation everywhere, the same darkness, the same sense of being oppressed—all these dreadful things had existed, did exist, and would continue to exist, and in a thousand years life would be no better. He did not want to go home" (7:345). He perceives history through his sense of the oppressive cold, compounded by his feeling that it was oppression that killed Christ. He does not see, however, that he may have changed the face of nature through his all-encompassing vision of misery, cold, and oppression. What he sees instead as he trudges along that dreary Chekhovian road, is the silent, empty, lonely marshes. He is returning, unwillingly, to what he had left, and as he does so he notices the change in the weather that had "at first been fine and still" (7:345). He recognizes the cycle of return in his own journey, but not that of crucifixion and resurrection. Ivan's perception of Good Friday renders a change in his perception of history, as well as the weather—that Chekhovian barometer of perceived environment. But at the same time he sees history and the future remaining oppressively stable. The change which has come over him finds its correlative in the story of Peter's refusal to recognize Christ.

As he returns home the old widow Vasilisa and another woman are warming themselves dreamily by a blazing fire. Vasilisa does not at first recognize Ivan, although he has been gone only since morning. He comes to warm himself by the fire and relates the story of Judas's betrayal of Christ and Peter's refusal to recognize Christ. The setting of Peter's expiation and redemption is, in Ivan's imagination, the same as their own present situation: " 'On just such a cold night as this the apostle Peter warmed himself by a fire,' the student said, stretching his hands over the flames. 'So it must have been very cold. Ah, what a terrible night, grandmother! It was an extraordinarily long, sad night!' " (7:346). As he finished the story with Peter in the garden weeping silently alone, Ivan hears the old woman weeping as well. It is an epiphany in which Ivan is struck by the similarity, not between the crucifixion and the present world of misery, but between Peter and this old woman. Ivan now believes that "it was clear that the story he had been telling them though it happened nineteen centuries ago, still possessed a meaning for the present time—to both these women, to the desolate village, to himself, and to all people" (7:348). In this moment Ivan is transformed. His vision shifts from Christ to Peter through the joyful weeping of an old woman: "And suddenly his soul was filled with joy, and for a moment, he had to pause to recover his breath. 'The past,' he thought, "is linked to the present by an unbroken chain of events all flowing from one to the other.' And it seemed to him that he had just seen both ends of the chain, and when he touched one end the other trembled." Each note, each theme, each different key affects the entire piece as they all stand in relation to one another. Earlier, when Ivan had been unconcerned and unaware of the religious significance of the day, he saw the world as still and fine; later, knowing that it was Good Friday, he viewed the world only in terms of Christ's crucifixion; but now, when he sees and hears Vasilisa weeping with joy at the expiation and redemption of Peter, the full weight of the recognition of his own part makes him totally aware of the significance of both the past on the present and the present on the past. Earlier, he had believed that only the past could influence the present, but now he is able to see that the weeping of an old woman in the present is able to alter his view of the past, which in turn again transforms his view of the present. The cycle is complete when he realizes that Vasilisa has been affected by a story in the past. The cascading sensations of past/present that crashed down with such tragic force on Varka now in Ivan drive toward a more hopeful climax: "it occurred to him that the same truth and the same beauty which reigned over humankind in the garden and in the courtyard of the high priest had endured uninterruptedly until the present time . . . and the feeling of youth, health and vigor and the inexpressible sweet expectation of happiness, of an unknown and secret happiness, took possession of him little by little, and life suddenly seemed to him ravishing, marvelous, and full of deep meaning." Ivan now perceives the unchanging links of history, but through his altered eyes history has itself been reshaped. He still does not recognize, however, the profound force with which one tug of the chain can radically transform the other end. The ironies of change become manifold: nature is transformed so that it can reflect Ivan's state of mind, which sees no change in the oppression of man throughout the centuries; Christ alone appears to be on Ivan's mind, but he tells the story of Peter; Vasilisa sees history from a different point of view, altering Ivan's vision of the present, so that his view of the past changes.

Varka, Egorushka, and Ivan are all swept into a swirl of impressions they do not understand. They begin to respond to fluid time, while sensing that the vast swarm of accumulating spatial images must be reduced, juxtaposed, and synthesized if they are to find a balance between change and changelessness.

By 1897 Chekhov was beginning to sort out his multidirectional middle period. "In the Cart" becomes the bridge to his last great stories of impressionism. It is a very important piece that is often overlooked in favor of the tentatively impressionistic *futliarnost'* trilogy ("Man in a Shell," "Gooseberries," and "About Love") or the traditionally realistic "Peasants" and "In the Ravine."[14]

"In the Cart" opens with a progression from objective description to subjective rendering, producing the Chekhovian subjective objectivism: (1) "At half past eight in the morning they drove out of town." (2) "The paved road was dry, a fine April sun shone strongly, but there was still snow in the ditches and forests. Winter, vicious, dark, long, had just ended, spring had suddenly arrived." (3) "But for Maria Vasilevna sitting now in the cart, nothing new or interesting was offered by the heat, nor the languid, limpid forest warmed by the breath of spring, nor the black flocks flying in the fields over huge puddles that resembled lakes, nor the wonderful, unfathomable sky, into which it seemed that one could plunge with such joy" (9:244). The first line, so simple and convincing in its precise omniscience, counterpoints the heavily subjective, adjectival quality of detailed nature in the third part of the passage. Part two acts as the transition between the change from winter to spring and between pure description and Maria's perceptions of the day. But even within her subjective view there exists a contradiction that will lead to her later privileged moment. Nothing is new or interesting, but her rendering of this nothingness (rendered, of course, through the central consciousness of third person) is vivid, varied, and alive. She feels the heat, senses the new warmth of "the breath of spring," sees the movement of the "black flocks" and the "wonderful, unfathomable sky." This sky even "seemed" to her something into which she could "plunge with such joy." Her actual impressions are at odds with her beliefs about her life—she believes her existence, therefore nature, to be tediously unchanging, and yet she perceives both the dark languidness and the unfathomable joyousness of nature's impressions.

The importance of the subjectively objective central consciousness becomes quite evident in this instance, providing perceived impressions without the perceiver's knowledge of what they are and what they mean for her life. It sustains the fissure between the *voir* and *savoir* of an incipient, expanding consciousness and secures the constant flow between multiple points of view. This fluid perspective between the subjective and objective makes the source difficult to locate, thereby rendering the ambiguous reality of impressionism. In Chekhov's early stories the perspective was usually unequivocal, but Chekhov began to increase the factors in impressionism's commitment to epistemological indeterminacy. The fragments of the past, the sameness of the journey, and the dreams of the future combine with the sensory stimuli of nature in transition and the movement of the cart to bring Maria to a moment of stasis—a stunningly compressed epiphany at a railway crossing that is the result of her rearrangement and synthesis of all these components.

Her personal past has become detached from her and is rendered through the distant language of a fairy tale: "Once she had a father and mother" (9:245). Her reality of the past becomes "as vague and formless as a dream." And even the most objective record of it, a photograph, begins to disintegrate: "Of her former possessions only the photograph of her mother remained, but the dampness of the school had faded it, and now nothing but the hair and eyebrows could be seen." Subject and object have become one. The past fades, leaving only the present.

This journey becomes fused with all the others into what she sees as a life of unending tedium: "She had gone so often to the town for her salary that she could not count the times; and whether it was spring, as now, or a rainy autumn evening, it was all the same to her—" (9:244). This journey, this life, this boredom becomes a time void. She does not live in or through time, but exists detached and suspended so that nothing touches her: "she felt as though she had been living here for a long, long time, for a hundred years." Yet at the same instant she wishes to speed up time, to control it by ending this journey as quickly as possible.

As the trip continues, Khanov, a fortyish landowner who had been last year's school examiner, suddenly emerges beside the cart. And just as suddenly, Maria perceives him in terms of a past, not a present, sensation—the exam papers that smelled of wine. Maria had been concerned with neither education nor her pupils, only examinations. One set of exams had been no different from this trip, just one of many and all the same. But now she begins to see other qualities in Khanov, as she plunges into the layers of perceptual immediacy: she sees him as handsome, strong, "but there was something barely perceptible in his gait which revealed a person already touched by decay, weak, and nearing the end" (9:247). With this newly discovered perceptual acuity she suddenly fuses the past with the present through an impressionistic association: "The forest suddenly smelled of wine." No longer is the past lost in the flatness of indistinguishable presents. Her multisurfaced view of Khanov is the result of a past sensation associated with him—the wine-tinted examinations—superimposed on a present sensation associated with the monotony of nature—the forest's smelling of wine. Past and present, man and nature commingle in a particularized impression. Maria is beginning to break the pattern of her one-dimensional, timeless and changeless life.

In order to complete the *durée* she must dream of a future. However, new dimensions stimulate fears of the unknown: "Fundamentally, life was so arranged and human relations so complicated, so utterly beyond all understanding that when you thought about it you were terrified and your heart sank." At this moment Khanov leaves. Her sense of loss triggers, first, confusion and a series of fragmented images, then, as the wind blows the sound of his carriage to her, all "these thoughts become mingled with others. She wanted to dream of his beautiful eyes, of love, of the happiness that would never come to her. . . . And if she were to become his wife?"

Maria's life had been one of exactitude, one that denied the past, accepted no future, and refused to acknowledge the exigencies of immediacy. All three become galvanized into a life of nothingness. Winter turned to spring, darkness to light, and sights and sounds changed along the road, but not for Maria. The road serves as both unchanging entrapment, "Here was her past and present, and she could imagine no other future than the school, the road to town and back, and again the school and again the road" (9:244), and also liberation, through the constant movement that only now and for no particular reason forces Maria to deal with the changes that confront her. As the trip becomes more uncomfortable, she becomes physically more sensitized: a man she knew materializes beside the cart and she sees "the barely perceptible"; they stop at a tavern and she hears the "roar" of conversation, the "banging" of a swinging door, and the "confusion" of men shouting.

As they continue Maria sees Khanov in the distance crossing the bridge. This again triggers heightened awareness. The river that she had crossed so many times before suddenly becomes (for the reader) Heraclitean and seasonally cyclic: "In the summer the river was only a shallow stream which you could walk across easily. Usually in August it was dried up, but now, after the spring floods, it had grown to be a torrent of swift, cold, muddy water fifty feet wide" (9:250). One obstacle after another forces her out of her dull, languorous life. While there is no indication she understands that "you cannot step into the same river twice; for fresh waters are ever flowing in upon you,"[15] she does "feel a sharp chill at her feet." Her consciousness is becoming finely attuned to the images, sensations, and dreams of past, present, and future. But since the cart has been in constant motion, she has not had the moment of stasis in which spatialized time draws out of the flux a privileged moment.

Suddenly, the "barrier was down at the railway crossing" (9: 251). Before the train begins to pass she sees the town, the end of this journey, in the objective detail and warm tones of an impressionist painting: "the green roof over the school, and the church with its blazing crosses that reflected the setting sun; and the station windows were ablaze too, and pink smoke rose from the engine." But Maria's frame of mind from the trip continues to linger over this picture providing a contrasting overtonal harmony: "And it seemed to her that everything was shivering with cold." Now the train begins to flash by and its windows, reflecting the same blazing light, "hurt her eyes." It is movement that forces her to react to the sensory world and it is movement within stasis that will allow her to create an impressionistic synthesis of past, present, and future. Her mother, who represents the lost past, and Khanov, image of the unattainable future, materialize within the painful rush of the train, the present. All exist for her as subject and object coalesce in a transient epiphany:

Here it was—the train; the windows reflected the blazing light, like the crosses on the church; they hurt her eyes. On the platform of one of the first-class carriages stood a woman, and Maria Vasilevna glanced at her as she flashed by: mother! What a resemblance! Her mother had had just such luxuriant hair, just such a forehead and that way of holding her head. And with amazing distinctness, for the first time in those thirteen years, she imagined vividly her mother, her father, her brother, their apartment in Moscow, the aquarium with the little fishes, everything down to the smallest detail; she suddenly heard the piano playing, her father's voice; she felt young, beautiful, well dressed, in a bright, warm

room surrounded by her relatives; a feeling of joy and happiness suddenly
overwhelmed her, she pressed her hands to her temples in ecstasy and
called softly, imploringly:

"Mama!"

And she began to cry, not knowing why. At just that moment Khanov
drove up in his carriage, and she, seeing him, imagined such happiness as
had never been, and smiled and nodded at him as an equal and an intimate, and it seemed to her that the sky, the windows, the trees, were
glowing with her happiness, her triumph. No, her father and mother had
never died, she had never been a schoolteacher, that had been a long, oppressive, strange dream, and now she was awake. . . .

"Vasilevna, get in!"

And suddenly it all vanished. The barrier rose slowly. Maria Vasilevna,
shivering and numb with cold, got in the cart. (9:251–52)

This remarkable passage brings to fruition Chekhov's long
struggle with the various elements of impressionism. In this
silent instant, Maria Vasilevna experiences the pure impressionistic moment, the *moment bienheureux*. In a sense, Chekhov's
career seemed to have been pointed toward this passage. In
"Sleepy" Varka has an epiphany, but it is quite different in that
she reduces all the impressions which beset her into one image
that triggers action. Maria Vasilevna, however, brings together
images she had lost or could not grasp by creating and having
created for her an instant of full, rich life. The impressions she
had denied herself come to life. They are acts of perception that
combine subject and object, while blending the past and future
into an atmospheric moment of presentness. And as in all impressionistic moments, this one, like the train windows that
trigger it, flashes past and vanishes into both time and space.

This moment is carefully framed by the railway crossing barrier that forces her to stop, while it allows the train to pass. Thus
the relativistic motion of both Maria and her environment is
momentarily stayed. This gives her a respite from total flux, allowing her to see movement in relation to a fixed body. She can
then come to grips with herself. The experience is agonizing—
she must endure the actual sensory pain of "blazing light." The
impressions that flash by release, not simply associations with
the past (the connections remain unexplained), but the instan-

taneously ambiguous perceptual existence of her mother: "a lady . . . mother! . . . what a resemblance!" This impression touches off memories of the "smallest detail" with "amazing distinctness." Nevertheless they remain impressionistically fragmentary and incomplete. Then from her visual imagination, she hears (actually?) a piano and her father. These moving images develop a core of stillness, as though commingling the past with the present creates a stasis of spatialized time. From this center radiates the now changed mood of Maria, rendered through her perceptions of objects. She sees herself in a "bright, warm" room and "a feeling of joy and happiness" washes over her. The cold, shivering world has been left, momentarily, behind.

Suddenly Khanov again emerges, but this time she sees him only in terms of her future happiness. Then "it seemed to her that the sky, the windows, the trees, were glowing with her happiness, her triumph." The cycle of that *durée* becomes complete. These thoughts of the future provide a past that never died. The moment is total and complete, except for the Chekhovian irony that leaves Maria stranded in the cruel inevitability of the impressionistic moment; it lasts only a moment. The moment she begins to think that her past life was a "long, oppressive, strange dream" and that only now in this epiphany has she awakened, at that very instant she is awakened to the *reality* of that "dream." In her desire to distinguish between the indistinguishable, the dream and the reality, in her desire to hold onto that moment by making it everlastingly timeless, she breaks the spell; the spell is broken. She destroys the experience by asking too much of it, and at the same time it comes to an abrupt end because it must, as all moments do. Will it irrevocably change her life? Chekhov, the impressionist, does not know. What he does know, he tells us: "Maria Vasilevna, shivering and numb with cold, got into the cart."

This delicate control over the impressionistic method made Chekhov ready, in his last, painful, bittersweet years, carefully and slowly to write his most important impressionist stories.

* 4 *

Chekhov the Impressionist
1899–1903

I * "THE LADY WITH THE DOG"

"The Lady with the Dog" (*Dama s sobachkoi*), written in 1899, represents Chekhov's finest impressionistic achievement. It is carefully constructed to surround every impression, thought, and feeling with the opacity of ambiguity and change. It is now a critical commonplace that Chekhov propelled himself into the vanguard of literary modernism when he spun those delicate threads of ineffable indeterminacy in *The Three Sisters* (1901) and *The Cherry Orchard* (1904). These plays are generally acknowledged to have laid the foundations for the theater of the absurd.[1] When played well they project the existential problems of being and becoming, phenomenologically perceived reality, ambiguity of speech and gesture, constant miscommunication, fragmentation of present surfaces, tension between metric and human time, multiple perspectives, and change. Too often Chekhov's stories of this period are overlooked in the rush to crown him the father of the modern theater. Chekhov's craft and vision as a short story writer certainly did not falter as he constructed his impressionistically modern plays. Rather, his continuing development as a writer of intricately impressionistic stories led to his rapid eminence as a major modern playwright.

The dominant themes of Chekhov's last two plays display the tensions between change and stasis and the differences among characters perceiving change. At the center of this issue is the epistemological question of how one knows what change is. These problems are the very essence of literary impressionism. And it was in this sphere that Chekhov intensified the impressionistic artistry of his finely-honed final works. In "The Lady with the Dog" change becomes both affected by and acts on passing time and timelessness. Time and change determine the deceptive line of demarcation between dream and reality, the elusiveness of love, and the phenomenologically ephemeral interface based on the fluctuating skittishness of subject and object.

Dmitrii Dmitrich Gurov, the central consciousness of this story, indolently lounges on the esplanade in Yalta, passively overhearing gossip about "the lady with the dog." This vague bit of description leads to a drifting, unsatisfying love affair between two bored, inert people. The past pervades their relationship, just as it affects the perceptions of Gurov: he both forgets and remembers those aspects of his other affairs that might allow him greater convenience and moral lassitude in this present liaison; his image of both himself and Anna Sergeevna is largely informed by his past philandering with women whose "lace on their lingerie seemed to him to resemble fish scales" (9:361); as the affair continues, Gurov forgets in winter Moscow what their relationship had been in summer Yalta.

Gurov's perception of passing time determines the quality of their affair. Through the prism of his jaded cynicism he sees their relationship as a way of both filling a time void and, like Varka and Egorushka, killing time. Later, however, when he longs for Anna, time becomes forcefully transient: the train vanishes, the seasons change, and the mirror startles him with the extent of his gray-headedness. Complementing this quality of fleeting time is the distinct imagery of timelessness: the sea at Oreanda, the hellish circles of "oppressively hot" Yalta that make the city appear "quite dead" (9:362), and the elements of repetition that Gurov sees as his history. Meanwhile Anna is driven to repeating the words "always" and "never."

This story conveys an elusive surface fragmentation that had not been so fully realized by Chekhov before. Gurov perceives only bits and pieces of both his past and present. Initially he sees only a lady with a dog, later he grasps other details, but he always seems to veer away from perceiving a total human being. Gurov relies on impressions, signs, gestures, mannerisms,

and expressions to form a suggestively incomplete and unreliable composite of Anna: he sees what it is safe for him to see; he
sees so that he can keep himself at an emotional distance from
her; later he sees her with "love"; when she is gone, his vivid
memory recalls an image of her that "seemed to him lovelier,
younger, tenderer than she had been" (9:365); at the theater
when he first sees her again, she strikes him as a "little, undis-
tinguished woman, lost in a provincial crowd" (9:368), and yet
that image fills him with happiness. Gurov sees and feels impressionistically, so that this "love" story, filtered through his
consciousness, becomes a broken mass of sensations, punctuated
by flourishes of conscious oratorios.

Love becomes the perfect impressionistic subject, because it is
so responsive to change, so evanescent, and so dependent upon
the subjective perceptions of both lovers. Karl Kramer puts it
this way: "Perhaps in Anna, Gurov has found the only real love
of his entire life. . . . Is this a new experience for Gurov, or is it
merely a repetition of the emotional tangle he has been in so
often before? Gurov himself is unable to answer and thus the
narrative which describes their relationship is itself ambiguous."[2] Do we know what love is, does Gurov know? Present
perceptions of past experiences, fluctuating impressions of the
present, a chameleonic lack of identity, an inability to know
what Anna feels, and a belief that happiness is somehow linked
to love, all conspire to throw the avowed subject of this story,
love, into doubt. It becomes virtually impossible to make any
definitive statements regarding Gurov's contradictory claims
that this affair is no different from his others and that this is the
first time he has ever been in love. Chekhov has so constructed
this story that it is both one impression of an affair sandwiched
in among many, many others to be remembered at some future
date as simply "another episode or adventure in his life" (9:
364), and an entire string of separate impressions, each changing so quickly that it is real only for the duration of its existence.
All impressions, then, vanish into the opaque past.

While each impression has a feel and mood all its own, so has
the entire story and each of its four parts. "Sleepy" projects a

mood of desperate sleeplessness, "The Steppe" is pervaded by the musical undulations of sights and sounds, and in "A Dreary Story" the encroaching darkness hangs heavily inert. "The Lady with the Dog" exudes the drifting indeterminacy of an oddly errant relationship. Part One suggests the languid filling of time, Part Two, the oppressive atmosphere of timelessness, Part Three, the winter grayness of loss, and Part Four, Gurov's and Anna's drift toward their uncertain future. Chekhov created these overtones through the shift away from description and toward the metonymic rendering of atmosphere.[3]

Gurov is a chameleon. He has been in Yalta only two weeks and has "become used to the place" (*privykshii tut*) (9:357). Chekhov's choice of words implies that Gurov rapidly accommodates himself to his environment and just as quickly becomes bored by it. He adapts so completely that he retains no fundamental identity. He has cut himself off from his past, his family, and his home. And yet almost immediately he begins "to take an interest in new faces." The vital, almost eccentric imagery he endows Anna with—her beret and white Pomeranian—becomes a way of immersing himself in a new, fresh identity.

The lady with the dog has an anonymity about her that must attract a man of no identity. She has no past, no name, and must be bored if she is in Yalta alone. They talk, eat dinner, and walk to the sea together before he even learns her first name and patronymic. Only much later does he learn her seemingly disembodied German surname. It is as though Gurov wishes to project onto her the most superficial, anonymous, and nonhuman characteristics. In this way she will make no demands on his need for distance and self-delusion, allowing him to fluctuate at will between romantic idealism, cynicism, and indifference. What he sees, then, are only the most striking and fragmentary physical features, the ones that lead to caricature and in no way reveal her humanness. The title of the story itself maintains the ironic distance Gurov hopes to sustain.

His view of the past further establishes his need for both indifference and vitality. And he surveys his past looking for ways to approach this new affair, he repeats the fact that "bitter experience" (9:358) has taught him about women. These experiences, the causes of which remain unknown to us, have led him to believe that women are both an "inferior race" and that he cannot live without them. He also remembers that "every fresh intimacy, which at first seems to give the spice of variety, ends by introducing excessively complicated problems, and creating intolerable situations." Gurov traps himself in a self-defeating cycle: to destroy boredom he seeks out new adventures and "fresh intimacies" that will force him to forget his past, and yet once he has forgotten, the freshness vanishes and becomes "excessively complicated," threatening his isolation and indifference. This cycle presumably continues ad infinitum, because Gurov has devised a foolproof system of selective forgetting: "But with each new encounter with an interesting woman those experiences somehow slipped from his memory and he wanted to live, and everything seemed so simple and amusing." This process allows him to mingle his embittered indifference and his "elusive" charm into each affair. But it also leads to a life of nothingness, punctuated only by those momentary interludes that seem to offer vibrancy. He severs himself from the past in order to feel the moment, but only succeeds in killing time, including the moment.

When he slips back into the boring sameness of endured time he perceives the moment cynically. The past has taught him to distrust the present, but the present drives him to perceive the past with equal distrust. Gurov is trapped in the suspended ambiguity of a time void, wedged between time and timelessness, past and present, the moment and the *durée*. When at the end of the story Chekhov captures Anna and Gurov in the image of two migratory birds "caught and compelled to live in different cages" (9:372), the cycle of self-deception born of isolation becomes complete. It is then possible to see that within this entire affair, one which seems so fraught with longing and sadness, so intent on finding happiness in love, Gurov may simply have followed the pattern of his numerous earlier "adventures."

From the beginning their relationship is established on the basis of time:

Gurov: "Have you been in Yalta long?"
Anna: "Five days."
Gurov: "And I am dragging through my second week."
There was a short silence.
"Time passes so quickly, and yet it's so dull here," she said not looking
at him. (9:359)

This tediously laconic conversation begins their liaison. If this
form of communication, filled with silence and lack of contact,
is mutually attractive, then it is difficult to see how they could
expect anything more of love. It indicates they will move
through "love" as they have through life, passing through the
silences they hope to fill. Gurov's question is both an admission
of ennui and a plea to infuse his life with vitality and immediacy.
Her perception of time displays a peculiar twist, in that
when life is dull one usually thinks of it as dragging by. It is as
though she embraces boredom in order to speed time through
the void of her life. Time reaches out for them both, affecting an
effort at human contact in their enduring but unendurable lives.
And over this stand the numerous silences that further reinforce
the yawning gulf between them.

Part Two frames Gurov and Anna in exteriorized change as
they isolate themselves in the clutching timelessness of oppressive
heat. It opens on the note of passing time—"a week had
passed since they met" (9:360)—but it is, in fact, a time void.
Nothing has happened, so there is nothing to record. This
method of narration reflects the impressionist style of bypassing
the usual "events" in life: births, marriages, consummations,
deaths. The deliberate force of these ellipses focuses attention on
the flow of nuances and oblique epiphanies of life. Chekhov even
intensifies this notion through the actual delineation of purposeful
vacuums that fuse timelessness with passing time. His characters'
weary futility suggests that what is rendered for us is as
pointless as what is not.

While in Part One Gurov and Anna consciously satisfied with
boredom the subjective changes demanded by passing time, in
Part Two change becomes objectified in an evening to morning,
summer to autumn progression. Meanwhile, the heat seems to

hold them in mirage-like stasis. The stillness, monotony, waiting, silences, and isolation all contribute to the images of timelessness. Gurov and Anna are snared in the oppressive circles of an inferno: Anna in the midst of her first affair believes that she has "fallen" (*tochno k svoemu padeniiu*) and that "the devil made me do it" (*nechistyi poputal*) (9:362); Gurov becomes bored with her rambling protestations of guilt, and later, while watching the sea, thinks only of images of eternity.

Finally, after they return to the esplanade, the inferno imagery is sealed by their vision of the town looking quite "dead" (*imel sovsem mertvyi vid*). Their affair is controlled by the self-deception inherent in their insular and dissimilar experiences. This leads to Gurov's plaint: " 'I don't understand,' he said softly, 'what do you want?' " Not only can he not conceive of her needs, but he does not even know how to react to her. Should he reveal his boredom or try to "understand" through intonation, at the very moment his words belie his tone?

Gurov and Anna lose their ability to see clearly as they become further embroiled in this affair. Gurov's view of Anna is in continual flux. In the beginning she is simply a lady with a dog; then her "expression, bearing, dress, and the way she did her hair, told him that she belonged to the upper class, was married, was in Yalta for the first time and alone, and was bored here" (9:358). After his first meeting with her he felt there was "something pathetic about her" (9:360). Later, after he makes love to her, he sees the "timidity, the awkwardness of inexperienced youth" and that "there was something touching about her" (9:361). He then becomes bored with her. In the second half of the story, when he is in Moscow, he imagines her "lovelier, younger, tenderer than she had been" (9:365), and when he finally sees her at the theater she becomes "this little, unremarkable woman, lost in the provincial crowd, with a vulgar lorgnette in her hand" (9:363). But this time he thinks of her as filling his whole life. Anna, for her part, symbolically loses her lorgnette after she first meets Gurov, and later, when they meet at the theater, she holds another lorgnette in a tight grip,

as if determined not to lose it again because of him. Their relationship continues and the lorgnette again disappears.

When sight abandons Gurov as he first kisses Anna, his perceptions shift and he "drinks in the moist perfume of the flowers" (9:360). Later, as the lights from the train carrying Anna
away vanish and the sounds fade into that silence which seems
to define their relationship, he fills the void with sounds, not
sight. He hears the "cry of the grasshoppers and the buzzing of
the telegraph wires" (9:364). His perceptual world seems transformed, and as he realizes it he senses a return to reality. (But
in Chekhov's late impressionism the line between dream and
reality has become virtually nonexistent.) Gurov may feel that
he has "just waked up," but there is ample evidence that his
"dream" may simply have been another in a long series of self-
delusory affairs, each about as real as the fish scale lingerie.
Chekhov's method approaches the surrealism of Dali or Buñuel
with the "strange images" and inexplicable shifts in a character's perceptual world.

This dream motif in Chekhov's progression became more pro-
nounced as the dreams themselves became less distinguishable.
As his vision matured he came to understand that all subjective
images are phenomenologically real. In "Sleepy" the dream
images of Varka's past have a texture more real than the vapor-
ous haze of the cottage. Early in his career Chekhov began to
work with dream images that had the clearly defined contours
of unreality. He evolved to the point where the division between
dream and reality became unrecognizable. The impressionists
needed to create sensory reality while giving subjective shape to
time and space. Yet their equally strong desire to lay a foundation of subject matter that did not strain credulity provided the
perfect vehicle for a cautious venture into surrealism. Chekhov's
impressionism is partially, then, the fusion of realism and surrealism, resulting in "poetic realism."[4]

In the beginning of Part Two as Gurov and Anna aimlessly
wander the pier in silence, their impressions begin to increase.
Anna seems to search the darkened faces, as though waiting for

someone. Her sense of vague longing and her inability to focus on anything that has identity drives her closer to Gurov. He suddenly and for no reason kisses her—but then looks to see if anyone has seen them. They go to her room and consummate their affair. The oppressive heat and the perfume overwhelm him, and he escapes into the past as a way of distancing himself from the powerful impressions of the present. He "preserves the memory" (9:361) of three kinds of women who make no demands on his need for emotional disengagement. It makes no difference whether they once existed or have been invented; they have shaped Gurov's present attitudes. Based on these memories he momentarily sees Anna's inexperience as refreshing and her seriousness as inappropriate.

The image she has formed of herself will not allow him to frame her in his past nor escape from it. She confronts the moral situation of their affair. But what she is really doing is facing him with those aspects of his own life that he has avoided: she feels she has been deceiving herself; she wants "to live! To live, only to live" (9:362). His reaction is again self-deceptive avoidance: he eats a watermelon with affected boredom. He wants to respond to immediate sensations, not moral platitudes. Chekhov shows us both the dangers of living impressionistically without consciousness and of seeking answers to definitive pronouncements, as Anna does. Neither of these two ill-suited lovers can reach across the void to each other. They scream to one another in silence.

After this strange, obliquely fragmented, mistimed, and misfelt consummation, they drive to Oreanda to watch the morning sea. As they sit silently on a beach overlooking the sea, Chekhov forces the powerful impressions of the moment upon them. But this time Gurov does not respond; instead he (through an almost authorial distance and tone, used ironically by Chekhov) begins to think philosophic thoughts. Through this transiently impressionistic imagery of morning mist and motionlessness, he contemplates what he believes to be the indifferent and eternal universe that rolls like the sea over every individual. It would be tempting to take this internalized pontification of Gurov's seriously and proclaim that here is his moment of synthesis, the broad view of timelessness surrounded by the beauty of momentarily captured impressions. But he destroys it with an uninterested dismissal of Anna's attempt to reach him through shared perceptions of the loveliness. " 'There is dew on the grass,' said Anna Sergeevna after a silence. 'Yes, it's time to go home' " (9: 363). Gurov is bound by time, even as he speculates on timelessness. And from that instant until the lights from the train disappear, leaving Gurov alone in the autumn chill, their affair seems propelled by the sameness of scheduled time: "Then they met every day at twelve o'clock. . . . Almost every evening at a late hour they would drive somewhere, to Oreanda or to a waterfall; the trip was always a success, the scenery invariably impressed them as beautiful, majestic" (9:363–64).

Yet inserted between these two expressions of monotony, Chekhov creates for Gurov an impressionism of tedium that leads to a change in his perception of Anna: "complete idleness, these kisses in broad daylight exchanged furtively lest anyone see them, the heat, the smell of the sea and the continual flitting before his eyes of idle, well-dressed, well-fed people worked a complete change in him; he kept telling Anna Sergeevna how beautiful, how seductive she was" (9:363). Why Gurov would respond to such dullness with such vibrancy is beyond Chekhov's and impressionism's purview. This is a world of indeterminate causes—which is, of course, the stuff of poetic realism. As in Proust and James, Chekhov's impressions, significant or not, strike at the most gratuitous moments and often lead to the most unlikely and ambiguous reactions. Change is never measurable, only sensed in the mutual and completely amorphous relationship between subject and object. Chekhov, then, stands back and attempts to render Gurov's "change" through an objective stance, realizing, of course, that he is simply providing a neutral perspective for the examination of phenomenological ambiguity. Does Gurov change? Is this "complete change in him" (*tochno pererodili ego*) more definitive because it is stated explicitly? In Chekhov's late impressionism there is simply no way of telling, since each moment is so self-contained, making

no particular progression toward a character's final state of being.

Anna's husband writes that she must return. As they leave,
Anna describes their parting in those grand romantic absolutes:
"It is fate. . . . We are parting forever, it has to be, for we should
never have met. Well, God bless you" (9:364). Gurov says nothing. Chekhov renders only his sensory responses to their parting.
It is as though he feels their separation more strongly than he
would have himself believe—and perhaps more than Anna, although we have no access to her consciousness. He feels the enveloping darkness cloak him in loneliness and longing. Then he
snaps himself out of this "dream," thinking that this may have
been no more than "another episode or adventure in his life, and
it too was already ended, and now only the memory remained."
His self-protective, intellectualized shell returns as he attempts
to analyze his attitude toward Anna with that deceptive honesty
which passes for enlightenment. He has deceived himself, not
her. He struggles to rid himself of his sensory impressions, because they penetrate his layers of unchanging and self-justifying
consciousness. There is no escape, however, because he notices
the "scent of autumn in the air" and proclaims to himself that
it is "time for me to go north, too. . . . High time."

Part Three develops a major shift in imagery, signaling a possible change in Gurov: winter in Moscow at home. But the open,
fresh whiteness of snow, the cultural bustle of the city, and the
winter routines of home only bring out the chameleon in Gurov
again: "Little by little he became immersed in Moscow life" (9:
365). The same pattern in his life holds: images call back the
past, he initially hungers for the new and fresh, and he falls into habitual tedium. Yet Gurov now for the first time begins to
project a future in relation to Anna. He believes that she will
become "misty in his memory, and only once in a while will
she appear in his dreams with her touching smile, as will the
others." But this does not happen. Instead he finds his memories
of her insistently vivid and close to the present, until finally she
seems actually to be following his every movement, even peek-

ing out at him from the bookcase and fireplace. While this is no quasi-ghost story, it is very similar to the transformation of memory into a living presence in James's "The Jolly Corner." Once more Chekhov has tied a character's progression toward an epiphany to the recognition of the total *durée*—past, present, and future. Gurov had lived only for the past and present, which is why Anna's constant questions about a future became such a source of nagging irritation.

But Anna no longer exists for him in the present. He cannot passively wait, in the manner in which he had previously styled his life. For the first time (perhaps?), Gurov must search for what he has lost—and in a sense this resembles Proust's search for lost time, because it is the memory of Anna that he looks for, however distorted. He doesn't really hope to find the reality, for that would only mean continuing their monotony. He cannot allow this present image of the past to remain unfulfilled and futureless: "his memories turned into dreams, and in his imagination the past would mingle with the future." He tries, as Riabovich did in "The Kiss," to make Anna and love more real, more palpable, but no one wants to listen. He travels to her town in search of her. As he leaves he asks himself why he is doing this: "What for? He did not know himself" (9:366–67). Suddenly the whiteness of Moscow becomes drenched in gray. Nowhere in the story is colorlessness used so intensely: the hotel floor is covered with a gray army cloth, the table is gray with dust, in front of Anna's house is a long gray fence, his bed has a cheap gray blanket covering it. This grayness is the colorless stretch of reality representing the boredom of their relationship.

Gurov finally meets her at the theater, but only after registering the overwhelming impressions of provinciality she is surrounded by and that are in part reflected in her. As they hurriedly exit to the corridor, his fear produces another wave of sensory impressions. He "suddenly recalled how when he had seen Anna Sergeevna off at the station he had told himself that it was all over and that they would never meet again" (9:369). Chekhov never recorded that thought of Gurov's, so we have nothing to check it against, but we do know that these are precisely the thoughts that Anna expressed to Gurov. Again Chekhov has placed our perspective in ambiguous limbo. We don't know whether to believe Gurov's memory or not. His last thought at this moment provides the link to a future and drives the story toward its uncertain conclusion, as Gurov thinks, "but how distant the end still was" (*No kak eshche daleko bylo do kontsa*). The final lines of the story repeat that image, but from a position only slightly more distant, "that the end was still very far away" (*chto do kontsa eshche daleko-daleko*) (9:372). Gurov becomes increasingly concerned with the future, as his past begins to fade. No longer does he make the associations that place Anna among his other affairs. Gurov impulsively kisses her in the corridor of the theater as he had earlier on the pier at Yalta. In horror she projects her life of unhappiness into the timeless stream: "I have never been happy, I am unhappy now, and never, never shall I be happy, never" (9:369–70). She leaves him standing alone on the stairs, as he had been left on the railway platform in Yalta. This time she presents him with a future, however tenuous, by saying that she will come to Moscow.

Part Four, the final section, like Part Two opens with the impression of passing time, as Anna begins to visit Gurov in Moscow, "every two or three months" (9:370). She gives a medical excuse to her husband who (and here, Chekhov in one phrase creates a paradigm for the entire story) "believed and disbelieved her."

One day while walking with his daughter, Gurov answers with authority and without hesitation her question about why it thunders in the winter. He, like Nikolai Stepanovich in "A Dreary Story," is able to explain natural phenomena, but unable to understand his own life. What he does not realize is that in Chekhov's universe they are equally indeterminate. The single-faced truth of nature that Gurov perceives is as simplistic as the "two lives," one secret and one open, that he sees himself living. Nature and man are multifaceted and continually changing. Life may not be so easily compartmentalized. Any moment, glance, tone, and expression may reveal a glimpse of only one of many surfaces. For in the subject-to-object relationship what is communicated may or may not be what was intended, but even an instant of miscommunication may be truthful—it is, after all, real.

What Gurov and, in fact, all of Chekhov's impressionist characters face is a crisis of faith, or to put it in terms of Gurov's consciousness: "Judging others by himself, he did not believe what he saw" (9:371). He cannot believe himself, so he does not believe Anna, relegating her to the level of all those other deceptive women, "the inferior race." This, of course, leaves the reader in a similar morass. The flux of time, the changing demands of spatial perception, and the continual interface between subject and object, all make for an ambiguous world. Impressionists attempt to steer their characters toward survival, toward that particularly Jamesian balance between a naive perceptual belief and an expanding yet skeptical consciousness. Gurov had been all skepticism, because he could not conceive of a future that would turn his sardonic indifference into love. For love in Chekhov is nothing more than an absurd belief in an ephemeral and infinite future, which may transform the past and present into a thing of perceived beauty.

Gurov sees a definitive end to their affair, but only in some uncertain and distant future. He cannot understand it himself and refuses to tell Anna. At this moment, when he embraces her in a gesture of soothing diversion and studied indifference, he catches sight of himself in the mirror. In that quick, unexpected glance he finds his epiphany in the existential confrontation with time and mortality. Proust's Marcel had seen himself aging for the first time in the face of Gilberte's daughter. Gurov also understands that same principle. The gray hair and the younger woman in his arms force the recognition that, in Proust's words, time is "colorless and inapprehensible. Time, so that I was almost able to see it and touch it, had materialized itself in this girl, slowly moulding her into a masterpiece, whilst on me too parallelly, it had done its work, but without, alas! a master's touch."[5] The gray of Gurov's head matches the gray of his favorite of Anna's dresses. These become woven into the texture of the grayness pervading his search for her. It is all colorless time. This grayness has been the "inapprehensible" slippage of time, the boring sameness of their lives, but now the grayness of his head presses upon him the *belief* that "he had fallen in love, really, truly—for the first time in his life" (9:372).

From that moment, as time stops for him, as he looks at its passing without indifference, the narrative switches from Gurov's consciousness to statements of "they": they believe Fate had meant them for each other; they could not understand why each had a spouse; they forgave each other for their pasts and their present. And finally, in a very important statement, "they felt that this love had changed them both" (*chuvstvovali, chto eta ikh liubov izmenila ikh oboikh*). K. M. Vinogradova has pointed out the two other versions Chekhov had considered for the last few words: that this love, (1) "had made them both better" and (2) "had changed them both for the better"; finally he simply settled for (3) "had changed them both."[6] It seems clear that this paradigmatic progression shows Chekhov, the impressionist, struggling to maintain the non-didactic, ambiguous artistry of impressionism. Now "they" have changed. Have they? How have they? It makes no difference, really, because they believe they have. Yet this surge of togetherness and open compassion is in itself subject to the rush of time and indeterminacy. So as Gurov and Anna struggle to reshape the confining contours of their relationship, Gurov in frustration asks, "How? How? . . . How?" The subtle time shifts and unintelligibility of the last lines suggest that their lives will be spent in an unending and definitively unsuccessful search for the answer to Gurov's "hows?" Gurov and Anna face a future of uncertainty, based on a past that makes little sense, and a present of vibrantly fleeting instants and continually tedious unhappiness. Yet by the end of the story they seem to have accepted a present futureness, they seem to have stepped into the *durée* and are able to believe in its continuity. This is the heart of Chekhov's impressionist vision.

II * "THE BISHOP"

One of the most sadly neglected impressionist stories is one of Chekhov's greatest. "The Bishop" (*Arkhierei*) (1902) forces ontological ambiguity to the limits of human existence. The question is not whether Gurov loves Anna Sergeevna, but whether Bishop Petr actually exists. The problems of perception become greater, because the point of view is more tenuous.

While many critics have looked upon this story as a simple, realistic portrayal of a Russian bishop,[7] there are those who have noticed the complexities. Dmitri Chizhevsky, in one of the pioneering surveys of Chekhov's impressionism, states that "Chekhov places stress on the fact that sensations, experiences, are in continual flux, in a process of change. Above all, he tried to record the fading of experiences and events. . . . The motif operates most strongly at the end of Chekhov's last story [*sic*] 'The Bishop.' "[8] Nils Åke Nilsson also noticed the impressionism of Chekhov's story: "This interplay of rhythms is emphasized by something which could be called an impressionistic or a 'bloc technique.' Such a technique, a result of Čechov's demand for economy and objectivity, consists in placing small complete scenes next to each other without any comments."[9] And finally, in the best effort to come to terms with Chekhov's impressionism, Karl Kramer ends his book with the observation that "ambiguity is a concomitant of Čexov's impressionism; whenever our focus shifts from what is to what it seems to us to be, we have opened the floodgates to a deluge of possibilities, none of which can ever be certainties. . . . 'The Bishop' is an appropriate story with which to end an account of Čexov's studies in the tenuous and uncertain nature of man's existence in a world whose exact proportions he is incapable of ascertaining, and where all truths are relative."[10]

In this story, Bishop Petr's actual existence is called into question through the multiple perspectives of a multidimensional past. The Bishop forms the center of consciousness, and yet we enter into his sphere of perception only after a short introduction that is clearly outside his "distorted" subjective vision. And the story is completed after his death, with his mother's waning efforts to keep not only his memory but also his existence alive in the face of neighborly skepticism. Chizhevsky says of this that "in this way 'reality' recedes into the background, and the events which apparently constitute the causes or motivations of experiences have an effect only in the form which they assume, as they are broken up and reshaped in people's psyches."[11] Since memory forms the structure on which the ambiguity of the Bishop's existence is based, the perceptual filter through which the past is seen is open to distortion. But just as Proust never questioned the "reality" of his distortions of the past, so Chekhov refused to allow a definitive choice to be made regarding the "Truth" of windmills and knights. He avoids the problem of illusion/reality by believing, just as the impressionist painters did, that appearances *are* reality and that perceptions are phenomenologically subject to the seeming caprices of both subject and object. Chekhov, in refusing to relinquish empirical epistemology, forced his characters to accept the ambiguity of existence, thereby driving them to hang on to the validity of their immediate perceptions. Since these perceptions are subject to the vagaries of time, it takes faith to continue to believe in existence—not simply the existence of one's dead son, but the existence of one's perceptual reality.

When we can test the perceptions of one character against those of another, we face not simply the epistemological issue but the ontological as well. In this story the weight of perceptual consciousness falls on the Bishop, yet in a stunningly subtle shift of perspective Chekhov permits the mother a moment of subjective perception while her son, the Bishop, still remains alive: "And it seemed to her that he had grown thinner, weaker, and more insignificant than he had ever been, and she forgot he was a bishop" (9:430). By taking the narrative away from the

Bishop for a moment, Chekhov grants the mother her own perceptual and narrative validity, forcing us, then, to question her final perception. The logical extension of this story might then follow this pattern: if the memories of Bishop Petr are subject to the distortions of present experience, and if these memories fade and vanish, then it is possible that after the Bishop's death his existence will become nothing more than a memory for others. We must question his existence, since it appears to be based on his mother's memory, just as we were skeptical of his remembrances. The Bishop's memories never existed except perhaps in the imagination of a lonely, poor peasant woman. The Bishop himself, in whose existence we believed, disappears by the end of the story. Past and present, memory and existence flow together in this Proustian vision of "pure time." In "The Bishop" Chekhov concedes that, intellectually, the epistemological and ontological ambiguities of life, death, and memory are irresolvable.

The one means of resolving these indeterminacies of existence resides in faith, and it is the collapse of faith in the modern world that has all but obsessed the greatest twentieth-century writers. A major theme in many of Chekhov's stories ("The Kiss," "In the Cart," and "The Lady with the Dog") centers on the dreams that could have become reality if only people had been able to continue to believe in them in the face of confusion, emptiness, and the passage of time. A number of characters experience a moment of happiness, because for an instant they believe they had been loved or kissed. So long as they maintain a faith in the existence of that moment they are able to keep it alive. But as its reality evaporates into the temporal distance, they falter and lose their power to believe. Only dissolution and nothingness remain for those characters who have neither the faith to believe that the past is the present nor the strength to hope for a future moment of happiness. This conviction Chekhov had carried through so many stories on a secular level becomes transformed into a superimposed religious allegory in "The Bishop." The allegory, however, serves only as a symbolic structure for man's need to animate his images through a secular faith. The full dramatic scope of these modern literary and human concerns explodes in the final moments of this remarkably polymorphic story.

The first two chapters of this story occur on the eve of Palm Sunday and on Palm Sunday itself, recording through the Bishop's memories his rise to eminence. His ascension resembles the journey of Christ to Jerusalem. The Bishop dies on the day before Easter and on Easter Sunday the town comes alive with the "deep happy notes of the church bells . . . birds were singing, and the bright sun was shining. The great market square was full of noise . . . in a word, everything was gay and happy just as it had been during the previous year and as it doubtless would be in the years to come" (9:430). The Bishop's resurrection takes the form of nature, the town, and its people. Though Bishop Petr may be forgotten, his memory and spirit are renewed in succeeding bishops, all of whom perform the same functions and represent the cyclical recurrence of infinite existence. The Bishop's death brings a new beginning, just as winter hails the spring and silence tolls for the noise of life. Each Sunday after service when Bishop Petr rides home in his carriage he feels, sees, and hears the same sounds and sights that will vibrate with life after he has died. These images of regeneration and hope reinforce the cyclical pattern of both the story and Chekhov's belief in changeless change: "The Bishop got into his carriage and drove home, listening to the joyous and harmonious chimes of the heavy church bells, which he loved and which filled the whole garden in the moonlight. . . . The breath of spring could still be felt in the soft cool air. . . . Bathed in a clear and peaceful moonlight, the pilgrims were trudging home through the sand on both sides of the carriage. All were silent, deep in thought. Everything around looked familiar and friendly and young—so that *one longed to believe it would endure forever*" (9:417; italics mine). The bells continuously toll for matins, vespers, and mass as though representing the continuity of existence. Faith is necessary for existence, and existence is necessary for the renewal and continuity of hope; the cycle must be complete.

While the endless procession of bishops will give meaning to Bishop Petr's death, he must also find an identity for his own existence. He must discover a meaning for his present life if he is to retain the hope for his and the world's resurrection, or at least its renewal. It is in this quest for a unique identity that his very existence is called into question. His happiest memories appear to be of childhood, before he became a priest, and he longs to find that self hidden beneath the cloaks of his office. His moments of most intense isolation occur when he senses his mother's inability to respond naturally to him, because he wears the vestments and carries the aura of The Bishop. It is only when he is dying that his mother "forgot he was a bishop, and she kissed him as though he were a child very close and dear to her" (9:430). It is then that she recognizes in him what he has been longing to be: her son. Yet the inability of people to see in a man more than one surface forces upon him the identity of a bishop. His dual identity as son and bishop drives him to abrupt changes in mood, because he involuntarily responds to the way he sees people perceiving him. He feels kind and gentle when he believes he is simply a man who can minister to his flock as a man. But when he notices his congregation responding to him only as a bishop, he reacts with the arbitrary disdain of a man of power. The role takes over the man, and Chekhov has continued his vision of man as chameleon. The Bishop's attitudes toward his past are controlled by the memory fragments that cast him in the role of either a son or a bishop.

His existence and his identity hinge on his mother's ability to hold on to her memory of him as a son. She, however, wants to preserve both images: "And sometimes she will pause and talk with the other women in the fields about her children and grandchildren and about how she had a bishop son" (*syn arkhierei*) (9:431). In the mother's description of her children and grandchildren Chekhov left no question as to their existence. She specifically refers to them in the present tense, but when she speaks of Bishop Petr it is in the past perfect, indicating she may have had but no longer has a "bishop son." That event, his existence, is completed and isolated in the past. She would never question whether she had a son nor would her friends, but they are tentative regarding the existence of a bishop who was also her son: "And here she would speak timidly, fearing that they wouldn't believe her. . . . And as a matter of fact not everyone did believe her." The possibility of the mother, a peasant woman, having a bishop for a son is too overwhelming in its social incongruity; more importantly, it is as though bishops cannot exist as human beings, so that she could not have had a son who was also a bishop. Bishops are an office, vestments, rituals, and spiritual manifestations. Individual bishops are forgotten, because their identities are wedded to the concept of the infinite continuity of bishops. Bishop Petr's mother lacks the faith of Mary, who was able to fuse the image of her son with that of a spiritual son of God and man.

The analogy is apt, for in this understated allegory, Bishop Petr is Christ. Often, in fact, Father Sisoi, in ambiguous phrases that seem to be both exclamatory pleas to God and addresses to the Bishop, shouts: "Lord Jesus Christ! . . . A thorough rubbing will do you good! Lord Jesus Christ!" and "I'll be leaving tomorrow, your Eminence, because I've had enough of it. Lord Jesus Christ! Well, that's how it is!" (9:429). The Bishop's death before Easter allows him to rise on Easter Sunday and become one with the world of man, God, and nature. The juxtaposition of the death of the Bishop and the rising of Christ provocatively suggests that Bishop Petr be taken as the risen Christ: "The Bishop was dead. . . . The next day was Easter" (9:430). The point of the story is not to affirm that Bishop Petr is Christ, but to demonstrate the unstable ontological difficulties of maintaining a sense of identity about oneself when one is both a man of flesh and the embodiment of spirituality, particularly when one lacks the faith to maintain an identity in either state. At the same time, this story is about the Bishop's and his mother's distortions of perception. The anguish of existence appears through prismatically perceived identities refracted by ambiguity, indeterminacy, and a lack of faith.

Bishop Petr perceives a dual world, the world of a bishop and of a man. The bishop's world "was like being in a fog" (9:416).

He sees through the labyrinth of centuries of bishops past and future, so that "it seemed that those faces—old and young, men and women—were exactly the same. . . . He could not see the doors through the haze, the crowd kept moving and it looked as though there was no end to it and there would never be an end to it." As he lives through time, in the vestments of a bishop, the void of unchanging continuity often seems unendurable. How can he feel the growth of his identity when he inhabits an office of stasis and when his flock all seem forever the same? Here the fog of timelessness is painful. But after the service, which embodies stasis, the Bishop rides home and sees white walls, white crosses, white birches, and listens to the "joyous and harmonious" (9:417) chimes of church bells. He longs for all this freshness and joy to last forever. And in this hope he confronts the ambiguity of timelessness: the church service where he must accept the role of bishop is unendurable in its endlessness, while nature in its rebirth makes him feel his organic humanness and fills him with the desire to stop this same endless cycle and hold on to its natural beauty; at the same time nature and its vitality "seemed now to be living its own life, incomprehensible, but close to mankind." The Bishop's relationship to both the church and nature is ambiguous and incomprehensible, and so are his two identities.

His entire existence becomes precarious and unstable. His mother "suddenly appeared to him as though in a dream or delirium . . . or perhaps it was only an old woman who resembled his mother" (9:416). As he questions her existence, so does the reader, until her presence is confirmed by a lay brother. Bishop Petr's perception of the past is equally ambiguous, as memories flood his consciousness only to be both revered and questioned: "Dear, precious, unforgettable childhood! Why was it that those far-off days, which would never return, seemed brighter, gayer, and richer than they really were. . . . And now his prayers mingled with memories" (9:418). Many of Chekhov's characters are faced with the dilemma of whether to believe in the past and see it as a moment of immediate experience, or believe the past can never return and all that is left of it is

one's highly distorted dreams which have little to do with reality. The past represents both remembered recreation and loss.
Those memories of the past have also become part of his prayers
for the future. Imagination and perception in the present have
fused the great polarities of destruction and creation, past and
future. Yet a day later these cycles of change are called into
question when the Bishop's mother, who saw him for the first
time in nine years, says, "dear Lord, you hadn't changed even a
little bit" (9:421).

His mother's appearance in the narrative further unsettles an
already unstable situation: to her, Bishop Petr seems not to have
changed, although time alters all things; at the service she wept,
"though God knows what I was weeping for"; she is not clear on
whether to address her bishop/son formally or familiarly, feeling "as though she was more like the widow of a deacon than his
mother"; as she reared her children when she was young, so
now does she take care of her grandchildren (the cycles of gen-
erations seem not to have altered her); and finally, talking of a
grandson's decision to study medicine, she says, "He thinks it's
the best thing, but who really knows?" The Bishop's mother refuses to recognize change and allows herself to succumb to the
chaos of the unknown. She does not believe in anything—not a
strong legacy to pass on to her son, who himself seems to suffer
from the same weakness. The moment Bishop Petr recognizes
this transient form of indeterminacy in his mother, his "mood
abruptly changed. He gazed at his mother and could not understand how she had come by that timid, deferential expression of
face and voice, and he could not understand what lay behind it,
and he did not recognize her" (9:422). If his identity is in question, so is hers. The relativism of dual points of view places the
issues of identity and indeterminacy into open conflict: two
characters in flux multiply the surfaces of existence, while
dramatizing the chasms of unexplored knowledge that lie between each.

Bishop Petr's perceptions of his surroundings change with
his shifts in mood. When he cannot understand his mother's
identity, he begins suddenly to suffer from a headache, his legs

become wracked with pain, "the fish he was eating seemed stale and tasteless," he notices in his guests silences and long faces. There has been no apparent cause for this change, yet his mental state and his environment have become one. As the moonlight disturbs his vision, he begins to fade into his past. He remembers his first days as a rector, when he was happy and the "days flowed so peacefully and pleasantly and seemed to stretch far into the future with no end in sight." He has so surrendered himself to his past that he actually becomes a part of it, losing his present identity. He begins to recall memories, so the past now comes to have a number of levels which exclude the present: "He remembered how homesick he had been for his native land, and he remembered a blind beggar woman playing on a guitar underneath his window and singing about love, and whenever he listened to her, he always found himself for some reason meditating on the past. Eight years slipped away before he was already fading into the far off mists as though it were a dream" (9:423). In this remarkable passage, past and present become confused, sliding through one another so that the fragments of the past become fragments of the present, and it all seems like a dream. The power of this passage, woven together with the threads of indeterminacy, dreams, and memories, finally calls into question the Bishop's identity, and, ultimately, his existence.

Could not this reverie have been the dream of a mother who wishes that in her dull, peasant life she had borne not simply a son, but a "bishop son"? If she can dream of a famous son who has finally, just before his death, come to see that "his old mother had changed—had in fact changed more than most" (9:424), that the past had been "vivid, beautiful and joyful" (9: 425), but that this past was also "in all likelihood as it had never been," then she can continue to live a life of sadness and joy, incomprehension and dignity, hope and hopelessness through him, her son, the Bishop. Her son becomes a vicarious existence through which her life becomes richer and fuller. He exists as an instrument of his mother's wish-fulfillment. It is important that when the Bishop is dying the point of view of the mother be expressed, so that she can resolve, for a moment, the human side of the identity she created for him. He is her son for that moment before his death, justifying for her, after his death, his existence as both a son and a bishop. He is her Christ: he can give her faith; he can allow her to believe in him.

Time, however, begins to erode the dream of a bishop/son: "In a word, everything was lighthearted and frolicsome, just as it had been during the previous year and as it doubtless would be in the years to come. A month later a new bishop was installed, and no one gave a thought to Bishop Petr. Soon he was completely forgotten" (9:430). The possibilities of past memories that could create for the old woman a son who was also a bishop, now drift into the flow of passing time and destroy the memory. Chekhov's characters are rarely able to maintain their faith in either their dreams or their dreamlike realities. Time sweeps away and annihilates the existence of their beautiful moments. If time can dissolve what seemed to be, then perhaps it never was. The Bishop might have been only a passing impression that gave the old peasant woman a dignity she could never have attained without the miracle of memory. Time creates and destroys for Chekhov. Faith could stay the execution, but faith in one's own identity and in the reality of one's son is as difficult to maintain as a faith in Christ throughout the centuries, particularly in the face of skepticism: "And indeed there are some who do not believe her."

III * "THE BETROTHED"

Chekhov's final story, "The Betrothed" (*Nevesta*), was completed in 1903, just weeks after he had begun work on *The Cherry Orchard*. It is not his greatest story, but it is his most elusive, and therefore certainly his most misunderstood. For years it has been looked upon as his final pronouncement on Russia's future.[12] It is often set apart from the earlier stories. For, as Thomas Winner sees it, a new mood is represented by Nadia, who "asserts her right to a new life," while the other works often ended on "a sad note of realization."[13] Only Karl Kramer has observed the essential enigma of this story: "has Nadia escaped a narrowly provincial life and will she find some kind of more exalted existence, or is she condemned to an endless repetition of these awakenings and disillusionments? It seems to me both interpretations are equally tenable and this, of course, is at the heart of the story's ambiguity."[14] Considering that many critics view *The Cherry Orchard* as a "poetic comedy of exquisite balance" with "an embracing structure of comic-tragic ambivalence,"[15] it is surprising that "The Betrothed," with such strong connections to the play, is still perceived in a turgidly traditional light. Actually, Chekhov's last three stories evolve in much the same manner, project many of the same themes, offer the same tentative and ambiguous endings, and employ the same aesthetic: impressionism.

Gurov, Bishop Petr, and Nadia are all turned toward the rituals of new beginnings—a new face that will materialize into a first love, an Easter Sunday, a marriage. Yet none of these prospects become fully consummated. While Gurov proclaimed he had finally found a true love in Anna, the solipsistic quality of Gurov's history throws doubt upon his claim. Although Bishop Petr died on the Saturday night before Easter, it is possible he might never have existed. Nadia, too, changes her perceptions so often that when she refuses to marry, hoping instead to strike out on her own, we no longer feel it is a definitive act. She disavows that ritual of a new beginning in order to begin anew. The irony of her situation is sealed when she returns home to a pariah's welcome and the jeers of "The betrothed! The betrothed!" (9:449). She remains what she had tried to escape. Her flight had been so short-lived that it seems not to have existed, and is taken care of in two short lines dramatizing that void of passing time which also characterized "The Lady with the Dog": "Autumn passed, and winter after it. Nadia was already very homesick and every day she thought about her mother and grandmother, and she thought of Sasha" (9:446). Her first great excursion is characterized by the seasons of endings, autumn and winter, and is filled with thoughts for those representing stasis, her mother and grandmother. Sasha, her inspiration for transformation, is accorded only an afterthought. Given Nadia's reaction to this first and seemingly important break from provinciality, and given Chekhov's penchant for puncturing with devastatingly precise irony the pretentiously pontificated plans of his characters, it would seem difficult to claim that her "final" break toward that "new, broad, spacious life" (9:450) is any different from her earlier vision of an "immense, broad future" (9:445). In Chekhov's impressionistic fiction nothing is final. Marriage seems like a finality to Nadia; instead she, in effect, marries herself to continual beginnings.

The key to an understanding of this story rests in the realization that this is Chekhov's most perceptually solipsistic work. Since everything that seems to change is totally subject to Nadia's perception of change, "The Betrothed" becomes Chekhov's most completely self-enclosed, almost bracketed, examination of the phenomenological subject-object relationship. Chekhov is searching for the ultimate in elusive change, through the eyes of a young woman who sees her life progressing through the unending beauty of uninterrupted transformation. But she cannot at the same time reconcile herself to the fact that transformation means loss. Time cyclically returns all things to the same beginnings. This story, then, actually becomes Chekhov's final "statement" on the nature of change. Change is exhilarating and constricting, sequential and cyclical, static and dynamic, timeless and temporal, substantive and evanescent—and above all, impressionistic. Nadia is really the most completely impressionistic character in all of Chekhov's mature stories. But she has neither the complex consciousness of Gurov nor the ontological crisis of Bishop Petr. She seems to have more in common with the pure perceivers of Chekhov's early work, although she tries to give shape to impressions through time by conceiving of the differences between what has been, what is, and what will be.

This story's objectified elements of transformation are the seasons and the times of day, which Chekhov symbolically weaves through Nadia's own rituals of change. Before we are introduced to Nadia, Chekhov provides an ironic rhetorical flourish of mythic beginnings: "There was the feeling of May, sweet May! One breathed deeply, and hoped that not here, but somewhere beneath the sky, above the trees far beyond the city, in the fields and forests, spring was now unfolding a life of its own, mysterious, lovely, bountiful and holy, beyond the comprehension of weak sinful man. And for some reason one wanted to cry" (9:432). But even this passage contains the seeds of Nadia's dissatisfaction, that the "mysterious, lovely" life is unfolding somewhere, but not where she is. Her search for the future is as distorted as Gurov's belief in the tranquility of his past. Both deny the continuity of time and repudiate their perceptions of the present. The most profound irony in Chekhov is that while his characters respond impressionistically, they feel they must seek to redress the natural order of subjective time and their phenomenological impressions.

So Nadia, on the threshold of marriage and surrounded by spring, is unhappy, feeling that "somehow it seemed that just as now, her whole life would go on and on, without change, without end" (9:433). Were she to accept what she sees instead of believing only what she wants to believe, she could acknowledge the changes we see her perceiving. For instance, in the midst of her fears that if she married, "something indeterminate and dreadful" (9:436) would be awaiting her, she looks out the window into the garden and sees "the lilac bushes in the distance,[16] thick with flowers, drowsy and limp from the cold. A heavy white mist softly floats toward the lilacs, trying to cover them. Drowsy rooks are cawing in the distant trees." The shrouded, limpid, distant imagery reflects both her state of mind and the moment—"My God, why am I so miserable!"—and the state of the night. But as dawn approaches and the watchman's "tic-toc, tic-toc" (symbolic of passing time and change) has not been heard for some time, she begins to think of Sasha and his continual lectures on the need for her to break away from the provincial tedium of her life. She can't seem to banish Sasha's grating pontifications from her mind. Meanwhile, in the garden "the birds began to call, the mist lifted from the garden and everything was bathed in the sun's embrace, came to life and dewdrops glittered on the leaves like diamonds; and the old, long-neglected garden this morning seemed young, beautifully arrayed" (9:436–37).

This is perhaps Chekhov's most striking single example of impressionism. It makes palpable two juxtaposed spatial perceptions of nature held in perfect balance by the inner and outer worlds of one perceiver, while subject to change through time. Both the quality of light and Nadia's shifting moods crystallize the phenomenology of the *corps-sujet*. Nadia's consciousness penetrates the world of the garden, while the garden also penetrates Nadia's consciousness. They are both real and exist for one another. Chekhov is very careful to render the garden in credible, naturalistic terms, while showing the parallel changes in Nadia's moods. Does her mood change because she thinks of Sasha's energizing belief in self-revolution or because the dawn is breaking (both naturalistically and symbolically), or simply because subject and object are in gratuitous correspondence? Since impressionists refuse to deal in the roulette of speculative causality, there is really no way of knowing why nature and Nadia have found common coordinates. It is this continuously oblique unity that gives impressionism its open ambiguity.

The way Nadia sees and what she sees *suggests* that she *might* begin to move toward *some kind* of modification in her life. These qualifications point to a major technical and stylistic concern of impressionism, one which had been consistently but temperately used by Chekhov in his earlier work. Only in "The Betrothed" does its use become an unrelenting force in the intra-texture of the prose: "some," "somewhere," "someone," "something," "for some reason," "for no reason," "it must have been," "it seemed to be," "it seemed to her," "perhaps." Beyond the vast quantity of these authorial tropes are expressions that suggest the indeterminacy of the character's consciousnesses: "you don't know him," "Who knows!" "I don't know, dear," "Nadia began to feel that her mother did not understand her and was incapable of understanding her," "It was already clear to her that she no longer loved Andrei Andreich or, perhaps, she had never loved him, but how to say this, to whom should she say it, and what would be the use—she did not understand and could not understand," "and it was hard to tell whether he was joking or serious," "Nadia kept looking at him, but could not tell whether he was seriously ill or only seemed so to her."

Chekhov's ambience seems to be best described by Merleau-Ponty, who says that "instead of an intelligible world there are radiant nebulae separated by expanses of darkness."[17] In the world of Chekhovian impressionism, minutiae of perception are followed by vast silences, meaning and meaninglessness are yoked in the same instant, and both trivial and significant epiphanies are enveloped in epistemological indeterminacy. The ambiguity of impressionism finds its source in "the rejection of the clean cut distinction between the different aspects which constitute one and the same reality."[18] Nadia thinks that Sasha mouths the same old platitudes and yet he gives her inspiration for change; she believes nothing is different, but believes she is capable of creating a new beginning; she breaks away from the boring life of her hometown, but soon returns. At first she notices what appear to be negative changes in the town, but later when she goes up to her room she sees "the same bed, the same windows with the naive white curtains, and outside the windows the same garden bathed in sunlight, gay, and noisy" (9: 443). Nadia in her despair sees both the change and changelessness, the joy and oppression, the comfort and uneasiness of her return.

These paradoxes are so much a part of the impressionist aesthetic that they become the basic fabric of "The Betrothed." Near the end of the story Nadia's mother tells her that she has been thinking about philosophy and that "it seems to me that all of life must pass through a prism" (9:448). Nadia, like Gurov, is bored by this kind of talk. She interrupts her mother and the watchman passes with his tic-toc of passing time. Her mother tries again. She repeats the line about the prism and continues: "That is, in other words, life in consciousness must be divided into its simplest elements, like the seven basic colors, and each studied separately." Nadia falls asleep. The next lines carry her somnambulance through a time of changing change-lessness: "May passed, June came. Nadia had by now gotten used to the house." Nadia has become Chekhov's impressionist character *par excellence*. She simply flows through the prism without consciousness, never knowing whether she and/or her environment have changed. She never experiences the privi-leged moment that might crystallize her impressions; she re-mains in the swirl of relativistic flux to the end.

Despite the seemingly definitive upbeat ending, our memories of her continual vacillation and cyclic returns remain. Chekhov undermines the positive thrust by inserting a qualifying irony: she "left town—as she supposed, forever" (*kak polagala, nav-segda*) (9:450). Beginnings and endings, like life and death, are ambiguous, leaving only perception and belief, at their most subjective, to give shape to the fragments of time.

IV * IMPRESSIONIST DRAMA

Chekhov's last plays, *The Three Sisters* and *The Cherry Or-chard*, demonstrate more forcefully than any of his other work the conscious evolution of his impressionism. The strides he took toward modernism in his stories were matched by his experi-ments in the drama. But while his impressionist prose seemed neither to startle nor annoy, his efforts as a playwright were almost universally derided. As his aesthetic outlook became more completely impressionistic, it was natural that he would turn to the play as the perfect expression of those ideas. Impres-sionism, as we have seen in the analysis of Chekhov's prose, gravitates toward dramatic method.

One of the distortions of Chekhov's career centers on the either-or approach to his artistic development. Usually it is either his stories or his plays that are analysed, and often he is thought to have written stories and then plays. But Chekhov is reported by his brother, Michael, to have written plays while in grammar school,[19] then later he wrote farces. In 1884 he wrote two one-act plays. And in 1887 he wrote *Ivanov*, a play commissioned by F. A. Korsh for a major theater in Moscow. This is the same year in which he came to the end of his early period of impressionist prose and was ready to launch into "The Steppe" and "Sleepy." It is true that Chekhov's growth as an impressionist playwright lagged behind his progress in prose. It was not until the 1901 triumph of *The Three Sisters* that his impressionism really emerged on stage. Some of the blame can be placed on the sour reception of *The Seagull.*

But two more essential factors are responsible for the slow materialization of dramatic impressionism: (1) Theater was a popular form, attended, as Strindberg so acerbically noted, by the middle-classes, and they simply could not respond to plays that were not only anti-romantic and anti-melodramatic, but actually anti-naturalistic as well. After all, a play may be closer to life than a story, but people do not venture out of their homes and pay good money to witness a plotless and fragmentary piece of ensemble acting that carefully denies them an all-out release of emotions. Delicately changing moods, ambivalent reactions, and, to use J. L. Styan's term, "dark comedy," was not what moved the theatergoing public. (2) While drama seemed to be such a natural form for impressionism, the fine-spun threads that make it so fragile and ephemeral can actually mitigate its playing well. In other words, writing an impressionist play that could be acted out on the stage and understood by an audience was very difficult. And the theatrical conventions were carved in granite. I don't believe that the famous disagreements between Chekhov and Stanislavsky were the result of a total misunderstanding on Stanislavsky's part. It is very likely that Stanislavsky knew he must feed his audience their required portion of tragedy and weeping, that he must mediate between the impossibly divergent demands of both playwright and audience.

Chekhov is usually categorized in theater history as a naturalist, sometimes a realist. These are the labels that have plagued him in his prose as well. It is doubtful that these most hideously imprecise and virtually meaningless terms will die or go away. I am sure that there will be those who would wish the same of impressionism. But how can one justify a single rubric for such essentially different playwrights as Zola, Hauptmann, Schnitzler, Ibsen, Strindberg, Ostrovsky, Tolstoy, Turgenev, Chekhov, and Gorky, not to mention those out of the period, Shaw and O'Neill? Certainly Zola and Gorky were naturalists, and probably Tolstoy and Ibsen were realists—but Chekhov? Some moved through different phases, Strindberg, for instance. Yet the official triumvirate of theatrical naturalism is Ibsen, Strindberg, and Chekhov. I don't believe Chekhov's goals were ever naturalistic. He was trying to write *through* naturalism.

A good deal of the difficulty here has to do with the term *naturalism*. It seems to mean one thing in drama, another in prose; it has both a general meaning and a specific one; it can in the widest and loosest sense embrace drama and prose. Chekhov could only be included as a naturalist in its broadest meaning: an anti-romantic who attempted to depict the common occurrences of daily life with a maximum of scientific objectivity. The application of this term to the novel as it takes on more specific meaning confuses the issue: only those works that adhered to philosophical determinism could qualify. Based upon the positivism of Comte, the determinism of Darwin, and the methodology of Claude Bernard, Zola created his "experimental" novels and plays that found their characters in the bowels of the earth and subjected them to the overwhelming forces of destructive heredity and modern environments. Certainly this was not the aesthetic vision of Chekhov's plays. Naturalism in drama seems closer to the realism of prose: the plotless evocation of mood through the accumulation of common details enunciated in the trivial dialogue of everyday speech. But even this definition is potentially too subtle for most realism. Realists wanted "important" issues spoken of "realistically" by psychologically round characters. Chekhov was reaching for a much more tenuous reality—the reality of impressionism.

Once again, while there may have been no movement or consciousness of anything called impressionism, Chekhov was attempting something quite different from Ibsen, Strindberg, and other so-called naturalists. J. L. Styan and Maurice Valency have noticed the differences and mention Chekhov's impressionist qualities.[20] Martin Esslin and Tom Driver have noted the subjectivism in his objective realism, and feel that he is the forerunner of modern playwriting and theater of the absurd.[21] Yet for the most part Chekhov is still consigned to the naturalism he was trying to escape. It should be stated that many drama scholars define naturalism quite differently. Some try to squeeze Chekhov into the more traditional confines of prose naturalism. Others redefine naturalism in order to accommodate Chekhov's art. A more congruent approach would be to simply call his mature plays impressionistic.

One issue is clear: Chekhov the playwright has always been considered one of the giants of the theater. His plays, unlike his stories, have been carefully scrutinized. Had he been a novelist his prose reputation would have been just as great. But the essential growth and reputation of Chekhov as both short story writer and playwright rest on his continual return and struggle to reach for the techniques and vision of impressionism. The impact of Chekhov's dramatic impressionism was revolutionary, while his prose had been gradually moving in this direction for some time. Certainly Ibsen helped clear the way. Audiences knew what his plays were about; they were simply outraged at what they were about. Chekhov's plays were confusing because audiences could not put all the pieces together. They were not sure what they had seen, what it all meant, and what they were supposed to feel about it.

With so much written about Chekhov's plays, and since so much that has been written shows understanding of his modernism and methods, it is really only necessary to place his plays in the context of his impressionism. A close exegesis is unnecessary with a book as astute as Professor Styan's *Chekhov in Performance*. Act by act Styan pursues many of the essentials in impressionism, without, however, actually identifying *The Three Sisters* and *The Cherry Orchard* as the supreme examples of dramatic impressionism. And Styan points out a number of times that many of Chekhov's effects were honed in his years of story writing. So it would hold that his last two plays, written during his greatest impressionist prose period, would also reflect the maturity of his impressionism. It is with these two plays that we are primarily concerned.

The Seagull, while certainly a break from the conventional theater of the time, still contained the pistol that must go off in Act 4, the center stage for a major actress, and a symbol with a defined meaning. *Uncle Vanya* has elements of melodrama and farce and sees itself addressing an issue with naturalistic force. By 1901 Chekhov had already written "The Lady with the Dog" and felt himself to be in full command of his impressionist powers. The period between *Uncle Vanya* (1897) and *The Three Sisters* (1901) was the most critical stage in Chekhov's development as an impressionist. The growth of his prose from "In the Cart" (1897) to "The Lady with a Dog" (1899) was striking, but the leap he took from *Uncle Vanya* to *The Three Sisters* demonstrated the complete ripening of his impressionism.

The basic philosophic and aesthetic underpinnings of impressionist drama and prose are much the same. The shift to rendered atmosphere took an interesting turn in impressionist drama. Theater has always been the perfect medium for rendering rather than describing. Characters simply speak and sets are simply there. In this sense drama is inherently impressionistic. But at the same time playwrights felt the need to compensate for the potential ambiguity of rendering, making sure that symbolic action or narrative structure made clear their intentions. So on the one hand the drama served the impressionist need for presenting rendered experience, and on the other, there was the fear that a play of rendered atmosphere, the Chekhovian mood play, lacking action and eschewing "significant" issues, would be boring and misunderstood. This was the challenge Chekhov accepted—and paid for. His solution was to: (1) create an underlying mood so strong and pervasive that the audience could not escape its grip, (2) develop an intricate network of subtexts so the audience became simultaneously involved in a number of fragmented "plots" and relationships that deepened as they accumulated, and (3) commit himself to change through juxtaposition. This allowed the audience the propulsion of rhythmical movement, creating the impression of action.

The famous moods of Chekhov's plays grew out of these three principles. They emerged from the emphasis on means rather than ends,[22] effects rather than causes. He found that by creating characters who were at loose ends, or swept up in the swirl of daily trivia, or caught on the edge of conflicting interests, his plays would lose the precise definition of conventional drama, and such vague but deeply felt emotions as hope, happiness, despair, and regret would dominate. The plays would not, then, be about who loves or hates whom or how one acquires and loses power, but would instead be about hope and despair. Chekhov's plays were structured carefully but differently. Instead of building waves for the crash, Chekhov enunciates the ripplets of gesture and intonation, the orchestration of subtle, continuous change, the air of waiting, the suggestion of ambiguous meaning, the carefully placed "obliquely relevant, irrelevance,"[23] and the oddly charged silences. Dialogue and direction "take on that deceptive, Chekhovian quality of inconsequence by which the central mood of the whole group is filtered through a hundred details of the characters' speech and behavior."[24]

The atmosphere of a Chekhov play is always reinforced by the sets, which he himself took great interest in. He was precise in his set directions and was very upset when Stanislavsky continually insisted on heavy-handed symbolic objects and sounds. Chekhov's sets were designed to contribute to the mood rather than convey meaning. Everything in Chekhovian drama supports the moods of the play. The sets change and the moods of the characters change; sometimes the mood of the play is at odds with the moods of the characters. Or the mood of one character will run counter to that of another, and this may be interrupted by still another character's mood. For the audience this is a dizzying rollercoaster ride of emotions, but beneath, Chekhov is carefully constructing an underlying mood, one for each act, and finally, one for the entire play. This is what Chekhov's plays are "about." But it is also this complicated atmospheric structure that makes it so difficult for the actors and director to have it play well. Just the right sense of balance and tone is necessary. Like the fly in the delicate web, one false step causes the whole fabric to collapse around him.

Chekhov understood that drama could more accurately render his impressionistic need to record his characters' acts of perception. No longer was it necessary for him to steep his works in verbs of perception. On stage his characters were continually seeing, listening, smelling, touching. In most drama of the time characters responded as though they were products of the playwright's intellect and not of the perceptual world. The audience didn't experience their perceptions; they only saw them think or perceive symbolically. A second problem for Chekhov was that traditional theater too often filtered all perceptions through the main character. Attention was focused on center stage, and whatever character was there took the perceptions of others and transformed them into his own. So, in greater accordance with the prose concept of multiple perspectives, Chekhov developed the ensemble play. Here no one character's perceptions dominated. Each perception might stand in isolation, come in conflict, or merge with someone else's. The ensemble play had many of the characteristics of impressionist painting. It consisted of fragments of speech, much like the short brush strokes that both created bits of color and merged into the whole. The spatial diffusion of characters and groups of characters allowed the sets to surround them and become more a part of the gestalt than most plays where the set was only a backdrop against which the actors played. Again, as in impressionist painting, the fusion of characters to their environment became complete.

Chekhov found he could control the delicate balance between subject and object that was so necessary to the impressionist aesthetic. The danger in prose is for interiorization to become dominant; in drama exteriorization is inherently attractive. The drama Chekhov was breaking away from had resorted to soliloquies, choruses, or other internalizing devices as a way of rendering consciousness. To Chekhov's way of thinking these were unnatural and unnecessary contrivances. He knew that consciousness could be rendered without its pouring out of an actor. As a close observer of the world in which he lived he had seen people express consciousness in their relationships to objects, in their reactions to others, in their snatches of dialogue, and in their gestures, expressions, and mannerisms. Chekhov brought consciousness back out into the perceived world and his realization of impressionist drama helped him find a more perfect union between subject and object.

Perhaps the most striking aspect of Chekhov's late plays is their emphatic development of complex temporal patterns and spatial arrangements. It is here that Chekhov's major impressionist theme, change, and his most important method, juxtaposition, appear. Styan has fully understood these principles, carefully documenting them in *The Three Sisters* and *The Cherry Orchard*.[25] What remains is a need to enunciate their specifically impressionist qualities. In his prose, Chekhov fused subjective with objective time, space with time, and successive moments with duration. He has done the same in his impressionist plays. In the theater, Chekhov found new elements of subjective and objective time to juxtapose. He could more consciously exploit rhythm and pace and more explicitly manipulate the audience's sense of time. In both plays each character has a clearly delineated quality of subjective time. However, that quality is often defined by his relationship to clock time. Watches are consulted, clocks broken, days, months, and years counted. Meanwhile, the audience's own internal clock keeps it aware of the conventional length of time that an act and a play take. This is set off against the pace of each act, and is further complicated by Chekhov's insistence that the audience be aware of the different time schemes for each character. In fact, Chekhov's vaunted moods are often the product of his temporal patterns. And those patterns, so complex and varied, so steeped in the conflicting fragments of individual temporality, emerge to form a vague sense of time, a gestalt.

This temporal gestalt cannot be complete, however, without its complement, space. Prose is basically a temporal art, relying on the imagery of the imagination for its spatiality. Painting and sculpture are essentially spatial arts, clearly frozen in time but spatially present. Drama and cinema are the arts that most nearly combine both time and space as they are joined in the real world. Chekhov's sense of realism knew this, and it drew him inexorably toward drama. One of the reasons plays and screen plays are so dissatisfying to read is that the spatial quality that would be filled in prose is missing, or only suggested. In Chekhov's plays this is even more so, because he wrote so completely for a new kind of live performance. Reading Shakespeare one can revel in the language; with Ibsen the social issues are compelling. Reading Chekhov is like eating less than half a loaf; the dialogue seems mundane, the narrative line appears to be nonexistent, the social issues are buried beneath heaps of ambiguity, and the action is nil. In a Chekhov script there is only the barest suggestion of what might be, and that only if one conceives of the whole: the sets, the gestures and mannerisms, the groupings and regroupings of characters, the sounds and the silences. It must all work together or it does not work at all. Chekhov's plays direct themselves to the actors, the director, the stage designer, and, of course, the audience.

Chekhov had been developing a prose style that required a gestalt approach, and so in his final years he turned that energy and discovery to a new form: the gestalt play, the impressionist play. It was the concept of the ensemble that galvanized his methodology. Not simply would the actors on stage play as one, but all the elements of the play must be conceived of as one. And the fusion of space and time formed the central axis on which the ensemble turned. In *The Cherry Orchard*, for instance, Chekhov made space (the nursery) suggest time (the past, youth, innocence) and time (the destruction of the future) suggest space (the orchard itself, essentially offstage). Space like time is fragmented and continually being reformed, as instanced by the divided sets and fluctuating groups of characters. The ensemble amplified the spatiality of the plays, while their theme became that of time.

Time of every imaginable sort suffuses these plays, but, as in his prose, Chekhov juxtaposed duration with succession, the imperceptible undercurrent of past, present, and future with the powerfully fragmented sense of present moments. In his prose Chekhov used privileged moments to crystallize durational time into epiphanies of conscious awareness. In the plays no one character's consciousness dominates, so epiphanies are lost to them. Instead the audience sees time past, present, and future come together in eccentric moments of proximity. Suddenly— and often it will be a different moment for each member of the audience—the appearance together of a number of characters who each have dissimilar relationships to time will trigger a durational moment. At the same time this instant is no more than an instant, dissolving into the constant progression of fleeting presentnesses and reforming spatial groupings. And at other times when characters find themselves at temporal odds, which they always do, the audience only senses the fragmentary confusion of time. But these effects are always the result of Chekhov's careful fusion of duration and succession.

The impressionistic motifs of Chekhov's prose found their way into *The Three Sisters* and *The Cherry Orchard*. The silences that implicitly spatialized time and suggested meaning in the stories have been intensified in the plays. Perhaps no drama has ever been written with so many pauses directed by the playwright. They function differently in each situation, for each pause is filled in by both the audience's reactions and thoughts and the multiform suggestions created by the conflicting fragments of the actors' lines and feelings. The silences increase the vagueness and ambivalence of the play while they simultaneously enhance the audience's role as co-maker, or almost active participant. Chekhov has structured his plays so that every reaction is set against an obliquely conflicting reaction; we are meant to feel ambivalent toward every character, every line of dialogue, every human response, every scene and act, and finally, of course, toward everything in the play—even the play itself.

This ambivalence gives the plays their strange, uneasy sense of balance. The audience is continually caught between that Chekhovian blend of tragedy and comedy that is never really either, thereby driving directors, actors, and audiences to despair. Words are offset by actions, dreams by reality, offstage actions and noise are juxtaposed with those onstage, the naturalistic comes in conflict with the poetic, inertia struggles against purposeless activity. In many plays the point of such conflicts would be the resolving of them. Chekhovian impressionism, however, demands that nothing be definitive, so the curious and unsettling tension must continue, spilling out into the world beyond the play.

The feelings of the audience, then, are not only shared by the characters, but in fact define their lives. These characters either ambiguously succumb to the indeterminacy (Chebutykin's cheerful nihilism in *The Three Sisters* or in *The Cherry Orchard*, Charlotta's eccentric combination of magic, sanity, and absurdity, and, of course, the good-humored escapism of Gaev's imaginary billiard shots), or they attempt to overcompensate for their uncertainty with blustering clichés (Kulygin, Vershinin, and Tusenbach in *The Three Sisters* and the perpetual student of *The Cherry Orchard*, Trofimov). Not only does Chekhov humanize all his characters' faults, but he sets his characters into so many conflicting juxtapositions that our feelings toward them become doubly ambiguous. Our attitudes change almost moment by moment. This startling dramatic technique is at the heart of Chekhov's impressionist drama. Change and juxtaposition have always formed the center of impressionism and are completely interrelated. Juxtaposition creates change through the shifts in perceptual perspective it engenders. Change is what Chekhov's final plays are about. Changeless change envelops the characters. The three sisters, Olga, Masha, and Irina, are still in the provinces longing for Moscow, just as they were in the beginning of the play. Madame Ranevskaya will return to Paris just as she had left it, penniless and irrationally in love. These people, in fact all the characters in Chekhov's impressionist plays, show no basic change in character; there has been no fundamental movement in their lives. They perform the rituals of coming and going with much fanfare, as though to convince themselves that somehow their lives will change. And yet at the same time these plays are simply overflowing with changes of the moment. The sets change, the light within one act changes (essential to Chekhov's, shall we say, pure impressionism), moods change, time shifts, pace and rhythm accelerates, reactions, intonations, attitudes change—and all through the eternally complex structuring of juxtaposed elements.

The ambivalence of juxtaposition runs still deeper, for it defines the basic character of the play, its sense of purposelessness and inertia. It is, of course, the characters who create this quality, transferring it immediately to the audience. Not only are these characters always waiting for something to happen to their lives, but the abundant silences keep everyone waiting for the next irrelevant comment from a character who has no idea what came before the pause or where his words will lead. They find themselves isolated in the present. No one seems to listen to them, or if they do they respond as if they don't. They all yearn, to different degrees, for a past that is lost to them, a future that is unattainable, or a past-future about which they cannot make up their minds. Cut off from a temporal continuum they wander, wait, and utter inanities. They find themselves immersed in the fragmented details of social trivia and lost in a directionless present, yet they search for the unreachable past and future.

An example from *The Cherry Orchard* should help concretize Chekhov's impressionistic style and method. This piece of business occurs in Act One. Liubov Ranevskaya has returned from France to her childhood home. She is in the nursery and everyone is falling into the odd patterns of their lives, while Lopakhin attempts to explain the situation with the cherry orchard.

LOPAKHIN: Excuse me, Charlotta Ivanovna, I haven't had time to greet you. *(Tries to kiss her hand.)*

CHARLOTTA *(pulling away her hand)*: If I let you kiss my hand, you'd then want to kiss my elbow, then my shoulder.

LOPAKHIN: I have no luck today. *(All laugh.)* Charlotta Ivanovna, do a trick.

LIUBOV: Charlotta, do a trick.

CHARLOTTA: No need to. I want to go to bed. *(Leaves.)*

LOPAKHIN: I'll see you in three weeks. *(Kisses Liubov's hand.)* Until then. Time to go. *(To Gaev.)* Goodbye. *(Kisses Pishchik.)* Goodbye.

(Shakes hands with Varya, then Firs, and Yasha.) I don't want to leave. *(To Liubov.)* If you make up your mind about the summer cottages, let me know. I can arrange a loan for about 50,000 roubles. Think it over seriously.

VARYA *(angrily)*: Will you go away!

LOPAKHIN: I'm going, I'm going *(leaves)*.

GAEV: The boor. However, pardon me—Varya's going to marry him. He's Varya's little fiancé.

VARYA: Don't talk so much, Uncle.

LIUBOV: Well, Varya, I will be very happy. He's a good man.

PISHCHIK: A man, one must say in all truth—most admirable—and my Dashenka—she too says that—she says all sorts of things—*(snores, but wakes up immediately)*. At any rate, my dearest friend, could you oblige me—a loan of 240 roubles—tomorrow I must pay the interest on the mortgage.

VARYA *(alarmed)*: We can't. We can't.

LIUBOV: I really have nothing.

PISHCHIK: It'll turn up. *(Laughs.)* I never lose hope. There, I think to myself, all is lost, I'm ruined, then lo and behold—a railroad is run through my land—and they pay me for it. And then, watch, something else will turn up—if not today, then tomorrow—Dashenka will win two hundred thousand—she has a ticket.

LIUBOV: I've finished my coffee, now we can go to bed.

FIRS *(brushing Gaev, reprovingly)*: You've put on the wrong trousers again. What am I going to do with you?

VARYA *(softly)*: Anya's asleep. (Opening the window softly.) The sun's up already, it's not cold. Look Mamma. What beautiful trees. Heavens, the air. The starlings are singing.

GAEV *(opening another window)*: The orchard is all white. You haven't forgotten, Liuba? That long lane runs straight, straight like a tight belt. It glitters on moonlit nights. Do you remember? You haven't forgotten?

LIUBOV *(looking out the window into the orchard)*: Oh my childhood, my innocence! I slept in this nursery and looked out into the orchard from here, happiness woke up with me every morning, and then everything was just as it is now, nothing has changed. *(Laughs with joy.)* All, all white! Oh my orchard! After the dark, rainy autumn and cold winter, you are young again, full of happiness, the heavenly angels have not left you—If only this weight could be lifted from my breast, my shoulders, if only I could forget my past!

GAEV: Yes, and the orchard will be sold to pay our debts, strange as that may seem.

LIUBOV: Look, there's our mother walking in the orchard—in a white dress! *(Laughs happily.)* It is her!

GAEV: Where?

VARYA: Bless you, Mamma!

LIUBOV: There's no one, I imagine it. On the right, as you turn toward the summerhouse, there's a little white tree bending over, it looks like a woman—*(Enter Trofimov, in a worn-out student uniform, and glasses.)* What a wonderful orchard! Masses of white blossoms, the blue sky.

TROFIMOV: Liubov Andreevna! *(She looks around at him.)* I'll just pay my respects and leave at once. (Kisses her hand warmly.) I was told to wait until tomorrow morning, but I didn't have the patience—*(Liubov looks at him, puzzled.)*

VARYA *(through tears)*: It's Petya Trofimov—

TROFIMOV: Petya Trofimov, I used to be Grisha's tutor. Have I changed so much? *(Liubov embraces him, softly weeping.)*

GAEV *(embarrassed)*: No, now, Liuba.

VARYA *(weeping)*: I told you, Petya, to wait until tomorrow morning.

LIUBOV: My Grisha—my little boy—Grisha—son.

VARYA: What can one do, Mamma. It's God's will.

TROFIMOV *(gently, through tears)*: There, there.

LIUBOV *(softly weeping)*: My little boy was lost—drowned. Why? Why, my friend. *(More quietly.)* Anya's asleep in there, and here I am speaking loudly—making noise—Well, Petya? Why do you look so badly? Why do you look so much older?

TROFIMOV: On the train a peasant woman called me a mangy gentleman.

LIUBOV: You were just a boy then, a dear student, and now your hair is thin, you wear glasses. Are you really still a student? *(Walks toward the door.)*

TROFIMOV: I suppose I'll always be a student.

LIUBOV *(kisses her brother, then Varya)*: Well, go to bed—You've aged too, Leonid.

PISHCHIK *(following her)*: So that's it, now we're going to bed—Oh, my gout. I'm staying overnight. Liubov Andreevna, my dear, tomorrow morning—those 240 roubles—

GAEV: He's still at it.

PISHCHIK: 240 roubles—I've got to pay the mortgage.

LIUBOV: I haven't any money, my little dove.

PISHCHIK: I'll pay it back, dear—it's very little.

LIUBOV: Well, all right—Leonid will give—give it to him, Leonid.

GAEV: I'll give it to him; hold out your pockets.

LIUBOV: What else can we do, give it to him—He needs it—He'll pay it back. (11:320–22)

Perhaps the most striking quality of this scene's impressionism is the number of rapid mood shifts within such a short span of time. There are so many divergent forces impinging upon one another that the precarious balance can be radically altered with the introduction of any new element. The ensemble keeps changing. Charlotta leaves, then Lopakhin; Pishchik takes his place, the sun comes up, and Trofimov enters. Since impressionism is so much a matter of relations, each tug on the gestalt by a new component can totally alter the composition. In the beginning Charlotta plays off against Lopakhin, creating a mood of verbal slapstick comedy. When she leaves Lopakhin is caught in the fluster of transition. Should he leave or stay? Instead he introduces the serious matter-of-fact issue of the cherry orchard's future. But then, without discussion he leaves, allowing for a new mood change. Varya's anger and Gaev's indignation serve as the transition to another fleeting emotion, as Varya's future is touched upon. But Pishchik stops this with an out-of-the-blue, sleepy, and fragmented request for a loan. This engenders an ambiguous mood because Pishchik's comic absurdity evokes two serious responses: Varya's angry alarm and Liubov's sadly precise statement that she has no money. Undaunted, Pishchik falls back on his things-will-turn-out-for-the-best philosophy. But this only intensifies the viewer's ambivalence: it is dangerous, but silly; it is an affront to Liubov, but is comforting in its serenity.

Firs's absurd concern for Gaev's appearance provides the transition to the play's greatest moment of pure impressionistic lyricism. The light of dawn filters in the nursery. As attention becomes focused on the natural surroundings outdoors, the mood shifts toward internalization. Varya simply responds to the presentness of nature. But for Gaev and Liubov the scene outside triggers memory images. Yet superimposed on the past is the implicit uncertainty of the future. The slow change in light that Chekhov wanted now becomes a conscious part of the audience's *mise en scène*. The light allows for the whiteness of the spring cherry blossoms, but that whiteness is also a state of mind— Gaev's and Liubov's collective images of innocence. This is impressionism at its best. External and internal whiteness is fused in a phenomenological moment by the light. Both Gaev and Liubov become imagistic, Gaev with a metaphoric turn of mind and Liubov with an image (her mother dressed in white walking in the orchard) so powerfully real she puts it in the present tense, and Gaev asks, "Where?" The images of consciousness are real.

Liubov's reverie is almost a perfect paradigm of Chekhovian impressionism: she makes the past live in the present; she covers her canvas with a profusion of whiteness; she juxtaposes the warm whiteness of spring with the cold darkness of autumn and winter. But even more, Chekhov has Liubov articulate in virtually the same breath his dual attitudes toward change: "nothing has changed," but "after the dark, rainy autumn and cold winter, you are young again, full of happiness." Changelessness and change coexist. Both are true. In the next moment Liubov is wishing that this past, which has just provided her with a moment of happiness, could be forgotten so as not to burden her. This thought goes to the heart of Chekhov's profound understanding of human complexity. Liubov's remembrance of the past, which can give her a moment of present happiness, is heartbreaking because it is thrown into relief against the impending destruction of her orchard. If she did not remember the orchard, she would not care about its future, but then she would not have had that instant of joy the past had just given her. Time in Chekhov's impressionist fiction is a psychologically complex phenomenon.

Not only is each character's own relationship to time involved, but when these are set against the different characters' different time schemes, the ambiguity of time becomes intensified. (1) Lopakhin's present-tense punctuality would appear to be pragmatically businesslike, but his compulsive clock-watching seems to be more of an absurd social escape. (2) This intransigent present-tenseness develops as an opposition to Liubov's fluid and vague sense of past-present-future. (3) Trofimov feels he is above time; since intellect can transcend time, he has no use for it, but, of course, he finds himself continually entrapped by it. (4) Firs represents the fourth major strand of time, timelessness. He is so old that for everyone else he seems invisible, out of their realm of time. At the end of the play, when everyone has left, forgetting Firs in the house, he mumbles, "Life has gone by as if I had never lived" (11:360). All the other characters show interesting and conflicting variations on these four time schemes.

Returning to the progression of moods in this scene, Trofimov enters and breaks Liubov's bittersweet past-present images. She looks at him confusedly, as though in a relativistic time warp. Varya and Gaev add their own attitudes, hoping to distract Liubov from the painful connection they know Trofimov represents. His blundering helps Liubov fix on it; it is her drowned son, Grisha. The mood has changed to pure sadness. But instead of indulging in the self-pity of melodrama, Liubov immediately snaps out of it, thinking instead of not waking Anya with her talking. She shifts her care to Trofimov and then announces it is time to go to bed. But Pishchik, obtuse and oblivious to the end, asks again for a loan. This ends the scene on a note of comic absurdity, anger at his insensitivity, and pity at what Liubov must bear. She pays him and our emotions are at a loss. We have been tossed and turned through a maze of complex ambiguities. This is the essence of literary impressionism.

Part Three
Henry James

It is the art of the brush, I know, as opposed to the art of the slate-pencil; but to the art of the brush the novel must return.

Henry James

* 5 *

The Emerging Impressionist
The Portrait of a Lady and
What Maisie Knew

I * INTRODUCTION

> The power to guess the unseen from the seen, to trace the implica-
> tion of things, to judge the whole piece by the pattern, the condition
> of feeling life in general so completely that you are well on your
> way to knowing any particular corner of it—this cluster of gifts may
> almost be said to constitute experience, and they occur in country
> and in town, and in the most differing stages of education. If experi-
> ence consists of impressions, it may be said that impressions are ex-
> perience, just as (have we not seen it?) they are the very air we
> breathe.   Henry James, "The Art of Fiction"

James has rarely been considered an impressionist.[1] This is surprising, given his abundant use of the term "impression" in both
fiction and criticism, his long-standing interest in painting, and
fascination with pictorial tropes as metaphors for the process
of writing. He also expressed admiration for those passages in
Flaubert and Maupassant that capture both the impressionistic
play of light on objects and the shifting moods of a character.
But perhaps the deepest influence was an awareness of his
brother William's incipient studies into the phenomenology of
consciousness, the perception of sensations, and the pluralism of
time.[2]

For many years James gave a preeminent position in his
artistic lexicon to "impressions." James E. Miller, Jr., in his
edition of James's critical statements, says that impressions "became the law of the writer's life" and "in quantity and intensity,
became for James the lifeblood of consciousness."[3] Impressions
stand at the center of a process whereby life is experienced,

and, still further, art is created: perceptions yield impressions, which yield consciousness. James makes it clear that perceptions are the product of a uniquely subjective curiosity. Impressions occur through individualized perceptions and externalized experience, commingling with "myriad forms" and "immense sensibility." Impressionistic experience is "a kind of huge spider-web of the finest silken threads suspended in the chamber of consciousness, and catching every air-borne particle in its tissue."[4] It is consciousness of impressions that form the essence of James's impressionism. His many comments on the perception-impression-consciousness cluster further solidify his position as an impressionist. "The glimpse made a picture; it lasted only a moment, but that moment was experience. She had got her direct personal impression."[5] "I ought to endeavor to keep, to a certain extent, a record of passing impressions, of all that comes, that goes, that I see, and feel, and observe. To catch and keep something of life—that's what I mean. . . . It is too late to recover all those lost impressions . . . besides they are not lost altogether, they are buried deep in my mind, they have become part of my life, of my nature."[6] "Any point of view is interesting that is a direct impression of life. You each have an impression colored by your individual conditions; make that into a picture, a picture framed by your own personal wisdom."[7] "For if a picture, a tale, or a novel be a direct impression of life (and that surely constitutes its interest and value), the impression will vary according to the plate that takes it, the particular structure and mixture of the recipient."[8] This sampling demonstrates James's finely-tuned understanding of the delicate balance between the subjective and objective. Impressions *are* life. He never allows the reader to forget that impressions are "the real thing." Yet they are also highly subjective, momentary confluences.

James recognized, as Hugo Sommerholder puts it, that if "we are in such a mood that inner and outer worlds merge, then the conditions are ripe for the assimilation of the ego and the impressions from the outside world—and for the fusion of outer and inner space into one single space. The mood is the medium by which impressionist literature condenses itself."[9] An impression not only emerges from the coalescence of subject and object, perceiver and perceived, but in certain instances it produces a privileged moment. James believed that these supremely creative moments were the product of "all imaginative and projective persons who have had—and what imaginative and projective person hasn't?—any like experience of the suddenly-determined *absolute* of perception."[10] Often when he writes of impressions he is not speaking of his characters' but of his own. He wrote H. G. Wells that "it is art that *makes* life."[11] The impressions of an artist can be those of the "imaginative and projective" person. His own experiences with impressions, then, became a decisive factor in his creation of impressionistic characters. An analysis of his impressionist novels will reveal the pervasive power of those impressions on his characters' consciousnesses.

James's use of the term *impression* is usually grounded in a visual, painterly sensibility. It is often equated with "a picture." James had an "intense and lifelong" relationship with the visual arts, particularly painting.[12] And he made a conscious effort to graft his thoughts about painting onto his theory of fiction: "the abundance of art terms in his works of criticism is indicative not merely of his feeling a lack of a vocabulary appropriate to a serious discussion of fiction as an art but also of a visual orientation leading him to conceive of fiction and painting as analogous in aim and form and even competitive in the rendering of appearances."[13] But the questions remain: What painters, what styles, and what forms did James attempt to translate into his fiction? The answer is not an easy one, for his tastes in painting changed as his artistry in literature evolved. He was captivated by the "classical Renaissance and the painterly-picturesque styles," but as Winner also notes, he "had much in common with the contemporary impressionists in technique and thought but crucially differed from them in his formalism and traditionalism."[14] James's critical stance toward impressionist painting was initially hostile but grew into an enthusiastic, sensual embrace.

In a paper delivered to the Union College faculty in 1931,

Edward E. Hale remembers that an influential painter of the 1860s and '70s, William Hunt, instructed the two James brothers in 1859. In the 1870s he was considered to be an "impressionistic" painter by Bostonians. Years later James remembered Hunt's impact on him as "truly fertilizing."[15] James would certainly not have thought of himself as an impressionist writer in, say, 1874, the year the critic Louis Leroy coined the term *impressionist* from a pejorative review of Monet's *Impression, soleil levant*. But the roots already had taken hold. James's formalism and traditionalism probably forced him to temper the intuitive impressionism of his technique and thought. Finally, however, his impressionistic tendencies overwhelmed the formal structures of his novels and his cautious attitudes toward his artistic progression. He did not see himself standing against a puritan, bourgeois society that refused to acknowledge the fleeting incomplete sensuality of life. But the impressionist painters did. So it seems difficult for many critics to frame James and Renoir, for instance, in the same picture. But James began to concentrate on the same prismatic nuances that mark the finest achievements in impressionist painting. In *The Portrait of a Lady* James consciously used the language of painting. He also allowed galleries to stand as indices of Isabel's growth. Laurence Holland directly states the issue: *The Portrait* is an "achievement, to use the language of painting, of representational form." This novel has "a distinctly painterly objective" in that it does not imitate or refer to models of actuality but instead "*represents* them."[16] While *The Portrait* is deliberately painterly, its model is ultimately representational. The impressionism of this novel only seeps through the essentially static "portraits." It issues from Isabel's perceptual growth, culminating in her accidental glimpse of the intimate ambience enveloping Madame Merle and Gilbert Osmond in chapter 40. By the time of *The Golden Bowl* every impression shimmers through the filtered play of light, reflecting the continual kinesis between silent and expressively ambiguous relations.

Of his most influential predecessors, Maupassant and Flaubert, James was both critical and enthusiastic. He disliked their realism, their authorial intrusion, and their often stark subject matter.[17] But he admired their impressionistic tendencies—the hard surfaces, the control over limited point of view, and the courage of their perceptions.[18] So within the ugliness of *Madame Bovary*, James's eye picked out the

one little passage in which an agreeable "effect" is rendered . . . and it is the happy instance of the way in which this author's style arrests itself at every step in a picture. "Once, when it was thawing, the bark of the trees was reeking in the year, the snow was melting on the roofs of the out-buildings. She [Emma] was upon the threshold; she went in and fetched her umbrella and opened it. The umbrella, of iridescent silk, with the sun coming through it, lighted up her white complexion with changing re-flections. Beneath it she smiled in the soft warmth, and he [Charles] heard the waterdrops fall one by one upon the tense silk."[19]

It is not surprising that this arrested moment has such strong impressionist affinities when one considers that it emerges from an essay in which James argues that what "our eyes show us is all we are sure of."[20] And yet this certainty is only one of the many perceived surfaces, because "there is something else, be-neath and behind, that belongs to the realm of vagueness and uncertainty." He concludes that "we will 'render' things . . . as painters render them."[21]

Flaubert was not an impressionist, although some critics want to turn him into "the founder of literary impressionism."[22] Flau-bert was capable of impressionist passages, but his vision and method remained firmly grounded in nineteenth-century real-ism. His "God in Creation"[23] control stands in contrast to James's "muffled majesty of authorship" over which he only "ostensibly" reigns, and where he catches himself "shaking it off and disavowing the pretence of it while I get down in the arena and do my best to live and breathe and rub shoulders and converse with the persons engaged in the struggle."[24] Flaubert did, however, provide an incipient rendering of perceptual con-tours and the ambience of "changing reflections."

It was Eliseo Vivas who first grasped that what Henry and William had in common were major philosophic agreements reached quite probably without the force of direct influence. It

is not overstating the case to say that they were both phenomenological impressionists.[25] Henry found an aesthetic expression
for radical empiricism, while William's impressionism took the
form of studies into philosophy and psychology. Vivas puts it
this way:

> I seem to see between William's conception of consciousness and his phi-
> losophy of "pure experience" which is based on this conception, on the
> one hand, and on the other the mode of perception which became char-
> acteristically Henry's, an intimate relationship . . . each brother expresses
> in his own domain something which, I suspect, is somehow essential to
> the last half of the 19th Century, since it is not only found in pragmatism,
> and in the novels of Henry James, but in Bergson and elsewhere in phi-
> losophy . . . and also in the painting of the impressionists.[26]

The connection between Henry and William becomes fully realized in the context of impressionism. Only then is it possible to
see that the explicit concerns of William were borne out in the
fiction and criticism of Henry. William saw consciousness as "a
teeming multiplicity of objects and relations,"[27] not an entity
or substance, but a function or process. Henry's metaphor for
consciousness was an empty and bottomless vessel having impressions continually poured into it.[28] Henry's impressionism is
a process of becoming, marked by "relations" that "stop nowhere."[29] The central consciousness perceives juxtaposed objects. What is apprehended is not the clearly outlined contours
of a single object, but the penumbral interface of shifting relations. Vivas saw this link between the two brothers when he
described William's psychology through Henry's medium in
The Golden Bowl:

> Let us now attend to a man walking with his daughter on a Sunday after-
> noon in an old English garden. . . . Our psychological information, if we
> have been convinced by William James, will make us aware that what we
> observe from our point of vantage—the garden, the man and woman, their
> talk, the quality of the day, its light and warmth and fragrance—comes
> enveloped in an affective light which fuses the elements intimately. . . .
> If what we want is the reality of the scene, it is in its sensational flux that
> we must look for its true shape. Our problem then is to capture what we
> saw and heard in such a way as not to lose the fluid affinity that the things
> that make up the episode had for one another.[30]

Both Jameses believed in, as Henry put it, "the realm of vagueness."[31] William placed "the re-instatement of the vague" within the stream of thought that was so crucial to Henry's impressionism: " 'tendencies' are not only descriptions from without, but that they are among the *objects* of the stream, which is thus aware of them from within, and must be described as in very large measure constituted of *feelings* of *tendency*, often so vague that we are unable to name them at all."[32] Henry's impressionist novels are vast accumulations of tendencies that characters are unable to name; instead they sense impressions upon which they act. This vagueness that the Jameses responded to was not only impressionistically pictorial and psychologically sensorial, but infinitely pluralistic. This was the result of their philosophic and artistic attempts to break down the dualism of subject and object. William found such a polarity "a perfectly wanton assumption,"[33] while Henry's entire aesthetic was shaped by an expanding consciousness whose very act of perception is itself a form of expression.[34] Wallace Stevens saw this as the "vital engagement between man and his environment of the world."[35]

Perception serves as the creative center for both brothers. Each saw perception as the situational conduit to consciousness, which in turn produces the creations of imagination. Only through perception can the immersed consciousness probe the phenomenal world for information, for knowledge. But as the priest in Kafka's *The Trial* tells Joseph K., "The right perception of any matter and a misunderstanding of the same matter do not wholly exclude each other."[36] Perception does not always produce clarity of vision, but instead often leads to unreliability, uncertainty, and ambiguity. Henry's novels become renderings of bewilderment or, to put it in his words, the "great thing is indeed that the muddled state too is one of the very sharpest of the realities, that it also has colour and form and character."[37] Perception *is* the pluralistic activity. It is initiated by a kinetic subjectivity that points toward a shifting collection of objects: "Always immersed in an environing situation, the human being is constrained to construct its objects from a first, often confused, and always indefinite perception of a situational quality; and if this is a true picture of the matter, it can no longer be assumed that objects are the cause, even unknown, of our simple impressions."[38]

Perceptual indeterminacy and immediacy led the brothers into essentially similar conceptions of space-time. Both were Bergsonians[39] in that they saw time as a matter of perception, but they refused to describe time as purely durational. William, who erroneously but understandably wrote separate chapters on the perception of time and space, described time as both durational and successive: "It is only as parts of this *duration-block* that the relation of *succession* of one end to the other is perceived. . . . We seem to feel the interval of time as a whole, with its two ends embedded in it."[40] In other words, time is both an imperceptible stream and a cluster of discrete instants, spatialized and framed. This same concept lies at the heart of Henry's impressionism. The presentness of the moment spreads out into "a rearward and a forward-looking end," creating the "feeling of riding upon a palpable and appreciable present whose span comprises a bit of the past and a bit of the future."[41] This striking affinity between William and Henry plays a major and generally hitherto unnoticed role in the development of Henry's impressionism.[42]

In his notebooks Henry said of *The Portrait of a Lady* that it was both true and false that he had left Isabel Archer *"en l'air."* But, he continued, the *"whole* of anything is never told; you can only take what groups together."[43] A major portion of James's career after *The Portrait* was devoted to rendering a synthesis of epistemological indeterminacy, subjectively perceived time and space, and commingled subject and object into "that vague pictorial glow which forms the first appeal of a living 'subject' to the painter's consciousness"[44]—in other words, impressionism. This devotion was rewarded in *The Golden Bowl*. By the time he had completed this impressionistic *pièce de résistance*, he might well have written that the "whole of anything is *never known*, you can only take what groups together."

In *The Golden Bowl* James created the consummate impressionistic novel. It was the result of a vision that began with *The Portrait*. The seeds of James's impressionism are manifest in Isabel Archer's initial inability to see the nuances of complex appearances. But she changes from a deductive to an inductive knower; she comes to know based upon the relations that she sees; she learns in fits and starts, through momentary glimpses of perceived fragments and chance conjunctions. She is finally able to synthesize her vast accumulation of impressions by reading the ambient suggestions of her experiences. She begins to recognize that she has the "power to guess the unseen from the seen, to trace the implication of things."[45]

II * *THE PORTRAIT OF A LADY*

The Portrait is a novel of perception and change.[46] James is torn between the objective realism of carefully composed portraits and the subjective impressionism of Isabel's own shifting perceptions. Instead of the impressionistic fusion of subjective objectivism, there is a forced division in narrative method. Most classical cinematic narration captures the impressionistic style. The camera usually represents two points of view at the same time: the camera itself, mechanically recording from over the protagonist's shoulder or centering him in the composition, and the probing, selecting camera eye of the protagonist. Both involve the viewer in a more intimate perceptual identification.[47] This approximates the dramatic method James developed in his later fiction. In *The Portrait*, however, there is a certain uneasiness with respect to Isabel as the center of consciousness, even though James in retrospect admired its " 'architectural' competence."[48] It is as though the million windows in the "house of fiction" have here been reduced to three: the "I" of the narrator, the third-person narration, and Isabel. There is no question that the eyes have been multiplied by Madame Merle, Gilbert Osmond, Ralph Touchett, etc. In *The Portrait* these eyes are neither so multiplied that they blend into an impressionistic "spreading field" nor so controlled that Isabel becomes the center of an impressionistically perceived consciousness. This denies neither the many impressionistic portraits nor the powerful force of Isabel's perceptual disparity.

The opening passage is, in fact, the kind of pictorialism most critics point to when they describe literary impressionism. There is, for instance, a strong similarity between the "perfect middle of a splendid summer afternoon" (3:1) and Claude Monet's "Women in the Garden," painted in 1866–67. Zola said of this painting, that he had seen "a figure piece—women in light summer dresses picking flowers along the paths of a garden; the sun falls directly on their brilliant white skirts; the tree casts warm shadows like textile patterns on the path and across the brilliant white dresses. The result is quite singular. To dare to do something like that—to cut in two the material of the dresses with light and shade and to rightly place these women in a carefully kept flower garden—one must have a particular fondness for one's period."[49] Jean Leymarie noted that Monet "opened up an entirely new theme, that of garden spots in springtime, the quiet pastimes of a bourgeois afternoon, and in this atmosphere blossomed the Impressionists' finest, most characteristic works, which sealed the doom of traditional conceptions of form and color. Blue and green shadows flicker across faces in full sunlight, and women's silhouetted forms, unmodeled and volumeless, encased in white, tapering corolla-shaped dresses, flit amid the flowers and lend all their grace and animation to a light-filled paradise."[50]

For James, this paradise is English afternoon tea, the "little eternity . . . an eternity of pleasure." In this setting, "the flood of summer light had begun to ebb, the air had grown mellow, the shadows were long upon the smooth, dense turf. They lengthened slowly, however, and the scene expressed that sense of leisure still to come. . . . The shadows on the perfect lawn were straight and angular" (3: 1, 2). There is a similarity of style, atmosphere, and subject matter in these two pictures. But James, according to his own literary needs, has shifted the focus from stasis with implied movement (one woman in the background of Monet's painting shows slight movement and the shadows themselves suggest the passing of the day) to a decided emphasis on the waning afternoon sun, on the changes that are occurring. Early in his career James understood that literary impressionists must show the kinetic qualities of seemingly static objects and scenes, just as they press for changes in consciousness. It is important to remember that the impressionist revolution in painting had been about the need to capture the change and movement of immediacy. James's emphases were dictated by those impressionist elements that could be translated into his medium.

It is significant that the opening scene of *The Portrait* focuses on change and movement, because Isabel is prepared for stasis. She had painted the portrait of a lady placed in the midst of European society. It is a picture that cannot change. The conflict in this novel revolves around Isabel's a priori portraits and her struggle to maintain their exactitude in the face of time and changing relations.[51] Most of what she sees is determined by what she believes she should see. The opening scene, then, is drenched in irony. James subtly shows the movement of seemingly stationary pictures, so as to place Isabel at odds with reality. As she enters, James pretends (if read in only one way) to endow her with qualities of "clear perception."

He places the reader squarely in the center of a dilemma, and with the tantalizing mind of a mystery writer offers a few red herrings. Isabel believes two things: first, that she is a young woman who looked "at everything, with an eye that denoted clear perception" (3:18) and who had "a larger perception of surrounding facts" (3:66); and second, that she is prepared for change, that "there had really been a change in her life" (3:41), and that she "was in a situation that gave value to any change." It is too easy to believe in Isabel's powers of perception and desire for change. What she perceives is based upon "scanty evidence," theories, and romantic optimism. Her sense of change is limited to her Albany reverie in which she projects herself from her old world into a new, unlimited one (ironically, of course, she is leaving the new world and travelling to the old).

It is a romantic view of change, and occurs, significantly, when her eyes are closed. She cannot see what lies ahead, but since she thinks she can, she approaches empirical reality with the "fixed determination to regard the world as a place of brightness, of free expansion, of irresistible action" (3:68).

Isabel is trapped between the demands of a society that requires she see a world of clearly outlined shapes and her own instinctive impressionism that sees "too many things at once" (3:42), that leads "her into a thousand ridiculous zigzags" (3:67), and that produces thoughts that "were a tangle of vague outlines." But these kaleidoscopic impulses are always being corrected, checked, and followed by "a week of passionate humility." Thus her romantic need for grandeur, her cloistered reading of the German transcendentalists, and her fear of relativism all drive her away from seeing empirically.

She enters upon the sun dappled tea-time of Europe and proceeds to grossly misread the signs of this more subtle and sophisticated society. Ralph says to himself that she "doesn't take suggestions" (3:61). Though he might show her the ghost of Gardencourt that she wants to believe in, she would "never see it" because it "has never been seen by a young, happy, innocent person like you" (3:64). The more dangerous consequences of these misperceptions occur when she first sees Madame Merle and, later, Gilbert Osmond. She continues to misread their intentions, actions, and deeper surfaces, even after she has been warned and shown. Her stubbornness, born of pride and fear, makes her see these two people in her own way. Mrs. Touchett astutely notices Isabel's infinite capacity to see what she wants to see: "there's nothing in life to prevent her marrying Mr. Osmond if only she looks at him in a certain way" (3:395). And she does look at Osmond in a certain way. Her first impulse when seeing him "made it more important she should get an impression of him than that she should produce one herself" (3:356). But at this moment James backs away from offering us Isabel's impression directly. Instead he chooses to duck behind the narrator's analysis, that "Mr. Osmond, to do him justice, had a well-bred air of expecting nothing." (3:356). In other words, James is suggesting that Isabel does not really allow herself an impression. She suppresses her impressions in favor of a conceptualization, which she arrives at later and which fits her own preconceived needs: "Her mind contained no class offering a natural place to Mr. Osmond—he was a specimen apart. It was not that she recognized all these truths at the hour, but they were falling into order before her. For the moment she only said to herself that this 'new relation' would perhaps prove her very most distinguished" (3:376). She misreads people and situations because she simply does not see *them*. What she sees in Osmond is an idea and what she sees on first sighting Madame Merle is a set of preselected details.

Isabel, not knowing whom she has inadvertently walked in on, sees Madame Merle's "back—an ample and well dressed one" from a distance, as she played "something of Schubert's—Isabel knew not what" (3:244). Isabel is enchanted by the playing, but when Madame Merle effortlessly drops a French phrase, Isabel assumes that she is French, "and this supposition made the visitor more interesting to our speculative heroine" (3:245). Here Isabel appears to have accepted impressions. But there are many factors that transform this moment from an impression having a certain empirical truth to an image engraved on Isabel's consciousness. Isabel places far too great an importance on first impressions, and, in fact, "she had not yet divested herself of a young faith that each new acquaintance would exert some momentous influence on her life" (3:244–45). She also allows too many of those attitudes shaped in Albany to influence her impressions: if a well-dressed woman playing Schubert drops a well-placed French phrase with a certain panache, that woman must be French—and, therefore, a lady. When Madame Merle reveals that she is not French but American, Isabel's image has become so permanently etched that she simply fits the new detail into the same picture: "and as the opposite supposition had made her romantic it might have seemed that this revelation would have marked a drop. But such was not the fact; rarer even than to be French seemed it to be American on such interesting terms" (3:246). Isabel does not take impressions as they come;

she forces each one to fit into the prearranged picture, and, even further, she makes definitive judgments based on those perceptual shards. Finally, she stands by her portraits in the face of further empirical evidence. She does not paint her pictures *plein-air;* they had been conceived in Albany and painted in her imagination, with only the fewest details having been taken from nature. It is this dangerous lack of perceptual impressionism that casts her onto the shoals of distorted unity. She remains stubbornly monochromatic, and yet the very nature of her preconceptions gives her an openness. This oddly parallel growth brings her to the point in chapter 40 where she can absorb a multiplicity of fleeting impressions. She is then ready to confront actual perceptions. At this point Isabel's consciousness and James's art become one. It is a moment of impressionistic synthesis:

Just beyond the threshold of the drawing-room she stopped short, the reason for her doing so being that she had received an impression. The impression had in strictness, nothing unprecedented; but she felt it as something new, and the soundlessness of her step gave her time to take in the scene before she interrupted it. Madame Merle was there in her bonnet, and Gilbert Osmond was talking to her; for a minute they were unaware she had come in. Isabel had often seen that before, certainly; but what she had not seen, or at least had not noticed, was that their colloquy had of the moment converted itself into a sort of familiar silence, from which she instantly perceived that her entrance would startle them. Madame Merle was standing on the rug, a little way from the fire; Osmond was in a deep chair, leaning back and looking at her. Her head was erect, as usual, but her eyes were bent on his. What struck Isabel first was that he was sitting while Madame Merle stood; there was an anomaly in this that arrested her. Then she perceived that they had arrived at a desultory pause in their exchange of ideas and were musing, face to face, with the freedom of old friends who sometimes exchange ideas without uttering them. There was nothing to shock in this; they were old friends in fact. But the thing made an image, lasting only a moment, like a sudden flicker of light. Their relative positions, their absorbed mutual gaze, struck her as something detected. But it was all over by the time she had fairly seen it. (4:164–65)

Like so many of impressionism's privileged moments this one is accidental and silent. For the impressionists, as well as for the most modern of filmmakers, Jean-Luc Godard, "the immediate is chance."[52] What Isabel sees is a separate fragment of reality not determined by any other experience. So, by pure chance, Isabel silently stumbles upon a quiet moment between her husband and Madame Merle. As she rivets her eyes and whole sensibility upon a fleeting piece of a relationship, the sudden and accidental quality of the perception allows for no reliance on preconceptions. Yet she has been prepared for this moment by her unknowing accretion of earlier impressions, many of which she had rejected as either false or insignificant. Here James stresses the distinction between seeing and knowing. Isabel may have seen, but what she saw did not register in her consciousness. This fusion of perception and consciousness is as crucial to Isabel's growth as it is to James's impressionism. She is now ready for synthesis, and this chance image crystallizes that readiness. The knowledge she has acquired of European society's fixed social codes meshes anomolously with the intuitive associations affecting her personal affairs.

Isabel has wandered into a scene that galvanizes her past failures. With this shock of recognition her sense of passing time becomes momentarily lost. Instead she suspends time, spatializing it in her mind's eye with the full gestalt of its parts. What James has done in this scene is very close to Proust's forcing the fleeting present into the discontinuous past, or, put in Joseph Frank's terms, James has begun "to seize, isolate, immobilize for the duration of a lightning flash . . . a fragment of time in its pure state."[53] James, however, does not have Isabel attempt to transcend time. Her image, rooted in the reality of presentness and contiguous with her hitherto unrecognized past, is a jolt back into the proper sphere of duration. James and Chekhov agree that the failures of their characters' lives rest with a denial of durational progression. In order to reintegrate themselves into the *durée* they must stop and spatialize a temporal moment.

By freezing this scene Isabel will be able to both synthesize and analyze its implications and components at a later time. At first she only sees and senses the meaning of the colloquy. She

cannot fully understand its significance at the moment of perception. She will need the contemplation of a new reverie. The
flood of consciousness will contrast dramatically with her earlier
Albany reverie. She will also learn to rely on such previously
rejected reflectors as the Countess Gemini.

James suggests that this scene is an epiphany that can only
rivet itself to Isabel's consciousness by the force of its spatialized
presentness. As an emerging impressionist, James discovered he
could briefly submerge the flow of time by hypostatizing it in a
flood of arresting language: "she stopped short," "gave her time
to take in the scene before she interrupted it," "for a minute,"
"had of the moment converted itself," "instantly perceived,"
"arrested her," "lasting only a moment, like a sudden flicker of
light." These brush strokes suspend any action the way a thousand flickers of light on an impressionist canvas spread time
across the static picture. And yet, paradoxically, these same
strokes provide the dazzling movement of consciousness. Isabel's
perception of the pause of close familiarity both provides a static
void in language and sound and increases the powerful cross-
current between its significance and more intense absorption of
visual stimuli.

The bridges between these image fragments are rendered by
the impressionist through the emotional and sensory transitions
of central consciousness. To create this effect James shifted the
angle of vision from a description of the narrative action to the
effect rendered by this scene on Isabel's sensibilities. There is
little description of furniture, dress, or physical appearance.
These are not the items that register on Isabel's apperception.
Only what is felt is perceived. James controls the scene. The
Antonioni camera acts as a cinematic correlative to James's impressionism: objects appear blurred when they either are not
understood or are of no immediate consequence to the perceiver;
objects shift radically into focus with a sudden change of interest. James, the literary impressionist, however, is forced into a
slightly different sensory treatment. He creates the blurred, out-
of-focus effect of consciousness through such expressions as:
"She felt something new," "what struck Isabel first," "struck

her as something detected," "a sense that," "there was a vague doubt," "there was something in them that suddenly made vibrations deep," "she had not read them right," "it seemed to her," "it appeared that." These expressions intensify the commingling of subject and object. The focus is vague because James records only the briefest instant of an entire relationship. Isabel only sees and feels the flickering flash of bewilderment. But that is enough. Details are highly selective, randomly trivial, and crucially pertinent. What Isabel sees is no longer being selected by the controlled screenings of Madame Merle and Osmond. In this unplanned moment Isabel is free to absorb both what is, and what is for her.

But James refused to describe why Isabel sees what she sees. She notices Madame Merle's bonnet. Why? The impressionist brings the reader into the process of this world. He can ask why and feel responsible for imputing motive. The bonnet might simply have been of a striking color or it might not have seemed to suit Madame Merle at that particular moment. It is more likely, given the frame of reference James has provided us, that Isabel now senses that this unattached woman in the presence of a married man would not have a bonnet on her head. But this is a judgment we must make. The patterns of perception and James's own suggestions drive us to realize that what Isabel responds to is the anomalous. She has finally come to recognize the fixed standards of social convention against which she can perceive and test the infinite flux of human relations. She has no interest in the furnishings of the room or the other details that a realist would feel bound to describe. Since they do not exist for her at this moment, they are momentarily obliterated from her consciousness and our text. What is brought into focus instead is the illicit but totally comfortable sense of familiarity.

This scene is an impressionistic epiphany, to be sure, but it does not bring complete synthesis and understanding to Isabel. She must further restructure these fragments through her imagination in the rush of images brought on by her reverie in chapter 42. This reverie marks the extent of her growth as it stands in a before-and-after relationship to the Albany reverie. The

more recent one calls up the newly coalesced images of perceived experiences filtered through the richly prismatic depths
of her imagination. No longer does her imagination fly on un-
experienced expectations. She is now in a position to know. She
sees her relationship to Madame Merle, Osmond, and Pansy
more clearly. With this knowledge she is able to hear the Countess Gemini dot the i's for her and can evaluate the previous
attitudes and hints of Ralph and Mrs. Touchett. Isabel can fix
herself in relation to her world. Through these impressionistic
techniques James found a means for Isabel to perceive herself
and her world as it is.

But at the same time, Isabel's success signals a basic failure
in James's impressionistic vision. By the end of the novel the
gaps between what Isabel saw and knew and what others knew
have been completely closed. Isabel appears to know everything.
Had James fully understood impressionism's unending depths of
epistemological indeterminacy he would have left Isabel in a
state of wondering bewilderment. She knows too much. Isabel
has vanquished Madame Merle, helped Pansy, rejected Good-
wood, and ignored Osmond—and she has done all this because
she has complete knowledge about herself and them. The single
point of view, the unified consciousness, has replaced multiplicity by the close of the novel. The fragments have so cohered that
there is no room for unknowability: "She looked all about her;
she listened a little; then she put her hand on the latch. She had
not known where to turn; but she knew now. There was a very
straight path" (4:436). In James's later impressionism the path
will be not so straight. The gaps of unknowability will remain
open, unfilled, and visibly forceful.

III * WHAT MAISIE KNEW

James experimented with other modes, styles, and genres for
sixteen years before returning to impressionism. On the surface,
the heroines of his first two impressionist novels appear to have
much in common. Both Isabel and Maisie are on a journey of

perception, beginning in innocence and ending in perceptual acuity. They have been released into a confusing, complex, fragmented, multidimensional world of surfaces and adult duplicities. Their limited perceptions are tested in a crucible that combines elements too complex for their young sensibilities. Isabel begins from a fixed position of her own making, moves through an expansiveness based on inductively perceived experiences, and returns to a fixed epistemology. Maisie, on the other hand, is tossed into the flux of "new arrangements" without any preconceived notions, but with a great capacity for flexibility and absorption.[54] Her challenge will be to stay in the air, like the shuttlecock to which she is compared, without succumbing to the temptation of indiscriminate imitation. With so many unworthy models and such a great capacity for assimilation she must quickly learn not to fill her "vessel" at random. While Isabel needed to open herself to a variety of experiences, Maisie must protect herself from the tyranny of unselected experiences and values. Each faces the danger of believing she knows more than she does. But while Isabel prematurely sealed herself off from perceptual profusion, Maisie tries to stay the confusion of new arrangements.

As the novel opens, Maisie's world of parental stability has just been shattered. Her center has become unstable, ambiguous, relativistic, and random. Like all children, she wishes to find refuge in permanence, while testing the limits of change. But this process has been suddenly and capriciously inverted. James is testing Maisie to see whether she can find refuge from the chaos without isolating herself in a rigid epistemology and whether she can accept and transform the fragments of her world into a viable gestalt.[55] The challenge is greater and the stakes higher for this young girl, for she is younger and more completely abandoned than Isabel. She could drown without identity in an abyss of bewilderment.

The heart of this novel's impressionism is the shifting significance of parental relationships. Initially, a child believes in the inviolability of natural parenthood. In the modern impressionistic world this *donnée* will be shattered. Who stands in relation to whom and at what moment in time?—these are the questions of this novel. Or put another way, how should Maisie perceive someone who has been a governess one day and is a stepmother the next? This is compounded by the fact that there is a perfectly good mother who now seems to take little interest in motherhood, a father who keeps forcing relationships, and a friend of the new stepmother who seems more interested in fatherhood than the father. This, of course, is just the tip of the iceberg. But it does suggest Maisie's impressionistic problem (and the reader's, also). These new arrangements will be Maisie's, "to fit them together as she might" (11:6). She will have to read the gestures and expressions that lie behind the duplicitous bits and pieces of legal jargon and parental clichés. She will have to sense the dissolving and reforming relationships through the tinted clouds of tension. She will have to determine where she stands through a phenomenological reading of subject and object.

Maisie is tossed into a world of flux and indeterminacy, but she is there to perceive it:

> The child was provided for, but the new arrangement was inevitably confounding to a young intelligence intensely aware that something had happened which must matter a good deal and looking anxiously out for the effects of so great a cause. It was to be the fate of this patient little girl to see much more than she at first understood, but also even at first to understand much more than any little girl, however patient, had perhaps ever understood before. Only a drummerboy in a ballad or a story could have been so in the thick of the fight. She was taken into the confidence of passions on which she fixed just the stare she might have had for images bounding across the wall in the slide of a magic-lantern. Her little world was phantasmagoric—strange shadows dancing on a sheet. (11:9)

The multiple reflections of this novel are suggested in these opening lines. From her parents' point of view "the child," not Maisie, "was provided for." Only legally has she been provided for; by the end of the novel she will have been stranded, "orphaned," and unprovided for. The prismatic irony of these points of view will continue throughout the novel. The impressionistic thrust of this passage establishes the confusion of new arrangements, which suggests to Maisie both a vagueness ("*something* had happened") and a particularity (that it was important to her and that she must *look out* for the *effects*). Maisie sees more than she understands, so, like Proust's magic lantern, the images are not shaped by her own consciousness. At this point they are a disembodied phantasmagoria of objects separated from her being. Hanging in the balance will be "a young intelligence intensely aware." The kaleidoscopic refractions and geometric accretions of new arrangements will increase Maisie's bewilderment and wonder.

But James will throw the weight of the balance toward Maisie's forceful plasticity. She will see each fragment in the cascade of stimuli, and take each on both its and her own terms. Herein lies the heart of James's ambiguity. New arrangements have neither absolute nor a priori value or shape. If they seem to throw Maisie's world into chaos, then she must counter by forming her own relationships. It is a pragmatic world, so Maisie must grow pragmatic with it; she must find a balance between having her life arranged for her and arranging it herself. Eventually she will realize that there is no end to the surfaces of her parents and stepparents.

She is far ahead of many young intelligences, however, who immediately search for the causes of such effects. Somehow Maisie senses that inductive perception will hold her in good stead. She feels she must live in the presentness of new relations, while attempting to define them in terms of previous arrangements. This process helps prepare her for the next step of relationships. For James, as for Chekhov, life is experienced through the *durée*. Time is measured, not in increments of metric time, but through the shifts and fluctuations of sensations, impressions, and consciousness. As a result, elapsed time in this novel is vague. For instance, we are rarely told how old Maisie is as she passes through the various stages of youth. Henry James would agree with William that time's basic ingredient is "the specious present . . . a vaguely vanishing backward and forward fringe."[56] So for Maisie, "that lively sense of the immediate which is the very air of a child's mind the past, on each occasion became for her as indistinct as the future; she surrendered herself to the actual with a good faith that might have been touching to either parent." (11:14). Time shifts in *What Maisie Knew* are suggested through the vague relativism of "before" and "after," "earlier" and "later." Maisie exists in an intense present of memory and expectation in which every moment is a sum. It is a life of cumulative effects, which she often distends, as Isabel did, into agonizingly long moments of scrutiny. Duration is suspended between an indeterminate number of years in which Maisie's perceptions are played out *in toto* and those elongated moments when her perceptions are rendered in fleeting detail. Late in the novel she will begin to have the capability of synthesizing the "images and echoes kept for her in the childish dusk, the dim closet, the high drawers, like games she wasn't yet big enough to play" (11:12). She will learn to hold these "images and echoes" in her consciousness so that she too will be able to play the adult games. She will find many of the proper sums.

But the need to hold back while she still fills her vessel is painful. Because she cannot completely understand the meanings and directions of words, she responds to tones. But even tones can throw her off. She assumes that the nasty anger in one parent's tone is meant for her when it is actually being directed toward the other parent, through her. Maisie does not understand her role as the go-between, the shuttlecock. She assimilates all the points of view, all the tones of voice, all the gestures. Her pain is centered on the immediacy of indistinguishable impressions, but she is also storing away a "wonderful assortment of objects of this kind [that] she was able to discover there later, all tumbled up too with the things, shuffled into the same receptacle, that her mother had said about her father." With her "bewildered ears" (11:13) she records experience and with her "innocent lips" she plays it back. In the beginning of the novel she misses the underlying tone of voice in her play-back. So she learns to carry those tones with her, holding them until they connect to form an arrangement, but at the same time she reacts immediately, filling her vessel with impressions.

Tone in the impressionist novel is as important as the tints, values, shades, and harmonies of an impressionist painting. The impressionist aesthetic demands that if Maisie responds to tones, then James's prose must have tonal qualities. He understood the importance of this when he wrote that "the consistent, the sustained, preserved *tone* of *The Tragic Muse*, its constant and doubtless rather fine drawn truth to its particular sought pitch and accent, are critically speaking, its principle merit—the inner harmony that I perhaps presumptuously permit myself to compare to an unevaporated scent"[57] or "for Shakespeare's power of constitutive speech . . . as he passed from one application of it to another, tone became, for all its suggestions, more and more sovereign to him, and the subtlety of its secrets an exquisite interest."[58]

Maisie must learn to select from and distinguish between the myriad forms, structures, and shades of a tonal world. At first she doesn't understand her parents' tones because she is an innocent playing for no effect: "she was at the age for which all stories are true and all conceptions are stories. The actual was the absolute, the present alone was vivid" (11:14). But soon she begins to play with her doll in a way that prepares her for participation in the adult games. She at one point scolds her doll, "as she, Maisie, had once been replied to by Mrs. Farange: 'Find out for yourself!' She mimicked her mother's sharpness, but she was rather ashamed afterwards, though as to whether of the sharpness or of the mimicry was not quite clear" (11:34). Both the shame of ambiguous origin and the empirical testing of tone measure the growth of her consciousness. Later, having learned to play the games well, she will no longer rely on imitation. Instead, she will use her own tonal knowledge to play the various parents and stepparents into her hands. She will also discover the effects of silence and feigned stupidity.

Change haunts Maisie, whether it is in the tone of a voice or the change of a name. The fluidity of Maisie's world is signified by the abruptness of name changes. They signal new arrangements and force her to acknowledge the relativism of surface structures. No sooner does she become settled into the new "permanence" of a different parental union (or division) than she is confronted with another "permanent" relationship. Each name carries social and psychological codes that she must adapt to, while the old linger on and those yet to come hover in silence. James involved the reader in these travails through an intricate set of pronoun shifts: "There had been years at Beale Farange's when the monosyllable 'he' meant always, meant almost violently, the master; but all that was changed at a period at which Sir Claude's merits were of themselves so much in the air that it scarce took even two letters to name him" (11:161–62). Maisie's father, Beale Farange, at first is both "papa" and "he." Beale is slowly replaced by Sir Claude, Maisie's mother's lover and, later, stepfather. Sir Claude soon becomes "he." Maisie's mother, likewise, is both "mama" and "she," until she begins to disappear from Maisie's life and consciousness. Maisie's mother gradually becomes "Mrs. Farange." She is replaced by "Miss Overmore" who, as the governess and then stepmother, becomes both "Mrs. Beale" and the "she" of Maisie's life. Further confusion sets in when Sir Claude and Miss Overmore become lovers and try to force themselves as "papa" and "mama" on Maisie. Maisie rejects this, demanding either a communal foursome, which would include the dowdy new governess, Mrs. Wix, or Sir Claude alone as her suggestively incestuous father-lover. Mrs. Wix, with her "straighteners," signifying morally clear perception, finally straightens Maisie out. But while Mrs. Wix's moral rigidity may provide momentary shelter from the storm, it also begins to take on ambiguous value. What Maisie has learned by the end of the novel is that there must be a balance between change and permanence, relativism and the absolute. She knows that people exhibit varied surfaces in different situations and relationships. She balances this multiplicity by unconsciously devising a name-relationship scheme that provides her with an element of stability. While people's roles and names may change, Maisie structures these shifts so the emotional distance of each can be measured. Though "papa" or "mama" disappear, "he" or "she," no matter who it may be, will always indicate the emotional intimacy of a mother or father. Maisie has found stability within change. Mrs. Wix becomes the final "she" of Maisie's still youthful consciousness. James, however, makes it clear that while Maisie may have worked out a system, she will always find the relationships themselves ill-defined and confusing. Often she knows the words but does not understand the concepts; she knows what young and old mean only in relation to herself. What she does not know is that knowledge itself is relative, and that "everything had something behind it: life was like a long, long corridor with rows of closed doors" (11: 33–34). But she keeps herself afloat through a belief in her knowledge.

Maisie's reservoir of faith is tested in one of the most impressionistic scenes of this novel—a moment, like Isabel's intrusion on Madame Merle's and Osmond's private relationship, that through anomaly coalesces the many images and echoes of the past. The key difference is that during Maisie's moment we are meant to recognize how much she *doesn't* know, at the very instant she sees and knows more than ever before. Maisie and Mrs. Beale (once Maisie's governess, Miss Overmore) stumble upon Maisie's father, Beale, and "the brown lady" at the Exhibition. It is a scene that recapitulates the disorientation Maisie experienced when she and Sir Claude encountered her mother and the Captain at Kensington Gardens—unexpected relationships in unexpected places at unexpected moments:

Mrs. Beale hereupon, though discernibly disappointed, reminded her that he [Sir Claude] had not been promised as a certainty—a remark that caused the child to gaze at the Flowers through a blur in which they became more magnificent, yet oddly more confused, and by which, moreover, confusion was imparted to the aspect of a gentleman who at that moment, in the company of a lady, came out of the brilliant booth. The lady was so brown that Maisie at first took her for one of the Flowers; but during the few seconds that this required—a few seconds in which she had also desolately given up Sir Claude—she heard Mrs. Beale's voice, behind her, gather both wonder and pain into a single sharp little cry. . . . "Of all the wickedness—*Beale!*" . . . He had already, without distinguishing them in the mass of strollers, turned another way—it seemed at the brown lady's suggestion. Her course was marked, over heads and shoulders, by an upright scarlet plume, as to the ownership of which Maisie was instantly eager. "Who is she?—who is she?" . . . But Mrs. Beale for a moment only looked after them. . . . "The liar—the liar!" . . . Maisie considered. "Because he's not—where one thought?" That was also, a month ago in Kensington Gardens, where her mother had not been. "Perhaps he has come back," she said. . . . "He never went—the hound!" (11:171–72)

The pervasive blurs and startlingly sharp imagery are held in balance by the emotional resonances of Maisie's confused but acute vision and the Exhibition's swirl of finery. Maisie cannot perceive the human distinctions that rivet Mrs. Beale's attention because Maisie's vision is distorted by the tearful disappointment of yet another ambiguous promise made with little hope of certainty. Maisie sees only "a gentleman" and a "brown lady" through the confused filter of her tear-stained preoccupation with Sir Claude. Mrs. Beale, however, instantly recognizes both the figures and the relationship. The point of view, despite the sharp cut to Mrs. Beale's painfully muted outburst, remains Maisie's. Mrs. Beale's cry triggers in Maisie a new perception that quickly leaps beyond the simple recognition of her father. She focuses on the "upright scarlet plume," which bespeaks an interesting new relationship. What each sees across that crowded, moving, brilliantly colored room is colored by his own concerns: Maisie has no particular interest in why her father is here and not somewhere else, while Mrs. Beale's position as Mrs. Beale is vitally connected to that question. The rhythm of shifting time and space is strong, moments flowing in and out of intense sensation and perception. First there is the surge of swirling time and space around the Exhibition, then the timeless imagery of the blurred moment that hangs like the upright scarlet plume above the flux of movement. Suddenly Maisie and Mrs. Beale are returned to the crowd's immersion in space and time. As they move through the crowd their paralyzed prey stand frozen in timelessness, waiting for confrontation.

Maisie is unable to follow the informed content of the participants' silent battle, but she feels intensely its tone and tension. James, the impressionist, does not record the confrontation itself, preferring instead to capture its atmosphere through the consciousness of a bewildered perceiver. True to the social decorum of a public place, the battle is silent, but this does not lessen its violence. For Maisie, who would be lost in a verbal contest, the fierceness of "a glare of black eyes and a toss of red plumage" becomes a "muffled shock" (11:173). Such vast quantities of sensory stimuli impinge on her consciousness with such blinding speed that only later can she reconstruct her impressions. Often the attempt to give full shape to these moments results in a vagueness equal to the sharp synthesis: "It fell into place with all the rest that she [Maisie] had heard Mrs. Beale say to her father, but whether low or loud was now lost to her, something about his having this time a new one; on which he had growled something indistinct but apparently in the tone and of the sort that the child, from her earliest years, had associated with hearing somebody retort to somebody that somebody was 'another' " (11:174). While this echo of a word that meant nothing in the past emerges to form an association in the present, Maisie still "neither knew exactly what he had done nor what he was doing; she could only, altogether impressed and rather proud, vibrate with the sense that he had jumped up to something and that she had as quickly become a part of it" (11: 175).

Maisie's growth will be marked by the increasing sophistication of her impressionistic readings and responses. She will come to realize that how something is said carries more meaning than what is said, that tone suggests multiple meanings for different perceivers, and that the language of atmosphere is transmitted through the fragments of expression, gesture, and bearing. She will begin to see that words, like new arrangements, names, and ages, hold no absolute value. They must be weighed on the impressionistic scale that measures objective phenomena and subjective perception. All this is what Maisie knows!—or, rather, this is what she begins to know. But she holds onto the belief that she knows, even in the face of bewilderment and wonder. On the one hand, her blind faith hinders her ability to know, because in her need for permanence she sees the world through "straighteners," and yet that faith enhances her capacity for muddling through, for staying, like the shuttlecock she is, in the air and thus in the game. That faith gives this child, who is on the threshold of adulthood, life. Finally she chooses to stay with

Mrs. Wix, because Mrs. Wix has always given her the confidence to believe in her ability to know. This choice is a risk, however. A dangerous self-deception could prevent her from learning that she can *never* be "distinctly on the road to know Everything" or "that she soon should have learnt All" (11:281). This belief in the power of knowing throws the balance toward Maisie's dynamic quest "to learn and learn and learn" and "receive new information from every brush of the breeze."

* 6 *

Hesitation and Achievement
The Sacred Fount and *The Ambassadors*

I * *THE SACRED FOUNT*

The Sacred Fount is James's watershed novel, a work precariously balanced on the threshold of his major phase. James threw into this strange brew all the principles, motifs, and problems of his early impressionism. This theoretical outburst, so outrageous in its solipsism and yet so modern in its epistemology, transcends the joke James intended it to be.[1] In *The Sacred Fount* he shaped, however unintentionally, the aesthetic that would influence his two great impressionist novels, *The Ambassadors* and *The Golden Bowl*. A number of critics have approached *The Sacred Fount* through some of the isolated elements that we would now say constitute James's impressionism. But without the benefit of synthesis they have usually dismissed the novel as a fascinating mistake.[2] Instead, it should be looked upon as James's pivotal example of impressionism taken to extremes. Its theoretical quality allows us to demonstrate more thoroughly the aesthetic concerns of impressionism: the impossibility of determining the exact nature of change in a relativistic world; the fragmented indeterminacy of complex human relationships; the dangerous power of a priori belief as a design for human dynamics; the ensuing isolation when the design becomes more important than the testing of it; the breakdown of faith in one's perceptions and ultimately in oneself when faced with that isolation.

The narrator of *The Sacred Fount* finds himself caught, as Chekhov's bishop did, in the Kierkegaardian dilemma—how to maintain some kind of faith against the void. Isabel solves the problem too well, Maisie finds a positive balance, but the nar-

rator of *The Sacred Fount* slips from impressionistic control into
expressionistic nihilism. The narrator fulfills Maisie's negative
option; he comes to believe, self-delusively, that he knows All.
He is William James's absolutist. His quest for the truth casts
him into a rigid and symmetrical law of human change. He
posits a "vampire theory" for two couples and has confirmed
three fourths of the formula. What he is missing is "the right
woman—our friend's mystic Egeria,"[3] the fourth river in this
sacred fount of human dynamics. Henry James, however, is not
interested in his hero's quest for the truth; instead he is absorbed
in the process by which the narrator seeks out the truth. This
novel is really a mystery story, and James is as ready to lead the
reader down the garden path as Alfred Hitchcock is ready to
have us chase a "MacGuffin."[4] The narrator's vampire theory is
James's MacGuffin. The characters and even the reader may
pursue its solution, but it is irrelevant to the real concerns of the
work. James is not really interested in whether people find part-
ners who are depleted of or bequeathed age, intelligence, or
beauty. If the reader comes to identify too closely with the narrator's incomprehensibly labyrinthine obsession simply because
his perceptions appear to be the only perspective open to scrutiny, then the joke that James refers to will be on the reader.

What does interest James, however, is the process by which
one perceives change. The questions he raises are essentially the
ones he asked in *The Portrait* and *Maisie*, but framed more
explicitly. What constitutes human change? Is is possible to
determine objective change? Is change based upon new perspectives of spatial juxtaposition through time? With *The Sacred
Fount* James came to see what Chekhov had also discovered
in his later years, that change is ephemeral and ambiguous.
Change can take on many shapes and forms, but it must be confronted by anyone hoping to live through the relativism of time
and space. Isabel's sphere was less complicated and so more con-
trollable; Maisie found herself in a maze of adult games that
she hoped to stabilize but not assimilate; the narrator of *The
Sacred Fount* foolishly attempts to create his own "house of
cards" in an epistemological jungle where change leads both

nowhere and everywhere. He is aware of the infinite chaos that surrounds him and exists in his consciousness. To counter this morass he constructs a rigid superstructure of sheer faith with which to stave off the avalanche of change and indeterminacy. He fails because he obsessively reaches out and destroys the delicate spider web of experience, "which is never limited and never complete."[5] His prodigious mental powers are not equal to the task of adjusting to the accelerating multiplicity. He becomes, ironically enough, the instrument of his own defeat, because his attempt to repel the perpetual flood of change is based upon a theory of change that actually increases the variables and brings down upon him more confusion than he can possibly perceive, assimilate, and understand. His self-assurance is born of the same impulses that led to the positive choices of Isabel and Maisie, but his transformation from skepticism to blind insistence destroys the balance they so painfully fought for and won. He begins to accept what he has not observed, and in doing so rejects the impressionistic world James created for him.

He violently disrupts the balanced interface between subject and object, inner ego and outer world. His design hinges on the specific questions of whether Gilbert Long has been transformed from a dull to a clever man, and of who has transformed him, but it must also stand or fall on a series of changes that surround that structure. James, however, has created a novel that moves only to the tune of an anonymous, first-person narrator's perceptions and consciousness. The effect is to throw the narrator's structure into a solipsistic vacuum, forcing the reader to attune himself more acutely to the nuances of James's emerging dramatic method. The dialogue relieves some of the subjective isolation and provides a tension between the narrator's obvious motivational masks and the other characters' less visible subjective deceptions. But there is no objective relief. The narrator fails to achieve the frail balance because he cannot break out of his isolation: he enters the novel locked into a first-person narration; he projects a strongly personal attitude toward Gilbert Long; he does not recognize either of the Brissendens; he is the only guest at Newmarch who forms no amorous relationship;

he spends much of his time roaming the corridors and grounds alone; he is extremely wary of openly discussing his theories; and finally he leaves Newmarch alone, completely defeated after being accused of solipsistic madness by Mrs. Briss. Since his sensitivity prevents him from blatantly verifying his hunches and partial perceptions, his feelings for others actually isolate him further from the human community. And so his direct social intercourse breaks down into those Jamesian (and Chekhovian) ellipses, silences, and missed opportunities. He remains, as the reader does also, lost in the inner ego, trapped in a hopeless void of misinformation, screenings, and missing facts. The perceptions of the narrator remain forever ambiguous because he is either too sensitive, too genteel, too shy, too aloof, or too obsessed to verify what might be verifiable. But in an impressionistic world it is possible that the event or object of perception *was* ambiguous. The narrator remains an unreliable narrator, just as the world remains an unreliable world. To pursue the vampire MacGuffin is folly. But to examine why the narrator and his world remain unreliable is to penetrate to the heart of impressionism.

The mainspring of the narrator's obsession is memory. He is working under its double burden since he is narrating the entire event after some untold period of time and since much of what he believes at Newmarch is based upon his two-year-old memories of the Brissendens and Gilbert Long. His theory is based upon his memory of Long's snub of him and his inability to recognize the Brissendens. So the novel has the somewhat self-righteous yet desperately objective tone of memoirs, while it tries to capture the sense of immediacy and emotional involvement. But these are not memoirs; they are an attempt by the narrator to cathartically relive time. His lesson is that it is not enough simply to accept the surfaces of momentarily perceived impressions as truth nor is it possible to rely on those perceptions when they are subject to strange fluctuations and suspect emotional nuances of memory. The entire narrative becomes suspect in this heightened solipsism of time and space.

Time gives shape to the impressionism of this novel, for the narrator is clearly aware of the problems of memory, while he renders the "general effect" with the immediacy of detailed yet ambiguous concreteness. Memory, and certainly memory twice removed, becomes ordered, not serially but associationally, in a non-uniform flux of things hoped for and feared. It becomes fused and confused with hopes and fantasies that might be remembered as facts, but are based on lived-through modifications and reinterpretations and relived in the light of past losses, present pressures, and future dreams:

The day was as fine and the scene as fair at Newmarch as the party was numerous and various; and my memory associates with the rest of the afternoon many renewals of acquaintance and much sitting and strolling, for snatches of talk, in the long shade of great trees and through the straight walks of old gardens. A couple of hours thus passed, and fresh accessions enriched the picture. There were persons I was curious of—of Lady John, for instance, of whom I promised myself an early view; but we were apt to be carried away in currents that reflected new images and sufficiently beguiled impatience. I recover, all the same, a full sequence of impressions, each of which, I afterwards saw, had been appointed to help all the others. If my anecdote, as I have mentioned, had begun, at Paddington, at a particular moment, it gathered substance step by step and without missing a link. The links, in fact, should I count them all, would make too long a chain. They formed, nevertheless, the happiest little chapter of accidents, though a series of which I can scarce give more than the general effect. (13)

Memory does not exhibit the same ordered sequence as historically controlled events that move to the march of metric time. The narrator attempts to control his sense of loss and confusion through the illusion of total recall. He believes that if he could only relive the weekend at Newmarch, he could shape those events. Yet he was unable to maintain his own law of human dynamics. What he wants is a logical progression in his search for the truth; what he gets are subjective series of accidents that are as disordered and elusive as the memory from which they are recalled. He deceives himself into believing that his vast powers of recall and his ability to render minutiae can recreate the past as it actually was, not as it subjectively is. If he could only accept what he renders—the "snatches of talk," the "impressions," the "accidents," the surfaces that are the fragments of an impressionistic world—then he could live without the anguish of absolutism. He sees impressionistically and he renders what he remembers he saw, but he cannot believe in that reality. The narrator believes in the dichotomy between appearance and reality.[6] Rather than accept the perceptually impressionistic reality of the shifting, ambiguous relativism of fragmented appearances, he maintains a nihilistic faith in what he cannot perceive. This faith could represent the aesthetic needs of an artist,[7] but the narrator is only creating through the medium of his imagination and living through that vicarious, even voyeuristic, composition.

The primary issue of the novel and the key to the narrator's scheme, which he himself acknowledges, is change. Maisie, when faced with the reality that she was both a fixed and a changing point in space and time accepted and even vaguely understood that paradoxical relativism. She recognized the fluidity of multiple perspectives while she saw herself as the center of the universe. She did not attempt to resolve the problems of language and perspective as they related to age, beauty, love, and parenthood. She came to understand that as she moved through space-time as both its center and its peripheral satellite, words, concepts, and perceptions held different meanings and values for different people at different times and places. The narrator of *The Sacred Fount*, however, attempts to impose a reasoned solution onto the dancing contrariness of relativistic change. He forces a childlike egocentricity, a Ptolemaism, on the world he perceives, assuming that the Brissendens and Gilbert Long must have changed while he has remained constant in a world of timelessness. In his eyes, Gilbert Long *has* changed. Why? Not so that "he may seem different than when last we met, perhaps because I have changed and see him in a new light or perhaps I see him differently this time because he has graciously acknowledged me." As for Mrs. Briss: "I stared, then caught at her identity through her voice; after which I reflected that she might easily have thought me the same sort of ass I had thought Long. For she was simply, it appeared, Grace Brissenden" (3).

The narrator does consider her point of view, but seems unwilling to simply accept change as change. Everything that is not as it should be must then be something else, and he sees as his mission the creation of laws that will reach behind the illusions and serve up the reality. He is a romantic caught in the new world of impressionism. He has a desperate need to believe that he can only know the truth if he penetrates the surfaces of existence. But James himself cautioned against such an approach when he wrote that "Life is, immensely, a matter of surface."[8] The surfaces are more than enough for one man at Newmarch, for they multiply at a geometric rate. With each new relationship there develops a new surface and with each step toward the truth of that surface a new deception or fragment emerges, like Zeno's paradox, to keep the narrator always at arm's length from what he seeks. This world accepts subjectivism as *a* reality but not *the* reality. With his insistence on a unified, monolithic reality he can only bring his house of cards down around him.

If he were to completely isolate himself in his own subjectivism, he would be safe from the threat of relativism. But he feels he needs verification of his theories. This places him in the ambivalent position of knowing he can only find objective truth if he breaks outside of himself and tests his perceptions against multiple perspectives. He believes he can escape into his own truth, and that he will be right. He is caught between empiricism and solipsism. When he first tries to test his ideas on Gilbert Long he both faces the relativism and shrinks from it in horror. For he discovers in one short conversation that time and the spatial requirements of beauty and ugliness have no absolute values.

What in the world, in a year or two, had happened to her [Mrs. Brissenden]? She had changed so extraordinarily for the better. How could a woman who had been plain so long become pretty so late?

It was just what he [Gilbert Long] had been wondering. "I didn't place her at first myself. She had to speak to me. But I hadn't seen her since her marriage, which was—wasn't it?—four or five years ago. She's amazing for her age."

"What then *is* her age?"

"Oh—two or three and forty."

"She's prodigious for that. But can it be so great?"

"Isn't it easy to count?" he asked. "Don't you remember, when poor Briss married her, how immensely she was older? What was it they called it?—a case of child-stealing. Everyone made jokes. Briss isn't yet thirty." No, I bethought myself, he wouldn't be; but I hadn't remembered the difference as so great. What I had mainly remembered was that she had been rather ugly. At present she was rather handsome. Long, however, as to this, didn't agree. "I'm bound to say I don't quite call it beauty."

"Oh, I only speak of it as relative. She looks so well—and somehow so 'fine.' Why else shouldn't we have recognized her?"

"Why indeed? But it isn't a thing with which beauty has to do." He made the matter out with an acuteness for which I shouldn't have given him credit. "What has happened to her is simply that—well, that nothing has."

"Nothing has happened? But, my dear man, she has been married. That's supposed to be something."

"Yes, but she has been married so little and so stupidly. It must be desperately dull to be married to poor Briss. His comparative youth doesn't, after all, make more of him. He's nothing but what he is. Her clock has simply stopped. She looks no older—that's all."

"Ah, and a jolly good thing too, when you start where she did. But I take your discrimination," I added, "as just. The only thing is that if a woman doesn't grow older she may be said to grow younger; and if she grows younger she may be supposed to grow prettier. That's all—except, of course, that it strikes me as charming also for Brissenden himself. *He* had the face, I seem to recall, of a baby; so that if his wife did flaunt her fifty years—!" (5–6)

In this extraordinary passage the narrator is confronted by the basic problems that will frustrate his sacred search. He has encountered questions too relativistic and unknowable to be answered from a fixed position. He cannot rely on his memory to make clear the discrepancy in the chronological appearances of the Brissendens. There is no way he can objectively determine what the words "older" or "younger" mean when passed through the prism of the *durée*. The emotional and aesthetic complexities of taste throw "ugly," "handsome," and "pretty" into confusion when defined in the presence of another perspective, namely, Gilbert Long's. Had the narrator recognized, as Proust's Marcel finally did, that he too has aged and that his memory is subject to the whims of time, then he might be able to see that Mrs. Brissenden's "clock had simply stopped. She looks no older—that's all." It's not that she isn't older, it's just that aging is a conspiracy that we are all in together. But we *see* and *believe* that others age at different rates and always faster than we ourselves do. The narrator is also unable to fully comprehend the connection between age and beauty, although, true to form, he offers a theory. And finally, their conversation reveals a series of inexplicable temporal and spatial juxtapositions: the baby face of Briss when he was too old, and his stooped shoulders now that he is too young; his baby face next to Mrs. Briss's clothes made her look fifty, and those same clothes in relation to her newly rejuvenated physical appearance make her look twenty-five. The spatial incongruities compounded and set in relief against the temporal anomalies make for a labyrinth that only the innocent, inductive, and communicative Maisie could have navigated. The narrator of *The Sacred Fount*, isolated in his pride, reaching for more than he can humanly control, and forcing a faulty process of a priori induction onto a world that requires patience and perception, finds himself vanquished and alone with only his shrill cry of irrational faith to keep him alive.

The narrator faces much the same problem that plagued Maisie. Since the most obvious surfaces are often duplicitous (in *The Sacred Fount*, however, we don't even know this), both the narrator and Maisie must reach back and read the subtleties of tone. As the impressionistic world in which these characters live becomes more complex and the literature itself more sophisticated, tone becomes the central impressionistic aesthetic. Impressionist fiction becomes tonal poetry. In *The Sacred Fount* James's use of dramatic method and interior monologue dramatizes the manifest disparity of tonal language that exists between the narrator and the guests at Newmarch. So, in the final line of the novel, when the narrator recognizes that "what I too fatally lacked was her [Mrs. Brissenden's] tone" (319), he is confessing that he has failed. In seeking the answers to his questions, his obsessive crassness prevented him from capturing the subtlety of tone.

Mrs. Briss, on the other hand, has led him through a maze of ambiguous tones, leaving him stranded in uncertainty. In James's late fiction tone always reflects a state of consciousness that is never contained by only the one word, phrase, or conversation. The tonal aspects of any given moment are the accumulation of "echoes and images" that have been filtered through the brush strokes of James's vast labyrinth of time, space, and consciousness. This organic pointillism makes it extremely difficult for anyone writing on James to single out a quote without first providing a huge and unwieldy context.

If the narrator has failed to perceive the world accurately because *his* obsession, *his* isolation, and *his* memory have distorted reality, it is also the case that the reality he perceives, often very acutely, is simply unknowable. A perfect example of this indeterminacy occurs when the narrator and Mrs. Briss come upon May Server and an unrecognizable figure. Their distant perspective, and the tree which partially blocks their view, dramatizes the impressionist method, the narrator's *modus operandi*, and the conflict between his own and Mrs. Briss's way of seeing.

> She [Mrs. Briss] walked a few paces, as if to look about her for a change of company, and by this time had reached a flight of steps that descended to a lower level. On observing that here, in the act to go down, she suddenly paused, I knew she had been checked by something seen below and that this was what made her turn the next moment to give me a look. I took it as an invitation to rejoin her, and I perceived when I had done so what had led her to appeal to me. We commanded from the point in question one of the shady slopes of the park and in particular a spreading beech, the trunk of which had been inclosed with a rustic circular bench, a convenience that appeared to have offered, for the moment, a sense of leafy luxury to a lady in pale blue. She leaned back, her figure presented in profile and her head a little averted as if for talk with some one on the other side of her, someone so placed as to be lost to our view. (81–82)

This scene contains the compositional components of an impressionist painting: the clearly delineated angle of perception, in this instance height and distance; the quality of arrested time ("suddenly paused," and "checked"); the feel of immediacy ("made her turn the next moment to give me a look," and "ap-

peared to have offered, for the moment, a sense"); the perceptual obscurity of "something seen below" and "talk with someone"; the mood captured through suffused visual essence ("a
sense of leafy luxury to a lady in pale blue"); a particularized
perspective ("her figure presented in profile"); the implicit
color juxtaposition of tree trunk and leaves; the vague outlines
of suggestively rendered details. Unlike the spatial arts, however, this picture will continue to unfold and change as the two
observers' consciousnesses play over this scene. This seemingly
pastoral idyll exudes suspense, conflict, and indeterminacy.

They both agree on the "fact" that the lady is May Server,
but the partially hidden presence indicates an unknown relationship that might lead to the missing link, Gilbert Long's
"vampiral victim." Both Mrs. Briss and the narrator assume the
unseen person is male. The narrator, with unwarranted brava-
do, assumes further that he is M. de Dreuil. But Mrs. Briss, who
values empirical judgments, catches him up short with, "Are
you so sure? I don't make out the person . . . I only see she's not
alone" (82). Confronted by both the power of Mrs. Briss and the
unknown, the narrator backs off and settles for, "another man"
(83). Mrs. Briss then triggers his imagination by forcing the
conscious ambiguity of "It's *he!*" Her assertive equivocation pro-
tects her from committing herself to the unknown. But the narrator, unable to contain himself in this duel, responds, but this
time only slightly more tentatively, "Gilbert Long?" As items
of dress become known, the narrator continues to flailingly
assert conclusions, each time incorrectly. Finally "poor Briss"
emerges, and the narrator thinks: "That we should have been
confounded was doubtless but a proof of the impression—the
singular assurance of intimacy borne toward us on the soft summer air—that we had, however delusively, received" (84–85).
It was, impressionistically enough, intimacy and not identity
that was conveyed through "the soft summer air." Both knew
that. But Mrs. Briss knew that it was her husband first, only she
communicated it ambiguously to salvage her pride. She knew,
because with her intimate knowledge of her husband's gestures,
manners, dress, etc., she was able to know impressionistically,

while the narrator simply guessed. And now the narrator, who has not yet sorted out the anguish expressed by Mrs. Briss's "it's *he*," must assume that *both* were "confounded." The narrator does receive impressions, and correct ones, but in his continual attempt to force deductive conclusions onto an inductive process he both defeats himself and allows himself to be defeated by Mrs. Briss. He learns nothing from his theory, his law of the sacred fount, his "MacGuffin."

II * *THE AMBASSADORS*

The Ambassadors marks James's return to the pictorially scenic structure of *The Portrait* and a progression toward the impressionistic nuances of multiplicity and change. The perceptual maze is not as labyrinthine as it had been in *The Sacred Fount*. The relationships are less tenuous, with fewer combinations to rearrange. "Pictures" compose and decompose before Strether's eyes as he moves through the incredibly subtle relational network of Parisian society. While Strether, like Isabel, may seem to know "All" by the close of the novel, he is faced with a future that cannot qualify as a "straight path." Strether, older and more rigid, is less capable of absorbing and adapting to the accelerating world. He is confused by what he sees, what he fails to see, and what his expectations distort, just as Isabel was. His haunting sense of having failed at life leaves him defenseless, supported by neither the youthful ego of an Isabel or Maisie nor the theoretical chutzpah of the narrator in *The Sacred Fount*. Time, lost youth, and Woollett press on Strether's every perception. So while it might appear that James has regressively returned to the limited pictorial impressionism of *The Portrait*, he has, in fact, developed a fusion of impressionistic portraits and fragmented perceptual relativism. Strether's well-trained aesthetic sensibilities continually reform the world into the carefully composed design of the Lambinet painting he so loves, but lost. And yet in Paris, with his complex past returning, his future in doubt, and his present flooded with the fluid sensory stimuli of past, present, and future, Strether becomes submerged in the *durée*. He begins to perceive an impressionistic world impressionistically.

Strether returns to Europe after many years, with "such a consciousness of personal freedom as he hadn't known for years; such a deep taste of change . . ." (31:4). He has prepared himself to perceive in Chad the transformation that will justify his own need for change. He feels he has led a stultifying sycophantic life in Mrs. Newsome's Woollett. He has lost a wife, sacrificed a son, and pursued a tenth-rate literary career. His memories of Paris had been buried in the darkness of New England, but now everything requires a new look. This gives him a final chance to revolutionize his life. The seed for change had been sown thirty years ago in Paris, but had been stifled under the snow-cover of Woollett. Now, behind the role of emissary for Chad's return, Strether will attempt (without sullying his ambassadorial function) one last revitalization of his life. In his perception of Chad's change, Strether mirrors his own desire for change. So his quest reflects his "double consciousness" (21:5): his mandate to negotiate for the return and restoration of Chad and his sense that he is the ambassador of his own hopes for transformation. He finds himself caught between the two, but in true ambassadorial fashion he negotiates both. This double consciousness will thrust him into the middle of shifting perspectives. He will perceive the changes in Chad but not in himself. He will move from the naive perception of Chad's "virtuous" relationship with Mme de Vionnet to a realization that Chad is a selfish, brutal American. This "change" in Chad actually gauges the changes in Strether. And it is *this* relationship that Strether does not see. There is much more he does not see, at first, for he is "in the presence of new measures, other standards, a different scale of relations" (21:114).

Strether is driven by his failures in the past and the mortality of his future to squeeze every bit of existence out of a fragmented and bewildering present. For the first time in James's impressionist fiction, a character fully feels the weight of the past and the future, without sacrificing his need to live in the present. James found a way to allow the forceful past to be rendered in the present. At first Strether relives his past through watching Chad's Parisian life. Later, he will again experience the past-present through his fusion and transformation of the Lambinet into his impressionistic day in the country. He begins to see that he must not allow his past to remain dead and static. "His" Lambinet, for instance, can no longer symbolize what he had lost. He comes to learn, as Proust's Marcel does and Chekhov's characters don't, that the past must be energized through the present, and that it in turn will add a dynamic dimension to the present. The future also moves his present, because with his advancing age and awareness of death he senses that "something" will be for "the last time." Strether's new perception of time allows him to acknowledge momentary impressions as new life.

The first paragraph immediately sets in relief the "multiplicity of relations—between narrator and object, and between the ideas in Strether's mind—held in even suspension throughout the narrative," which explains "Strether's tendency to hesitation and qualification."[9] These qualities lead Ian Watt to classify James as an impressionist, one who became involved "in a very idiosyncratic kind of multiple Impressionism: idiosyncratic because the dual presence of Strether's consciousness and that of the narrator, who translates what he sees there into more general terms, makes the narrative point of view both intensely individual and yet ultimately social."[10]

Maria Gostrey will offer both Strether and the reader a more worldly and empirical perspective, not only of others, but of Strether himself. We are immediately struck by the contrast in ways of seeing as James quickly switches from Strether's vague and fragmented sensory impressions of Maria to her concretely detailed description of him. This shift signals the multiple perspectives that both Strether and the reader will have to absorb, learn from, and sort out. Each character will convey a point of view concerning Chad's alleged transformation and his relationship with Mme de Vionnet, and each will be colored by his own quality of personal involvement. Strether, the innocently limited but openly growing perceiver, will, in turn, graciously and unwittingly accept, rigidly and preconceivedly reject, qualifiedly listen, enthusiastically endorse, and reservedly scrutinize all opinions. He will change, and his transformation will involve loss but not failure.

Strether had lived so many years under the influence of Mrs. Newsome's rigidly moral prejudgments that he simply continues with the same cast of mind when confronted with new conditions. Mme de Vionnet, therefore, is "base, venal—out of the streets" (21:55), before he even meets her. But Maria Gostrey cautions him, just as Mrs. Briss checked the narrator of *The Sacred Fount*, when he attempts to impose these judgments on her: "Oh I don't know. One never does—does one?—beforehand. One can only judge from the facts. Yours are quite new to me" (21:54). James feels that both Strether and Maria are rigid in their view of what exists. Maria's invocation of the empiricist's prerogative forces her to abandon intuition and imagination, while Strether's method represents an equally limiting lack of actual perceptual experience. So Maria chides Strether for not being "sure," believing, as the realists did, that seeing renders unequivocal reality. But Strether needs her gentle pressure to crumble his Woollett-based foundation.

Strether's period in Europe, this second time, is a way of suspending time, so that he can sort out the pieces of his life and rearrange them. He begins to translate his Parisian idyll of thirty years ago into a vision of the future; he stretches the present in "the impulse to gain time" (21:9). By arresting and elongating each present moment between the past and the future, Strether believes he can stave off the forces of Mrs. Newsome. Vicariously, then, he can endow his lost youth and future hopes with images of renewal, represented by the seemingly transformed Chad, the eternally youthful little Bilham, and the frozen beauty of Mme de Vionnet. Strether's famous "live" speech to little Bilham becomes more than an existential exhortation for more meaning in life. It is a kind of internal monologue on his own need to realize the fleeting quality of time and a plea for immunity from its forward movement. What Strether does not recognize is that he is living through these people, hoping only to catch onto the caboose of their train of time. On the one hand he believes that "what one loses one loses" (21:217), and yet the passion of his speech suggests that he is trying to lose certain aspects of his past. The passion of belief is necessary for his emerging involvement in living, just as Maria's perceptual checks show him that Chad has not changed, that little Bilham is aging, and that Mme de Vionnet is, in fact, quite old. Time for Strether takes on that double-edged quality: when he suspends it, he robs it of its endurance and change and yet its transience taints the delight of each vanishing moment. Only when Strether learns to commingle his pasts (both Paris and Woollett) and his futures (both death and life) with his present (each present moment and the flow of presents), only then will he find a whole identity. When he realizes that he cannot live through others, he will no longer need the past he feels he has lost. He, like Proust, will transform that past into presentness.

But first he must be jarred out of his aged Woollett mentality. Chad becomes the vehicle by which he throws himself into a new vision of a radically youthful metamorphosis. As in so much impressionist fiction, a change in the direction of the human clock requires a sudden halting of the mechanism. Time must become hypostatized before it can change direction: "The fact was that his [Strether's] perception of the young man's [Chad's] identity—so absolutely checked for a minute—had been quite one of the sensations that count in life; he certainly had never known one that had acted, as he might have said, with more of a crowded rush. And the rush, though both vague and multitudinous, had lasted a long time, protected, as it were, yet at the same time aggravated, by the circumstance of its coinciding with a stretch of decorous silence" (21:135–36). This impressionistic moment, because it is Strether's own, is what begins to propel him into his new impressionistic world. Because he can stop time and respond to the "crowded rush" of the "vague and multitudinous . . . sensations that count in life," he has taken the first step toward the necessary "emotion of bewilderment" (21:136). This absolutely crucial moment signals "a phenomenon of change so complete that his imagination, which had worked so beforehand, felt itself, in the connexion, without margin or allowance." He is now in and of the impressionistic supersensual multiverse, absorbing, not escaping from, the relativism of sensory relations. He *sees* Chad and sees that Chad is not Chad, not the Chad of his imagination, at least.

In an impressionistic world, however, the question still persists, Who *is* Chad, then? James uses the double consciousness spoken of by Ian Watt to explode any certainty. A third-person narration is superimposed on the central consciousness: "perhaps he, Strether himself, was the only person after all aware of it [the change in Chad]" (21:137). This recalls the problem of solipsism raised by *The Sacred Fount*, while simultaneously delineating the epistemological difference between the two novels. *The Sacred Fount* explores the negative limits of knowledge; *The Ambassadors* asserts the positive. The narrator of *The Sacred Fount* sees a great deal, but we can never know whether what he sees is "the real thing." He prides himself on his powers of observation and continually asserts that he knows. But James has not constructed a world for an amateur Sherlock Holmes. This is an inductive world, where to assert what you know is not necessarily knowing, and where seeing does not always lead to knowing. The narrator negates knowing by asserting it too often and by refusing the perspectives of the other guests. In *The Ambassadors* Strether acknowledges his errors and therefore opens himself to perceptual relations. He learns that there is a progression from seeing to knowing. He sees Chad and Mme de Vionnet on the river but only later in Chad's apartment does he know about them. He learns that one cannot know without seeing and that seeing itself is not enough. Only through multiple perceptors, imagination, and conscious reflection can one know—but only enough to maintain an equilibrium in the ultimately unknowable, impressionistic world.

And yet the process of knowing is slow in coming to Strether. First he must divest himself of his Woollett-based moral preconceptions, then stop working deductively. He must also begin to sort out the valuable but extreme lessons of Maria Gostrey.

When, for instance, Maria reveals to Strether Chad's and little Bilham's deception, it "made Strether open his eyes. 'Do you *know* that?' 'I do better. I see it' " (21:133). Maria's perceptual empiricism is an important model for Strether, but he must also learn that to see is not better than to know. Seeing is not enough. His consciousness must be prepared to assimilate "fifty things." And little Bilham confronts Strether on this point: " 'you're not a person to whom it's easy to tell things you don't want to know. Though it is easy, I admit—it's quite beautiful,' he benevolently added, 'when you do want to' " (21:202).

Strether begins to open himself to seeing and knowing. The day in the country, so fully impressionistic, prepares him (and the reader) for the epiphany that will coalesce all the images of his trip to Europe and, in fact, his life: his view of Chad and Mme de Vionnet caught, impressionistically, on the river together. It is one of the great scenes in impressionist fiction and it has been carefully prepared for by James's controlled development of Strether's apperception. Had he taken this trip into the country earlier, it would have meant nothing, for he could not have experienced it impressionistically. The impressionism of this famous scene has been duly noted by some critics,[11] but never as an integral part of Strether's perceptual growth and never as a crucial component in James's own advancement toward a completely impressionistic vision of existence.

Strether's own train of time, which he finally catches, takes him "almost at random" (22:245) out into the countryside and into the Lambinet painting of his past, where he could "freely walk about" (22:247) in both time and his self-created painting. This painting is no longer the Lambinet of the French landscape school, but his own impressionist painting, reflecting his immediate state of mind. It is an accretion of all the "elements," emotions, sensations, and glimpsed fragments gathered during his three months in Paris. The scene is framed by the same kind of randomness that has characterized his new impressionistic experiences: the "random" selection of stations both from Paris and in the country and the "wonderful accident" (22:257) of Chad and Mme de Vionnet floating into view. In Paris there had been the "happy accident" (21:96) of sighting little Bilham on the balcony, the chance encounter with Chad that becomes one of "the accidents of a high civilization" (21:136), and the chance meeting with Mamie Pocock on the balcony that "represented the possibility between them of some communication baffled by accident and delay—the possibility even of some relation as yet unacknowledged" (22:147).

On the train Strether is still the "spectator" looking through the "little oblong window of the picture frame" (22:245). He is not yet at one with his environment. But this train will deposit him at precisely "the right spot" for his past, present, and future to coalesce into a Proustian privileged moment. He can now sense that the past he missed years ago in the form of the Lambinet will reappear, that "the chance of seeing something somewhere . . . would remind him" of the painting "he had quite absurdly never forgotten." This "composition" is rendered impressionistically indistinct by its obscure motives, the vague and fluid sense of space suspended in the "something somewhere," and time "absurdly" remembered. The ambivalence he has felt for a past that "beyond all reason and by some accident of association, was sweet" (22:245–46), prevented him from becoming totally integrated with his present. But now, alone and in the country, he will begin to steep himself in the present: he will immerse himself in his own painting, speak the language of the present (French), perceive the details of his surroundings, and force his past and future into impressions of immediacy.

Just as the impressionist painters sensed they were in the "right spot" to capture a particular atmosphere of color, light, and composition, so Strether stopped, "on catching a suggestion of the particular note required. It made its sign, the suggestion —weather, air, light, colour, and his mood all favouring—at the end of some eighty minutes; the train pulled up at just the right spot, and he found himself getting out as securely as if to keep an appointment" (22:246). By this time Strether has found the balance between chance that places him passively under the control of outside forces and the intuitive knowledge that this is the right spot. Impressionism fuses the passivity of chance (so

that he "found himself getting out") with the security gained
through many errors of perception, much pain, and an active,
open consciousness.

While still on the train he begins to experience his impressionist painting. He sees, hears, and feels the past harmonies of
detail and color that will be repeated in the country when he
leaves the train. The landscape Lambinet of his past becomes
the impressionist painting of his present: "It would be a different thing, however, to see the remembered mixture resolved
back into its elements—to assist at the restoration to nature of
the whole far-away hour: the dusty day in Boston, the background of the Fitchburg Depot, of the maroon-coloured sanc-
tum, the special-green vision, the ridiculous price, the poplars,
the willows, the rushes, the river, the sunny silvery sky, the
shady woody horizon" (22:246). A few moments later he is off
the train, and the experience of both the window-framed landscape of the train and the framed Lambinet of his past commingle with the unframed countryside. The repetition is a
striking example of Strether's immersion in the *durée:* "The
oblong gilt frame disposed its enclosing lines; the poplars and
willows, the reeds and the river—a river of which he didn't
know, and didn't want to know, the name—fell into a composition, full of felicity, within them" (22:247).

As he continues his rendering of this view he adds the colors
and details of his own impressionist painting: "the sky was silver and turquoise and varnish; the village on the left was white
and the church on the right was grey; it was all there, in short—
it was what he wanted: it was Tremont Street, it was France, it
was Lambinet. Moreover he was freely walking about in it"
(22:247). Time has become fused through space. Strether's
world is beginning to coalesce into the durational impressionism
of a painting that reverberates with the changed harmonies of
his experiences.

In the beginning of the novel Waymarsh was the "success"
while Strether considered himself "a perfectly equipped failure" (21:44). But now he "had the sense of success, of a finer

harmony in things" (22:248). The colors and components of his own painting that he can "freely" walk in, become one, imbuing the scene with dynamic harmonies of which he is a part. Strether, who had always felt himself to be the alien spectator, the man sent to do someone else's business, is now at one with himself and his surroundings. But he also recognizes that "his tension was really relaxed; the peace diffused in these ideas might be delusive, but it hung about him none the less for the time." His double consciousness that had brought him harmony also realizes the possible delusion and transience of this moment.

He continues in the impressionism of the day, until he finds himself, near dusk, at an *auberge* in a village "that affected him as a thing of whiteness, blueness and crookedness, set in coppery green, and that had a river flowing behind or before it—one couldn't say which" (22:252). Strether's ability to render the effect of essences is intensified when, after a momentary recall of the day's "other adventures," the harmonies of the day "somehow fell into a place in it" and there "was not a breath of the cooler evening that wasn't somehow a syllable of the text" (22: 253–54). The day, his life, his perceptions, and his knowledge of them are being "condensed" into a gestalt that stunningly, but with even greater compression, repeats the impressionistic essences of the scene: "Meanwhile at all events it was enough that they did affect one—so far as the village aspect was concerned—as whiteness, crookedness and blueness [notice the gestalt reversal of 'blueness and crookedness'] set in coppery green" (22:254). And so in this mood of "confidence" when he "had the *agrément* of everything" (22:255), "the picture and the play seemed supremely to melt together" (22:254). In this atmosphere of accord and slightly off-balance symmetry Strether can now read "an emptiness that made one of the boats suggestive" (22:255). He has prepared himself for "the full impression" of "the right thing" through three painful months of "inward exercise." This "chance in a million," this "wonderful accident," also occurs because the train had deposited Strether at "the right spot," so that his sharpened perceptions could now absorb "the right thing." Even though he is tired, he continues to look out at the boat until he sees "something that gave him a sharper arrest."

Time hangs suspended in this moment of consonance as Strether both waits for and actively perceives a picture filled "up to the measure" (22:256). The entire scene simply drips with the touches and tints, colors and objects that so fascinated the impressionist painters. And like Isabel's view of Mme Merle and Osmond, Maisie's sighting of Beale and the brown lady, and the narrator of *The Sacred Fount*'s observation of May Server and Briss, this picture is taken from a distant view with a particular angle of vision. They are all important moments that test each character's ability to impressionistically read an impressionistic scene.

This moment of Strether's demonstrates James's control over every element in literary impressionism: as the boat carrying Chad and Mme de Vionnet comes into view the "air quite thickened, at their approach, with further intimations; the intimation that they were expert, familiar, frequent—that this wouldn't at all events be the first time. They knew how to do it, he vaguely felt—and it made them but the more idyllic, though at the very moment of the impression, as happened, their boat seemed to have begun to drift wide, the oarsman letting go. It had by this time none the less come much nearer—near enough for Strether to dream the lady in the stern had for some reason taken account of his being there to watch them" (22:256–57). There is a powerful sense in this passage of what Strether both knows and doesn't know—and these elements are created through the language of impressionistic epistemology: "air quite thickened," "intimation," "he vaguely felt," "at the very moment of the impression," "seemed," "for some reason." What he knows at this point does not consciously apply to Chad and Mme de Vionnet, because he does not yet know who it is in the boat. What he does know is how to recognize the gestures and atmosphere of love. And this will carry him far beyond his involvement with Chad and Mme de Vionnet.

But he still must discover what their relationship is. The lady in the boat wavers just an instant. In that slight movement, that ill-defined gesture, everything that impressionism means in literature and everything that Strether has learned in Europe come together in a moment of time: "This little effect was sudden and rapid, so rapid that Strether's sense of it was separate only for an instant from a sharp start of his own. He too had within the minute taken in something, taken in that he knew the lady whose parasol, shifting as if to hide her face, made so fine a pink point in the shining scene. It was too prodigious, a chance in a million, but, if he knew the lady, the gentleman, who still presented his back and kept off, the gentleman, the coatless hero of the idyll, who had responded to her start, was, to match the marvel, none other than Chad" (22:257). This electrifying moment, for Strether, is just that, an instant of recognition that seems frozen and etched in his consciousness. At the same time James forces the issue of its transience: "sudden," "rapid," "so rapid," "for an instant," "within the minute." Space becomes linked to time through the echoes and harmonies of past images and gestures. Subject and object are fused through Strether's knowledge that it is Mme de Vionnet, at the same time that she knows it is Strether. She somehow communicates this knowledge to Chad, who keeps himself hidden as long as possible. Knowing is now connected to seeing, but Strether also knows more than he sees, because what he knows is the result of the full accumulation of past elements. While he knows a great deal, we are nevertheless aware of how much he doesn't know. He will have to wait, until at Chad's apartment he will know more. But seeing has led to knowing. What Strether knows is that change is continual, and what he has learned about seeing is put succinctly and tearfully by Mme de Vionnet: "It's how you see me, it's how you see me . . . and it's as I am" (22:285).

In his oscillation between the assimilation and rejection of shifting relations and values, Strether finally finds the balance and epistemological humility to deal with the future. When Maria Gostrey asks him, "to what do you go home?" he replies, "I don't know" (22:326). But when she makes one final plea for his love, Strether, who had consistently refused to acknowledge

such feelings toward him, this time replies, "I know. I know."
There is no longer the despair or idealization of the future. Instead there is a recognition and acceptance of the past and neither anguish nor guilt over the forces of the present. Strether sees
and understands what he cannot know and accepts what he can.
He accepts and rejects certain elements of the final composition:
that Chad is not "refined," but is a "brute"; that Mme de Vionnet is not young, and that he cannot accept her sacrificial offer
of herself, even though he is in love with her; that he does not
love Maria Gostrey, so must refuse her; and that he has a moral
obligation to return in his ambassadorial role to Woollett. He
has experienced the different rhythms of subjective time, thereby gaining the time he needed to resurrect his life without succumbing to the illusion of timeless enrichment. What he knows
is that he has "lived," and that living is seeing change where
and when there is change.

His final words—"Then there we are!" (22:327)—are those
of a pragmatist who has come to believe he basically knows
what his position is in relation to other human beings at a given
moment in time. He asserts stability while he acknowledges
flux. By the close of the novel he has experienced impressionism:
"a form and a surface," "lights which were faint and instantly
merged," "lines and tones" which had "quite melted away,"
sensations "both vague and multitudinous," the sense of "names
in the air, of ghosts at the windows, of signs and tokens, a whole
range of expression, all about him, too thick for discrimination,"
"an assault of images," "old ambiguities," "the change of position and of relation," "the flight of time," "proportions that
were changed," "of how many elements his impression was
composed," "some accident of association." The impressionistic
richness of these experiences led James to his impressionist masterpiece, *The Golden Bowl*.

* 7 *

James the Impressionist
The Golden Bowl

I * INTRODUCTION

The Golden Bowl is *the* impressionist masterpiece, because it holds in perfect control and brings to consummate resolution all the important elements of literary impressionism. No impressionist has found a more organic structure for conveying the epistemological problems[1] of multiple perspectives. The architectonic quality of the dual points of view is constructed through a brilliantly eccentric interface between subject and object. The continually off-center set of mistimed encounters provides Maggie, in particular, with a sense of time that she spatializes[2] in order to better engage the runaway *situation nette*. Finally, James's hard fought and painfully wrought "late style" serves as the perfect correlative for his now mature and unified vision of literary impressionism.

In this novel we and James's protagonists know both more and less about more than in any of his previous impressionist novels.[3] In the first half of the novel James renders the fragments of the golden bowl—Maggie, her father Adam Verver, and Charlotte—through Amerigo's eyes. In the second half Maggie reassembles the bowl into more than the sum of its parts; she includes herself in a newly-formed foursome. Her subjective limitations are just as great as her husband's, yet she has the additional task of perceiving deception without alerting the others to what she does and does not know. Maggie's half of the novel becomes (but only in concert with the Prince's half) the perfect impressionistic rendering of epistemological indeterminacy: who knows what? how do they know? why don't they know? how do they keep others from knowing what they both know and don't know? what are the consequences of knowing and not knowing? This novel is a more profound development of what Dorthea Krook described as "the epistemological theme" of *The Sacred Fount*.[4] In that novel one felt, as one often feels in the presence of Nabokov, that the issue of knowledge is a game. In *The Golden Bowl* there is no such thing as an unreliable narrator, because all errors of perception represent the seriously bewildering concerns of real experience, not illusions.

This is James's most carefully controlled novel of subjective objectivism. In creating the dual points of view James was taking a position regarding the subjectivity of the Prince's and Princess's perceptions.[5] The huge gaps between them in their knowledge bear this out, as we become involved in the problems of each. Because Amerigo has been shunted aside by Maggie and her father, Maggie does not really exist for Amerigo as a perceived entity, but only as a peripheral presence. Maggie, however, holds the entire foursome in careful view, allowing only the Assinghams to disappear slowly from sight. For the Prince, Fanny is so present that James justified a violation of literal point of view by taking us into the Assinghams' bedchamber for their continual rehash of events. Maggie, on the other hand, dismisses them as an obstacle to her attempted relational restructuring. The most striking quality of the dual points of view is the way it dramatically emphasizes the novel's subjectivity.

But at the same time, that world becomes objectified by the mere fact that one point of view acts as a check on the other. This allows us to believe we are experiencing a balanced reality, that we are privy to both the inside and the outside world, the subject and the object. One final device in James's objectification of his subjective method is the lurking presence of the unnamed "I," the almost forgotten first-person narrator who every once in a while reminds the reader that the Prince's point of view, for instance, has been distanced through a third-person narration. So with the "I" on one side and the Assinghams' midnight colloquys on the other, James has delicately widened and objectified the Prince's subjectively perceived rendering of the world. It is important to realize that these two objectifiers are largely absent in Maggie's half of the novel. She must learn to objectify her own world by working alone. She cannot rely on outside confirmation, if she is to reconstruct the closely held quartet without the other three hearing a false note. She must come to know objectively more through subjective means; she must listen to the strains of her own consciousness as she silently reads the muted notes of deception.

In the metaphor of the golden bowl James found an organic image for impressionistic alienation from and immersion in the swirling current of life. Through the golden bowl characters begin to see themselves and others as either subjects or objects. The bowl, like the people reflected in it, has no inherent value, but is both a subject and object against which its value fluctuates according to need. Each person in *The Golden Bowl* has, in the crassest terms, a market value. Both Amerigo and Maggie feel thought of, evaluated, and used as objects whose worth will enhance the value of the subject. The Prince often considers himself to be just another piece in Adam Verver's collection. He even asks himself what his value on the open market would be if he were to leave Maggie. Maggie, as if to reinforce his view, believes that her value to the Prince is that she increases his worth.

If the golden bowl serves as a reminder to these characters that they are objects, it also acts as a dynamic entity that sets in motion the search for the flaw, the crack beneath the surface of Amerigo's and Maggie's marriage. The gold of the bowl streams through the surface texture of their lives, while the gilt presses for a knowledge of what is beneath. The hard, pure crystal betokens what could have been, while the flaw describes what is. Finally, the three broken pieces present edges so sharp that Maggie can, significantly, pick up only two at a time. The golden bowl becomes the subject of this novel because it figuratively becomes the object controlling the characters' relations. It is what thrusts them into the flurry of their ambiguous and relativistic relationships. The bowl is both a symbol and an actual, active force. It represents the impressionistic dualism of a detached object and an engaged subject.[6]

The combination of perceptual point of view and dual perceivers serves to move *The Golden Bowl* toward the modernism of architectonically layered literature. Since each perceiver's consciousness shapes the contours of each half of the novel, the entire design is controlled by the confrontation between two different ways of seeing. And while there is no chronological overlapping, there is the sense that the two consciousnesses, Amerigo and Maggie, have at times met and become superimposed upon one another. There are memory playbacks from opposing points of view, and, of course, there are the Assinghams' detailed replays. So while Maggie's section essentially picks up where the Prince's had left off, the effect of multiple reflectors is to break down linear time. This is further enhanced by James's severe elimination of "events": Amerigo's and Maggie's wedding, the birth of the Principino, the mention of the number of years that have passed, and so on. The only chronology is that of perceived consciousness.

The most effective confluence of simultaneity occurs in the transition from the Prince's to the Princess's point of view. As Amerigo's half of the novel ends he has found himself at one with the perfect afternoon and will soon consummate his affair with Charlotte. Maggie's section begins with her waiting for him. There has been no chronological overlapping. But sensing that something is wrong and that she must act, Maggie waits for him, not at the usual Eaton Square, but at Portland Place. Without knowing it her wide-ranging consciousness fuses her awareness of trouble with the Prince's actions at a Gloucester inn. These reflections determine both her new course of action and the new direction of the novel: "She had but wanted to get nearer—nearer to something indeed that she couldn't, that she wouldn't, even to herself, describe; and the degree of this achieved nearness was what had been in advance incalculable. Her actual multiplication of distractions and suppressions, whatever it did for her, failed to prevent her living over again any

chosen minute—for she could choose them, she could fix them—
of the freshness of relations produced by her having adminis-
tered to her husband the first surprise to which she had ever
treated him" (24:10).

Maggie's decision to act, regardless of how blurred and bewildered the motivation, forces her to discriminate among impressions that once had no meaning for her. As the gestalt
psychologist, Wolfgang Köhler, notes, "Objects exist for us only
when sensory experience has become thoroughly imbued with
meaning."[7] Maggie is beginning to see what the relations are.
She is asserting herself as a phenomenological *tabula rasa*, a
fresh perceiver, no longer bound by contrived arrangements and
jaded by the perceptions of routine satisfaction.

So when Amerigo first enters the room where she has been
waiting, she puts her new perceptual awareness immediately to
work: "He had come back, had followed her from the other
house, *visibly* uncertain—this was written in the face he for the
first minute showed her. It had been written only for those seconds, and it had appeared to go, quickly, after they began to
talk; but while it lasted it had been written large, and though
she didn't quite know what she had expected of him she felt she
hadn't expected the least shade of embarrassment" (24:15).
What emerges from this silent moment is the impressionist's
predicament; her perceptual penetration is intensified because
she has been forced to look at the changes in her world, and yet
the closer she looks the faster she sees the image disappear. The
labyrinth of unknowability grows, increasing both the sharpness of the impression and the vagueness of the more complex
visual field.

As Maggie continues to watch closely, she gives a name to
something about which she is uncertain: "What had made the
embarrassment—she called it embarrassment so as to be able to
assure herself she put it at the very worst." In his look of embarrassment she finds her métier, her *modus operandi:* "With
the sense of it, on the spot, she had felt overwhelmingly that she
was significant." By forcing him to see her, to react to her, she
instantly realizes that she can become something other than an

object in the periphery of his vision. However, she is still in the presence of "some difference she couldn't measure" (24:16).

The Golden Bowl is the supreme impressionist example of abundant language used to render nonverbal experience. In this novel James created his most conscious and articulate characters. They dedicate themselves to seeing and knowing more and more, while they come to know less and less about more—and all this they do silently. For Maggie to confront an issue verbally she would have to be prepared for a verbal response, and that would throw her into situations where she would have to deal with verbal duplicity. *The Golden Bowl*, like Chekhov's late work, antedates the distrust of language so characteristic of the modernism of Kafka, Beckett, and Sartre. Yet while this novel presents one of the most dazzling displays of language, they are words that fill the vessel of consciousness. Only when consciousness has been filled to overflowing do the words spill out and spread over the phenomenological space between subject and object. Space, psychic space, becomes charged with the vibrations of silent consciousness. Only rarely (with the exception of Fanny Assingham, who is a creature of uninhibited word play) do people in this novel communicate meaningfully through words. *The Golden Bowl* is filled with the silences of what might have been said but wasn't, what might have been said if something had been said, elaborately soundless reflections, privileged moments, seconds and minutes of silent waiting, and encounters when characters send and receive impressions that communicate more than words ever could.

Most characters in impressionist fiction simply see and absorb change. They become the passive receptors of their sensory world. Maggie, however, transforms the impressionistic motif of passive waiting into a fluid relationship between waiting and pursuit. She not only accepts change, she affects changes in human relationships, even when she is not sure what the relationships are. She discovers that waiting can be pursuit. Though she must struggle from behind a veil of ignorance and naiveté, she learns to read the signs of duplicity and love. But finally, Maggie, more than any other character in impressionist fiction, works out of sheer faith. She believes that she must commit herself to love and innocence, even though she swims in a pool of deceit. No character has been more at sea in what she does not and cannot know. But she has the pragmatic will to believe in her ability to see just enough to adjust a set of tenuous relationships.

II * SENSATIONS AND CONSCIOUSNESS

While there is no hard evidence that James knew the work of the British empiricists Locke and Hume,[8] he might well have absorbed Hume's belief that impressions were distinct from one another, that they formed perceived fragments of knowledge. And yet at the same time James was influenced by his brother's and Henri Bergson's belief that there is a continuity in sensory experience, that we often perceive not the fragments but the entire sensory field. The result was a creative mix of nineteenth-century Sensationalist and twentieth-century Gestalt psychologies. Each placed great store in the role of the perceiver and neither attempted to separate sensations from perception. This became very important to James's fiction, for what interested him was the process by which characters turn sensations into consciousness through an application of freshly intense and intelligent perception.

What the Prince Sees

What Amerigo primarily sees is Charlotte and Fanny. But he also sees the objects of wealth, gold significantly among them, that the British Empire can offer. So that "his imagination, working at comparatively short range, caused him now and then to stop before a window in which objects massive and lumpish, in silver and gold, in forms to which precious stones contribute, or in leather, steel, brass, applied to a hundred uses and abuses, were as tumbled together as if, in the insolence of the Empire, they had the loot of far-off victories" (23:3). He sees a good deal of gold in his half of the novel. But it is Charlotte who rivets his attention. He really sees Maggie only once, and that is before he first sees Charlotte at Fanny's. From then on there is only Charlotte. When she enters Fanny's Charlotte makes sure she does not immediately address the Prince, so that he has all the more time to take her in. As he waits for Maggie at Portland Place, he vividly notices Charlotte from the window. Following their embrace and sealed pledge, Amerigo, at Adam Verver's party, is struck by "her intenser presence, her quieter smile, her fewer jewels" (23:322–23). Charlotte materializes in the window above him at Matcham with an "appearance of readiness not so much to join him . . . as to take with him some larger step altogether" (23:355–56). Finally, it is Amerigo who first intuitively "sees" the flaw in the golden bowl.

But the Prince is a very passive perceiver[9] whose perceptions can be manipulated by Charlotte. In the New York Edition, James divided the Prince's half of the novel into three books. Book One holds very close to the Prince's perceptions of Fanny, Charlotte, and the golden bowl. Book Two, however, subtly shifts from the Prince to Maggie and Adam. As this middle section obliquely veers outside the Prince's consciousness, it dramatizes his isolation from his wife and renders the unconscious conspiracy that marries Charlotte to Adam. This is also the only section that includes neither an Assingham midnight colloquy nor a Charlotte-Amerigo *tête à tête*. In effect this section has been taken from Amerigo, showing how little control he has over his perceptions. So, when Book Three opens with Charlotte majestically waiting on the staircase for the Prince to perform his duties below, we fully understand that while it may be the Prince who is doing the perceiving, it is Charlotte who is directing those perceptions. He completely loses his capacity for seeing with detachment when he becomes immersed in the harmony of Charlotte and the day at Matcham. In Maggie's half of the novel, her task will be to neutralize Fanny's seeing, redirect the Prince's perceptions by becoming an object of interest, and strip Charlotte of her power.

What the Princess Sees

By the time we finally see Maggie, her vision, which had seemed stupidly narrow from Amerigo's point of view, has begun to grow wider. She will be able to change the relational structures because she learns to envision a perceptual field, one in which she is included. She opens her senses to all the nuances that affect her: "It wasn't till many days had passed that the Princess began to accept the idea of having done, a little, something she was not always doing, or indeed that of having listened to any inward voice that spoke in a new tone. Yet these instinctive postponements of reflexion were the fruit, positively, of recognitions and perceptions already active; of the sense above all that she had made at a particular hour, made by the mere touch of her hand, a difference in the situation so long present to her as practically unattackable" (24:3).

The impressionism of this half of the novel is more striking, because if Maggie's perceptual awareness becomes heightened, so, too, does the Prince's; his need to cloak his relationship with Charlotte demands a closer watch on Maggie. So Maggie must constantly adjust to the changing conditions brought on by both "sides" seeing and countering. At first she sees herself as an "impenetrable and inscrutable" (24:4) pagoda, and then as the wheel of the family coach that stayed in place while the wheels of Amerigo and Charlotte pulled. These are images of stasis and passivity. She must change these conceptions of herself if she is to actively change the relationships: "She had seen herself at last, in the picture she was studying, suddenly jump from the coach; whereupon, frankly, with the wonder of the sight, her eyes opened wider and her heart stood still for a moment. She looked at the person so acting as if this person were somebody else, waiting with intensity to see what would follow" (24:25). Maggie, like most Chekhovian and Jamesian impressionist characters, now stops time before changing direction, then plays out the impressionistic balance between waiting and pursuit. Finally, she subjectively objectifies herself. Time stops so that she can detach herself from herself. She sees herself as somebody else, because her consciousness has grown to the extent that she can subjectively perceive the objective elements of her being. Maggie must act if she is to save her marriage, but she must act passively so as to not expose what she is trying to change.

Maggie becomes James's most convincing and complex *tabula rasa:* she sees herself; she sees the new arrangements and relations; she sees what others do not see and what they do; she sees what she does not need to see; she sees what she must not see without damaging her cause; she sees both literally and metaphorically; she sees from different perspectives; she sees what is both painful and pleasurable; she sees others seeing her; she sees Charlotte as both majestic and doomed; she sees Amerigo's embarrassment and sees that she must look away before he sees her seeing him; she sees that she cannot see what her father sees; and she sees Fanny struggling to know but not seeing enough to know. And so it is Fanny who, ironically, sees enough to state what James believes about Maggie: "You know because you see" (24:304). Maggie, however, returns with James's other equally valid belief: "I know nothing" (24:305). In overreacting, Maggie demonstrates her heightened consciousness and epistemological humility in the face of an impressionistic world.

III * INDIRECT LANGUAGE

Literary impressionists anticipated the phenomenological novel's distrust of language, but they did not believe that their characters should be driven into total silence; instead they "must uncover the threads of silence that speech is mixed together with."[10] At times, the impressionists and stream of consciousness writers seemed to be working toward the same goals.[11] But those writers more closely associated with stream of consciousness—Dorothy Richardson, Joyce, and Woolf—tipped the phenomenal balance toward the subject, toward interiorization. Their reality was more often the quality of presentness in objects and images that had once been or might be experienced, imagined, or dreamed—all thrown together into the flow of free association. Impressionists usually render the actual act of perceiving objects and images of consciousness. However, James's and Chekhov's characters do engage in moments of interior synthesis.

Yet the line of phenomenological modernism—Kafka, Sartre, Beckett, and Robbe-Grillet—returns to the impressionists rather than stream of consciousness writers, because impressionists are always immersed in the physical world of time and space. As that world became more complex and multifaceted these writers realized they must find a language for their characters, a language that could at least partially reveal the nonverbal aspects of communication. It is this view of the new impressionistic world that has made cinema the most effective art form to continue what the impressionists began. Merleau-Ponty has described the process this way: "What if language expresses as much by what is between words as by the words themselves? By that which it does not 'say' as by what it 'says'? And what if, hidden in empirical language, there is a second-order language in which signs once again lead the vague life of colors, and in which significations never free themselves completely from the intercourse of signs?"[12]

If *The Golden Bowl* is one of the most difficult works of fiction in the English language, it is because James created a monumentally complex example of this "second-order language." It is a language that follows the perceptual contours of the duplicitous Prince, whose perfect taste and *politesse* eliminates the possibility of direct speech. Together with Charlotte's fluent cleverness, wit, and beauty, the two characters develop a sophisticated sign language that enhances James's impressionism. It is a language of gesture, glance, mood, tone, and pitch, and it increases their illicitness while brooking no indiscretion. But it does not match—because they underestimate—the high order of Maggie's resourcefulness, commitment, and intelligence. She learns to read their language without their really knowing whether and how much she knows. It is a war of nerves and each skirmish increases the complexity of their "second-order language."

This form of language throws into relief the inability of characters to know precisely. Verbal language attempts to codify and reduce the ambiguity of consciousness. The impressionists believed that language had become an instrument of abuse and manipulation, that it could no longer convey the deep structures of consciousness in action. And at the same time these were writers, artists who had to find linguistic ways to convey nonverbal experience. This is not to say, of course, that other writers have never had to confront this problem, but with the advent of "the supersensual multiverse" this issue became exacerbated. James tried to deal with this paradox by searching for language that forced upon the reader the ultimate in ambiguity and unknowability. At the same time, he strove to find language that would transmit the labyrinths of consciousness with great precision. For all his uses of the abstract, the general, and the intangible,[13] James, like Proust, moved round and round an object or image, then doubled back in an effort to surround what is being rendered with a plenitude of precise suggestiveness.

In the silences between people James fills what have so often in literature, but never in life, been voids: "Mrs. Assingham, for answer, only looked at him, and this the next instant had apparently had more effect than if she had spoken" (23:39); "as after this they awaited their friend in silence the effect of the silence was to turn the time to gravity" (23:44); "so their queer minute without words told him" (23:51); "so much mute communication was doubtless all this time marvellous" (23:155); "it was in their silence that the others loomed, as she felt" (24:54). These silences permeate both the Prince's and the Princess's narratives, creating an intratexture of indirect language that verbally renders nonverbal experience.

James discovered that these silences could best be communicated through metaphors, or as Bergson was to later put it: "Comparison and metaphor will here suggest what cannot be expressed."[14] Many of the impressionistic effects of James's late works were sustained by his use of metaphor. He was able to fuse disparate sensory impressions and convey both the abstract and the palpable qualities of an object or image, while he searched for the clarification of the unknown. Metaphors also act as thematic indices for Amerigo's and Maggie's ability to see and act on relationships. And finally, James's metaphors enhance his impressionistic lyricism, his poetic realism, as they color the contours of perceptual atmosphere and abstract conceptualization.

The Golden Bowl abounds in such glittering and extended metaphors as the ship and boat for those two explorers Amerigo and Adam, the pagoda, wheel, telescope, and hard glass for Maggie, the bird in the gilt cage and the silken noose for Charlotte, and the bridge game for the relations that seem to be out of Maggie's control. But it is the "as ifs" that form the basic fabric of James's figurative language. One example that occurs at a dramatic moment links the silences of both Maggie and the Prince. Amerigo enters to find the golden bowl shattered and Maggie picking up the pieces: "She had proceeded without words, but quite as if with a sought effect—in spite of which it had all seemed to her to take a far longer time than anything she had ever so quickly accomplished. Amerigo said nothing either—though it was true his silence had the gloss of the warning she doubtless appeared to admonish him to take: it was as if her manner hushed him to the proper observation of what she was doing" (24:182–83). This fascinating phenomenological passage represents their first real instance of reciprocal communication. Time is both elongated and truncated for Maggie. The action of picking up two of the shattered pieces seems to take a long time in terms of the intensity of her effect and his perception of it. At the same time, it is completed quickly in relation to her sense of how long it seems to take. Distended time is subjectivized through the object of her perceptions, Amerigo, while the actual physical act is shortened because it does not preoccupy her. It becomes a detached action.

The "as ifs" carry out this same effect by calling into question the issue of detached objectification and subjective unknowability. The first "as if" asks if Maggie is conscious of this effect, while she is clearly looking at herself looking at him who is looking at her. The second "as if" *seems* to come more from his point of view as he sees that her manner forces him to look at her in a particular way. These "as ifs" work to produce the multiple perspectives so important to the impressionism of this novel: "A good metaphor produces thereby 'shifts in attitude.' "[15] It is not surprising that Maggie's narrative contains more metaphorical configurations than the Prince's. Maggie changes the course of events and shifts her own mode of thinking. Amerigo's mind is less flexible and not as imaginative, therefore less metaphoric. James uses metaphor in *The Golden Bowl* to dramatize distinctions between characters, supply images for linguistically untenable situations, evoke sensory experiences, and synthesize impressions.

IV * SPATIAL TIME

James is rarely thought of as a creator of privileged moments. Yet both he and Chekhov anticipated Proust, Joyce, Rilke, and Faulkner. This is not to say that writers as diverse as Wordsworth and Tolstoy had not shaped moments when characters become isolated from time, while being transported into a realm of spiritual resurrection. James's moments, however, tend to be more experiential and less transcendently "meaningful." They are periods of heightened sensory awareness and expanded consciousness. There is usually a change in perception. It is unlike the Romantic epiphany where a perceiver discovers that an object has become invested with its now unveiled "true meaning." Instead, the perceiver discovers a new sensory perspective based on a new synthesis of already experienced fragments. It is usually triggered by an accidental juxtaposition of elements in a silent situation. The intensity of focus is so great during these instants that the rest of the external world seems to evaporate, leaving—in James, at least—the two perceivers locked into a detached pocket of phenomenal reciprocity.

The effect of this is to stop narrative time dead in its tracks. This results in a detailed scrutiny of its spatial elements. The moment appears to take on a significance disproportionate to its actual passage through the durational world. In James this elevation seems commensurate with the increasingly sensitized consciousness that is expanding to absorb and surround the object of consciousness. A Jamesian epiphany is not "the ecstatic identification of the self and the world."[16] Instead, it is a phenomenological union whereby the phenomenon of perception is experienced and is itself experience, and the perceiver becomes the crucial link between the two. This relationship cannot be examined without the writer's and the character's plucking it out of the stream of time and spatializing it. Time takes on a new order—a phenomenological one—that flows between the reader and the work, the author and the characters, and the characters themselves. This moment, this new temporal order ends as abruptly as it began and reemerges with both narrative and subjective time.

Since these moments of spatialized time are wedded to heightened consciousness, it is not surprising that the Prince neither participates in nor precipitates many of them. And those that he does experience are always shared by Charlotte, not Maggie. They are, in fact, created by the active, yet accidental, entrances of Charlotte. The first such instant occurs when Charlotte enters Fanny's drawing room and allows Amerigo's consciousness to float over her presence. She shows her spatial self in the light of their past relationship and uneasy present. The second moment is "the exceptional minute, a mere snatch, at the tail of the others, on the huge Portland Place staircase" (23:91). The Prince "prolonged the minute" and the "items of his consciousness had clustered so quickly that by the time Charlotte read them in his face he was in presence of what they amounted to" (23:95). This third frozen scene gives a symmetry to the second, because it too frames Charlotte, majestically situated on a "monumental" staircase above Amerigo. But this time it is Charlotte who is in control of the perceptual vantage point, and she sees herself the way the Prince does. She "created, for a number of seconds, an arrest of vibration" in which "it all hung together, melted together, in light and colour and sound" (23:246).

James's instinct for the dramatic saved the richest and most impressionistic privileged moment for the end of Amerigo's narrative. This is important, for it measures the distance Maggie will have to make up in her narrative, because it is the perfect consummation of Amerigo's and Charlotte's relationship. It begins as a day in the country, and, not unlike Strether's impressionistic day, reveals the many components of illicitness. James captures the vague emotional sensations of the Prince's many detailed impressions. For the first time really, the Prince is "in possession" of both the day and his perceptions: things "melted together, almost indistinguishably, to feed his sense of beauty" (23:351); "this offered a certain sweet intelligibility as the note of the day? It made everything fit" (23:352); "the upshot of everything for him, alike of the less and the more, was that the exquisite day bloomed there like a large fragrant flower that he had only to gather" (23:355).

"But it was to Charlotte he wishes to make the offering." And almost immediately she appears above him framed by a window:

They were conscious of the same necessity at the same moment, only it was she who as a general thing most clearly saw her way to it. Something in her long look at him now out of the old grey window, something in the very poise of her hat, the colour of her necktie, the prolonged stillness of her smile, touched into sudden light for him all the wealth of the fact that he could count on her. He had his hand there, to pluck it, on the open bloom of the day; but what did the bright minute mean but that her answering hand was already intelligently out? So therefore while the minute lasted it passed between them that their cup was full; which cup their very eyes, holding it fast, carried and steadied and began, as they tasted it, to praise. He broke however after a moment the silence. (23:356)

This frozen, silent, spatialized moment is a perfect example of the elements of impressionism. The instant has been suspended and framed on both ends by moving time. It represents the reciprocal fusion of subject (Amerigo) and object (Charlotte), and, since multiple points of view have been allowed to enter the Prince's sphere, object (Amerigo) and subject (Charlotte). Amerigo is able to read Charlotte's signifiers ("the very poise of her hat, the colour of her necktie, the prolonged stillness of her

smile"). In a brilliant use of metaphor, the sensations of sight
and taste are united through an elongated moment that seals
their union. It is a self-consciously framed picture, an impressionist painting.

Maggie's privileged moments are more numerous and more
complex than the Prince's. Significantly, they begin to occur
only after Maggie has groped and stumbled through half of her
narrative. She begins to see and know only when the Prince
walks in as she is picking up the pieces of the golden bowl. From
that electrifying moment until she has rearranged the foursome,
Maggie, like Marcel at the party of the Princesse de Guer-
mantes, experiences a quite rapid series of privileged moments.

The most important of these occurs during a bridge game at
Fawns. Adam and Fanny, Amerigo and Charlotte are the players. Bob Assingham keeps to himself and Maggie sees this as a
perfect opportunity to be alone with her thoughts. But she realizes that each of the players is concentrating on her rather
than on the cards. For a moment she feels a rush of vertiginous
power and control. As she sits outside their game she knows that
she could "sound out their doom in a single sentence" (24:233).
She gets up and passes behind each player, silently bending "a
vague mild face upon them as if to signify that little as she followed their doings she wished them well" (24:234). And each
in turn meets her eyes, which leaves her "with the strangest of
impressions—the sense, forced upon her as never yet, of an appeal, a positive confidence, from the four pairs of eyes, that was
deeper than any negation and that seemed to speak on the part
of each for some relation to be contrived by her." Then she goes
out onto the terrace and looks in at them through the windows.
This allows her a more veracious view, while it also isolates her
from them: "It was as if the recognition had of itself arrested
her—she saw as in a picture." (24:236).

The overt rhythm of movement and arrest has begun. It will
shape the impressionism of this scene, as it has the entire novel.
Charlotte seeks out Maggie as the other three continue the hand.
Maggie sees her coming, and it "was an impression that fairly
assailed the Princess and to which something of attitude and

aspect, of the air of arrested pursuit and purpose, in Charlotte, together with the suggestion of her next vague movements, quickly added its meaning" (24:238). This is a perfect moment of James's mature impressionism. The contours are blurred, the motion hypostatized, and the meaning suggested. The confrontation between Maggie and Charlotte which had been building for so long is now being played out in the best of James's muted impressionism. These are two highly intelligent and complex consciousnesses gingerly moving toward one another. They both have more to lose through direct articulation of their grievances—which, it must be remembered, neither is sure of. So impressionism defines this oblique standoff. It consists "of the unuttered and unutterable, of the constantly and unmistakably implied" (24:240).

As they move closer to one another, "the intensity of their mutual look might have pierced the night" (24:241). Maggie enters into the pure realm of subjective timelessness as she becomes phenomenologically wedded to Charlotte: "How long had she stood staring?—a single minute or five? Long enough in any case to have felt herself absolutely take from her visitor something that the latter threw upon her, by this effect of silence, by this effect of waiting and watching, by this effect, flagrantly, of timing her indecision and her fear" (24:242). James further unites them in their confrontation through the most controlled commingling of points of view. He has prepared us for this kind of moment by allowing us to have had access to Charlotte's perceptions throughout the novel. Now, while we are strictly held by Maggie's perceptions, her consciousness so flows into Charlotte's that it seems as though we are engaged in both at the same time: "By the time she [Maggie] was at her companion's side, for that matter, by the time Charlotte had, without a motion, without a word, simply let her approach and stand there, her head was already on the block, so that the consciousness that everything had gone blurred all perception of whether or no the axe had fallen." They are both lost and immersed in the impressionistic world. They have been bracketed, and can know very little outside of what their perceptions—now blurred

—tell them. At the same time, they are reading more intensely the inscrutable signs. They see more and they see less; they know more and they know less about more.

They must widen their perspective; they must see and acknowledge that there are multiple perspectives. So for a moment Maggie and Charlotte watch the card players: "Side by side for three minutes they fixed this picture of quiet harmonies, the positive charm of it and, as might have been said, the full significance—which, as was now brought home to Maggie, could be no more after all than a matter of interpretation, differing always for a different interpreter" (24:243–44). This stunning moment culminates a more important impressionistic vision than we have seen before. It is a whole complex of privileged moments that move both Maggie and Charlotte toward each other. A bond is formed between them as they each see what the other sees. Maggie learns that she is not alone in what she doesn't know, because she now sees and knows that the "significance" of anything is "a matter of interpretation, differing always for a different interpreter." This isolates her, but with Charlotte standing by her side seeing the same phenomenon, they each know just enough to perform the acts of selflessness needed to repair the now altered golden bowl of their lives. In *The Golden Bowl* James refined and enriched the techniques and vision that had shaped the impressionism of his earlier novels.

Afterword

✳

Chekhov and James

Both James and Chekhov followed remarkably similar patterns in the development of their literary impressionism. They were first drawn to impressionism through their experiments with children and adolescents as the purest perceivers confused by the raw impressions of a complex world. But both James and Chekhov were torn by the tensions between realism and impressionism. So for a time they reverted to what they thought were their social responsibilities, which they felt could best be conveyed through the authorial "objectivity" of realism. Then, on their journey back to impressionism, they both attempted play-writing as a way of expressing their new concerns for the impressionistically non-didactic dramatic method. Both efforts were immediately rejected by the public and the critics. James discontinued this endeavor by redirecting his ideas into the impressionistic novel. Chekhov quietly continued writing plays until Stanislavsky made them melodramatic and naturalistic enough to gain acceptance. But Chekhov, too, found impressionistic prose to be an entirely satisfactory medium for evoking his new vision of the new world—the impressionistic world.

This is a world where characters must learn to change and adapt to a changing environment. They must learn to see and to know through inductively perceived impressions, while they also become painfully aware of the subjective limitations of knowledge. They perceive ambiguous surfaces that only reveal more surfaces, as they come to realize that appearances are the only reality. This complicates the structures of their lives, for they can no longer believe in Truth but only in the many truths that are "a matter of interpretation, differing always for a different interpreter." And these truths are only fleetingly experienced in a momentary coalescence of fragmentary impressions. These privileged moments usually vanish before their full

meaning is grasped. So the characters are often left with the
tenuous reality of memory as they struggle to maintain a faith
in the presentness of their experiences. The experiences rarely
have definitive causal lines, and as a result they become discrete
moments of accidental immediacy. Time is, therefore, both successive and durational, popping up as frozen spatial images cut
off from the flow of past-present-future, then becoming reim-
mersed in the *durée*. This ambiguous, relativistic, and tenuous
nature of experience drives the author to render perceptually
blurred bewilderment, rather than either the subject or the object. What is rendered is the mood, sense, feel, and atmosphere
that exists between perceiver and perceived, subject and object.
Literary impressionists discovered a new way to depict a new
way of seeing and knowing. Literary impressionists discovered
modernism.

Notes and Bibliography

*

Notes

INTRODUCTION

1. K. E. Senanu, "Anton Chekhov and Henry James," *Ibadan Studies in English* 2 (1970): 182.
2. James/Turgenev, Crane/Tolstoy, Thoreau/Tolstoy, Whitman/Dostoevsky, Melville/Dostoevsky.
3. Sharon Spencer, *Space, Time and Structure*, pp. xix–xxiv.
4. Maria Elizabeth Kronegger, *Literary Impressionism*, pp. 17, 20, 89; Herbert J. Muller, "Impressionism in Fiction: Prism vs. Mirror," *American Scholar* 7 (1938): 355; R. M. Albérès, *Histoire du Roman Moderne*, pp. 191–92.
5. Beverly Jean Gibbs, "Impressionism as a Literary Movement," *Modern Language Journal* 36 (1952): 175–83.
6. Henry Adams, *The Education of Henry Adams*, p. 382.
7. Albérès, *Histoire*, pp. 184–86.
8. Joseph Warren Beach, *The Twentieth Century Novel: Studies in Technique*, pp. 332–36.
9. Ford Madox Ford, "Techniques," *Southern Review* 1 (July, 1935): 22, 24.
10. Muller, "Impressionism in Fiction," pp. 355, 356–57.
11. Arnold Hauser, *The Social History of Art*, 4: 134.
12. Ernest J. Simmons, *Chekhov: A Biography*, p. 496.
13. Dmitri Chizhevsky, "Chekhov in the Development of Russian Literature," in *Chekhov: A Collection of Critical Essays*, ed. Robert Louis Jackson, p. 54.
14. "Nonetheless, both authors increasingly move toward a phenomenology of mind at the very time when the possibility of a viable ontology appears to be unthinkable." Adams, *Education*, p. 458; John Carlos Rowe, *Henry Adams and Henry James: The Emergence of a Modern Consciousness*, p. 38.
15. Adams, *Education*, p. 457.
16. Kronegger, *Literary Impressionism*, pp. 26–27.
17. Anton Pavlovich Chekhov, *Polnoe sobranie sochinenii i pisem*,

[complete works and letters], ed. A. M. Egolin and N. S. Tikhonov, 15: 446. All subsequent quotations from Chekhov's works and letters will parenthetically incorporate the volume and page numbers of this edition within the text. All translations are my own.

18. "Zola's book *L'Oeuvre*, published in 1918, was, according to Benois, the first source of Impressionist ideas in Russia, where it was much read," Camilla Gray, *The Russian Experiment in Art, 1863–1922*, p. 40.

19. Richard A. Hocks, *Henry James and Pragmatistic Thought*, p. 15, quotes a letter from Henry to William: "Then I was lost in the wonder of the extent to which all my life I have (like M. Jourdain) unconsciously pragmatised. You are immensely and universally right."

20. Viola Hopkins Winner, *Henry James and the Visual Arts*, p. 51.

21. Dorthea Krook, *The Ordeal of Consciousness in Henry James*, p. 411.

22. Muller, "Impressionism in Fiction," p. 360.

23. Orm Øverland, "The Impressionism of Stephen Crane: A Study in Style and Technique," in *Americana-Norvengica*, ed. Sigmund Skard and Henry Wasser, p. 239.

1 * LITERARY IMPRESSIONISM

1. Calvin S. Brown, "Symposium in Literary Impressionism," in *Yearbook of Comparative and General Literature*, no. 17, pp. 80–81.

2. Ibid., p. 84.

3. Ibid., p. 80.

4. "It [impressionism] leans on the thought of William James, with his emphasis upon the marginal, incoherent, and inchoate elements of mental experience and his insistence that intellectual analysis of this experience breaks up the vital unity or wholeness that is its essential quality," Muller, "Impressionism in Fiction," p. 363.

5. William James, *The Will to Believe and Other Essays in Popular Psychology*, p. 17. "Nothing is more difficult than to know precisely *what we see*," Maurice Merleau-Ponty, *Phenomenology of Perception*, p. 58.

6. Kronegger, *Literary Impressionism*, p. 21.

7. Jean Mouton, "L'Optique de Proust, du regard à la vision," in *Entretiens sur Marcel Proust,* pp. 50–51.

8. Øverland, "The Impressionism of Stephen Crane," p. 240.

9. Maurice Merleau-Ponty, "The Primacy of Perception and its Philosophical Consequences," in *Readings in Existential Phenomenology,* p. 35.

10. Hauser, *The Social History of Art,* p. 224.

11. Ibid.

12. Ibid., p. 225.

13. Gaston Berger, "Phenomenological Approach to the Problem of Time," in *Readings in Existential Phenomenology,* p. 187.

14. Henry James, "The Art of Fiction," in *Theory of Fiction: Henry James,* ed. James E. Miller, Jr., p. 35.

15. Henry James, "Preface to *What Maisie Knew,*" in *The Art of the Novel: Critical Prefaces,* p. 149; and idem, "Preface to *The Ambassadors,*" *The Art of the Novel,* p. 321.

16. Henry James, "The Novel in 'The Ring and the Book,' " in *The Theory of Fiction,* p. 158.

17. Henry James, "Preface to *The American,*" in *The Art of the Novel,* pp. 37–38.

18. Henry James, "The Novel in 'The Ring and the Book,' " in *Theory of Fiction,* p. 158.

19. Henry James, "Letters, 1899, to Mrs. Humphry Ward," in *Theory of Fiction,* p. 155.

20. Paul Ilie, "Symposium in Literary Impressionism," in *Yearbook of Comparative and General Literature,* no. 17, p. 77.

21. It is not surprising, then, that both Chekhov and James tried their hand at variations of this genre: Chekhov in "The Swedish Match" and "The Shooting Party" and James in "The Turn of the Screw," "The Aspern Papers," and "The Jolly Corner," for instance.

22. Øverland, "The Impressionism of Stephen Crane," p. 250.

23. Percy Lubbock, *The Craft of Fiction,* pp. 17–18; Jean-Paul Sartre, *Situation II,* p. 93; Alain Robbe-Grillet, *For a New Novel,* p. 154.

24. Hauser, *Social History of Art,* p. 209.

25. "The act of perception is more important than either the perceived or the perceiver," Kronegger, *Literary Impressionism,* p. 40.

26. Maurice Merleau-Ponty, *Signs,* p. 16.

27. Øverland, "The Impressionism of Stephen Crane," p. 241.

28. Muller, "Impressionism in Fiction," p. 356.

29. V. H. Winner, *Henry James and the Visual Arts*, pp. 77–78.

30. See Merleau-Ponty, *Phenomenology of Perception*, p. xiv; and Chekhov's use of *ostrenanie*, Charles B. Timmer, "The Bizarre Element in Čechov's Art," in *Anton Čechov 1860–1960: Some Essays*, pp. 277–92.

31. Øverland, "The Impressionism of Stephen Crane," p. 260.

32. Henry James, *Partial Portraits*, p. 207.

33. Merleau-Ponty, *Phenomenology of Perception*, p. 333.

34. Roland Barthes, *Writing Degree Zero*, pp. 76–78.

35. "In his mature period the prime object of villainy is *futljarnost'*—encasing oneself physically, psychologically, morally, and spiritually in order to reduce the points of contact between oneself and the rest of the world." See Karl Kramer, *The Chameleon and the Dream: The Image of Reality in Čexov's Stories*, p. 62n.

36. Ihab Hassan, *The Literature of Silence*, pp. 174–200.

37. Merleau-Ponty, *Phenomenology of Perception*, p. 115.

38. Marcel Proust, *The Past Recaptured*, p. 140.

39. Sergio Perosa, "Naturalism and Impressionism in Stephen Crane's Fiction," in *Stephen Crane: A Collection of Critical Essays*, p. 80.

40. "German scholars in particular have formulated a system of *Stilentwicklung* where the development naturalism-impressionism-expressionism is depicted as a series of steps following one another in a thoroughly logical manner. The first, they say, is dominated by the outer world, the second by the meeting of the outer world and the inner Ego, and the third is wholly dominated by the inner Ego." Øverland, p. 240.

41. Kronegger, *Literary Impressionism*, p. 25.

42. Proust, *The Past Recaptured*, p. 132.

43. Hermann Bahr, *Zur Überwindung des Naturalismus*, p. 197.

44. See A. A. Mendilow, *Time and the Novel*; Hans Meyerhoff, *Time and Literature*; Robert Humphrey, *Stream of Consciousness and the Modern Novel*; and Shiv Kumar, *Bergson and the Stream of Consciousness Novel*.

45. W. H. Auden, "New Year Letter" (London: Faber and Faber, 1941), lines 440–41.

46. Joseph Frank, "Spatial Form in Modern Literature," in *The Widening Gyre*, p. 25.

47. Roger Shattuck, *Marcel Proust*, pp. 113–14.

48. Ibid., p. 117.

49. Merleau-Ponty, *Phenomenology of Perception*, pp. 411–12.

50. Bahr, *Zur Überwindung*, p. 198.

51. Wolfgang Köhler, *The Task of Gestalt Psychology*, p. 142.

52. Henry James, "Preface to *Roderick Hudson*," in *Art of the Novel*, p. 5.

53. Henry James, "Preface to *What Maisie Knew*," in *Art of the Novel*, p. 151.

54. E. F. N. Jephcott, *Proust and Rilke*, pp. 30, 28.

55. Henri Bergson, *The Creative Mind*, p. 222.

56. Ibid., p. 39.

57. Roman Jakobson, "Two Aspects of Language: Metaphor and Metonymy," in *European Literary Theory and Practice*, p. 124.

58. Ralph Freedman, *The Lyrical Novel*, pp. 1–41.

59. George Poulet, *Studies in Human Time*, pp. 34–35.

60. Friedrich Kümmel, "Time as Succession and the Problem of Duration," in *The Voices of Time*, p. 48.

61. Poulet, *Studies in Human Time*, p. 350.

62. Henry James, "The Story-Teller at Large: Mr. Henry Harland," in *Theory of Fiction*, p. 101.

63. Mendilow, *Time and the Novel*, p. 95.

64. Poulet, *Studies in Human Time*, p. 351.

65. Kronegger, *Literary Impressionism*, p. 60.

66. Hauser, *Social History of Art*, p. 170.

67. Øverland, "The Impressionism of Stephen Crane," p. 242.

68. Kronegger, *Literary Impressionism*, p. 60.

69. René Huyghe, "Shifts in Thought During the Impressionist Era: Painting, Science, Literature, History, and Philosophy," in *Impressionism: A Centenary Exhibition*, p. 15.

70. Ibid., pp. 14–32.

71. Henry James, *The Painter's Eye: Notes and Essays on the Pictorial Arts*, p. 28.

72. Henry James, "The Art of Fiction," in *Theory of Fiction*, p. 33.

73. Winner, *Henry James and the Visual Arts*, p. 51.

74. Henry James, *The Painter's Eye*, p. 28.

75. Maurice Merleau-Ponty, *Sense and Non-Sense*, p. 11.

76. Huyghe, "Shifts in Thought," p. 21.

77. John Rewald, *The Impressionist Brush*, p. 24.

78. Huyghe, "Shifts in Thought," p. 19.

79. Jules Laforgue, "Impressionism," in *Impressionism and Post-*

Impressionism 1874–1904: Sources and Documents, p. 16.

80. Henry James, *The Golden Bowl*, 24:306–7. All subsequent quotations from James's fiction—with the exception of *The Sacred Fount*—will parenthetically incorporate within the text the volume and page numbers of "The New York Edition," i.e., *The Novels and Tales of Henry James*, The New York Edition, 26 vols. (New York: Charles Scribner's Sons, 1907–17).

81. Rewald, *The Impressionist Brush*, p. 32.

82. Laforgue, "Impressionism," p. 16.

83. Merleau-Ponty, *Phenomenology of Perception*, p. vii.

84. Huyghe, "Shifts in Thought," p. 28.

85. Ibid., p. 31.

86. Laforgue, "Impressionism," p. 18.

2 * THE EMERGING IMPRESSIONIST

1. Thomas G. Winner, "Čechov and Scientism; Observations on the Searching Stories," in *Anton Čechov 1860–1960: Some Essays*, p. 326.

2. Kramer, *The Chameleon and the Dream*, p. 137.

3. Victor Terras, *Belinskij and Russian Literary Criticism*, pp. 162–63.

4. Winner, "Čechov and Scientism," p. 326.

5. R. M. Albérès, *Metamorphoses du Roman*, pp. 77–78.

6. Bergson, *The Creative Mind*, p. 239.

7. For relevant discussions of first- versus third-person narrations see: Henry James, "Preface to *What Maisie Knew*," in *Art of the Novel*, pp. 145–46; and Barthes, *Writing Degree Zero*, p. 38.

8. Robbe-Grillet, *For a New Novel*, p. 157.

9. Ibid., p. 163.

10. Timmer, "The Bizarre Element in Čechov's Art," pp. 277–92.

11. Ibid., p. 278.

12. Robbe-Grillet, *For a New Novel*, p. 19.

13. John Hagan, "Chekhov's Fiction and the Ideal of Objectivity," *PMLA* 81 (1966): 409–18.

14. Merleau-Ponty, *Phenomenology of Perception*, p. 151.

15. Robbe-Grillet, *For a New Novel*, pp. 51–53.

16. Barthes, *Writing Degree Zero*, pp. 4–5, 76–78.

17. Robbe-Grillet, *For a New Novel*, pp. 161–62.

18. Not all of Chekhov's impressionist stories are written in the third person, for instance, "Oysters" and "The Story of Miss N. N."

19. Thomas G. Winner, *Chekhov and His Prose*, p. 26.

20. Cornelis A. van Peursen, *Phenomenology and Reality*, p. 74.

21. Robbe-Grillet, *For a New Novel*, p. 155.

22. Poulet, *Studies in Human Time*, p. 295.

23. Kramer, *The Chameleon and the Dream*, pp. 47–59.

24. We are reminded here of the Kuleshov style of cinematic montage. This early experiment demonstrated that by intercutting—thereby juxtaposing—the same shot of an actor assuming a neutral expression with shots of a soup plate, a woman, and a corpse the viewers would notice changes in the actor's expression when there were none.

25. William Faulkner, *Absalom, Absalom* (New York: Random House, 1936), p. 261.

3 * ACHIEVEMENT AND HESITATION

1. Joseph L. Conrad, "Unresolved Tension in Chekhov's Stories," *Slavic and East European Journal* 16 (1972): 60. "By the end of 'Sleepy' we do not feel the same sense of frustration as at the close of 'Vanka.' Like Varka, the reader experiences a sense of relief, despite the horrible act brought on by the girl's maddening fatigue."

2. Gleb Struve, "On Chekhov's Craftsmanship: The Anatomy of a Story," *The Slavic Review* 20 (1961): 467–77.

3. Nathan Rosen, "The Unconscious in 'Vanka.'" *Slavic and East European Journal* 15 (1971): 451–52. Rosen, dealing only briefly with "Sleepy," fails to nail down the point that in killing the infant Varka has focused on and reduced all the fragments of a half-sleep unconsciousness, thereby transforming the image of infant/death into a conscious act.

4. This verb, *krichat'*, is very important in the associational connections which Varka makes. It is necessary to find a word in English that works uniformly throughout the story. A baby can cry or scream, but a cricket does not. The word I have chosen should fit with a baby, a cricket, crows and magpies, and the mistress—"screech." The clouds' screeching is, of course, Chekhov's emerging use of *ostranenie*. See Struve for his choice of "shrill."

5. For Chekhov's further development of this device and theme

see J. L. Styan, *Chekhov in Performance*, p. 243: "In *The Cherry Orchard*, time past, present and future are at the last one, the play's last act an integrated moment of revelation."

6. Frank, "Spatial Form in Modern Literature," p. 13.

7. Adams, *The Education of Henry Adams*, p. 461.

8. Laforgue, "Impressionism," p. 18.

9. Kramer, *The Chameleon and the Dream*, pp. 93–112.

10. Ibid., p. 113; Donald Rayfield, *Chekhov: The Evolution of His Art*, p. 92.

11. *The Chameleon and the Dream*, pp. 113–33.

12. Wayne Booth, *The Rhetoric of Fiction*, pp. 158–59.

13. Kramer, *The Chameleon and the Dream*, pp. 134–73.

14. Kramer does not cite the story; Hingley and Winner simply mention it in passing.

15. Heraclitus, in John Burnet, *Early Greek Philosophy* (London: Adam and Charles Black, 1908), fragment 41, p. 150.

4 * CHEKHOV THE IMPRESSIONIST

1. Martin Esslin, *The Theater of the Absurd*, pp. 68, 308.

2. Kramer, *The Chameleon and the Dream*, p. 171.

3. Winner, *Chekhov and his Prose*, pp. 37, 222.

4. William Earle, "Revolt Against Realism in the Films," in *Film Theory and Criticism*, p. 41.

5. Proust, *The Past Recaptured*, p. 259.

6. K. M. Vinogradova, "Stranitsa iz chernovoi rukopisi rasskaza 'Dama s sobachkoi,' " *Literaturnoe nasledstvo: Chekhov*, vol. 68, p. 140.

7. Ronald Hingley, *Chekhov: Biographical and Critical Study*, p. 175, says only that "The Bishop" is "a most sympathetic picture of a member of the clergy." Winner does not cite the story. Simon Karlinsky, *Letters of Anton Chekhov*, p. 441, notes that it is a "plotless and scrupulously realistic account of the last few days in the life of a high-ranking Orthodox Church dignitary of humble social origins."

8. Chizhevsky, "Chekhov in the Development of Russian Literature," p. 58.

9. Nils Åke Nilsson, *Studies in Čechov's Narrative Technique: "The Steppe" and "The Bishop,"* p. 68.

10. Kramer, *The Chameleon and the Dream*, p. 173.

11. Chizhevsky, "Chekhov in the Development of Russian Literature," p. 58.

12. This story has become a virtual Rorschach of causes and hopes: Vladimir Yermilov, *Anton Pavlovich Chekhov,* pp. 408–9; Virginia Llewellyn Smith, *Anton Chekhov and the Lady with the Dog,* p. 138; Hingley, *Chekhov,* p. 170; Rayfield, *Chekhov,* p. 239.

13. Winner, *Chekhov,* p. 225.

14. Kramer, *The Chameleon and the Dream,* p. 156.

15. Styan, *Chekhov in Performance,* pp. 244, 246–47.

16. Lilac for Chekhov is not simply a color, but an entire sensory complex that holds rich associations for his characters in a number of stories: "The Steppe," "The Kiss," and "The Lady with the Dog."

17. Merleau-Ponty, *Sense and Non-Sense,* p. 4.

18. Remy C. Kwant, *The Phenomenological Philosophy of Merleau-Ponty,* p. 9n.

19. Tom F. Driver, *Romantic Quest and Modern Query: A History of the Modern Theatre,* p. 236.

20. J. L. Styan, *The Dark Comedy: The Development of Modern Comic Tragedy,* pp. 78, 79; Maurice Valency, *The Flower and the Castle: An Introduction to Modern Drama,* p. 371.

21. Driver, *Romantic Quest and Modern Query,* pp. 221–22; Martin Esslin, *Brief Chronicles: Essays on Modern Theatre,* pp. 27–28.

22. Styan, *Chekhov in Performance,* p. 151.

23. Ibid., p. 163.

24. Ibid., p. 166.

25. Ibid., pp. 147–341.

5 * THE EMERGING IMPRESSIONIST

1. Edward E. Hale, "The Impressionism of Henry James," *Union College Faculty Papers* 2 (1931):3–17; Kronegger, *Literary Impressionism,* pp. 30, 32, 38; Louis Auchincloss, *Reading Henry James,* p. 13.

2. John Wild, *The Radical Empiricism of William James,* p. 408.

3. James E. Miller, Jr., *Theory of Fiction: Henry James,* p. 61.

4. Henry James, "The Art of Fiction," in *Theory of Fiction,* pp. 34–35.

5. Ibid., p. 35.

6. Henry James, *The Notebooks of Henry James*, pp. 23, 24.

7. Henry James, "1889 letter to The Deerfield Summer School," in *Theory of Fiction*, p. 94.

8. Henry James, "Guy de Maupassant," in *Theory of Fiction*, p. 64.

9. Hugo Sommerhalder, *Zum Begriff des literischen Impressionismus*, p. 16.

10. Henry James, "Preface to *What Maisie Knew*," in *Art of the Novel*, p. 151.

11. Henry James, "1915 letter to H. G. Wells," in *Theory of Fiction*, p. 91.

12. Winner, *Henry James and the Visual Arts*, p. vii.

13. Ibid., p. viii.

14. Ibid.

15. Hale, "Impressionism of Henry James," pp. 9–11.

16. Laurence Bedwell Holland, *The Expense of Vision*, p. 43.

17. Henry James, *Notes on Novelists with Some Other Notes*, p. 106.

18. Henry James, "Guy de Maupassant," in *Theory of Fiction*, p. 64.

19. Henry James, *French Poets and Novelists*, pp. 208–9.

20. Ibid., p. 201.

21. Ibid., pp. 201–2.

22. Kronegger, *Literary Impressionism*, p. 15.

23. Henry James, "Gustave Flaubert," in *Theory of Fiction*, p. 178.

24. Henry James, "Preface to *The Golden Bowl*," in *Art of the Novel*, p. 328.

25. Wild, *Radical Empiricism*, p. 408; Albérès, *Histoire du Roman Moderne*, pp. 184–85.

26. Eliseo Vivas, "Henry and William: (Two Notes)," *Kenyon Review* 5 (1943): 588.

27. William James, *The Principles of Psychology*, 1:224.

28. Henry James, "Preface to *What Maisie Knew*," in *Art of the Novel*, p. 143; idem, "Preface to *The Princess Casamassima*," in *Art of the Novel*, p. 63.

29. Henry James, "Preface to *Roderick Hudson*," in *Art of the Novel*, p. 5.

30. Vivas, "Henry and William," pp. 590–91.

31. Henry James, *French Poets*, p. 201.

32. William James, *Principles*, 1:254.

33. Ibid., p. 274.

34. Henry James, "Preface to *What Maisie Knew*," in *Art of the Novel*, p. 142.

35. Wallace Stevens, *Opus Posthumous*, p. 242.

36. Franz Kafka, *The Trial* (New York: Schoken, 1968), p. 216.

37. Henry James, "Preface to *What Maisie Knew*," in *Art of the Novel*, p. 149.

38. Eugene F. Kaelin, *An Existentialist Aesthetic*, p. 217.

39. Bruce Lowery, *Marcel Proust et Henry James*, p. 67. "Entre Henry James et son frère William; entre William James et Bergson; et enfin entre Bergson et Proust, ce dernier rapport étant le seul des trois ou l'on puisse vraiment parler d'influence:

William James—Henri Bergson
↓   ↓
Henry James   Marcel Proust"

40. William James, *Principles*, 1:609–10.

41. Ibid., p. 609.

42. Poulet, *Studies in Human Time*, p. 353.

43. Henry James, *Notebooks*, p. 18.

44. Henry James, "Preface to *What Maisie Knew*," in *Art of the Novel*, p. 141.

45. Henry James, "The Art of Fiction," in *Theory of Fiction*, p. 35.

46. Critics who have approached *The Portrait* from this perspective most successfully are: Holland, *Expense of Vision*, pp. 43–54; Tony Tanner, "The Fearful Self," in *Twentieth Century Interpretation of "The Portrait of a Lady*," pp. 67–82; Peter K. Garrett, *Scene and Symbol from George Eliot to James Joyce*, pp. 76–159; and Philip M. Weinstein, *Henry James and the Requirements of the Imagination*, pp. 31–71.

47. This is not the technique of the subjective camera which often mechanically and obtrusively becomes the literal eyes of the protagonist.

48. Henry James, "Preface to *The Portrait of a Lady*," in *Art of the Novel*, p. 52.

49. Emile Zola, quoted by Anne Dayez in *Impressionism: A Centenary Exhibition* (New York: The Metropolitan Museum of Art), p. 136.

50. Jean Leymarie, *Impressionism*, 1: 50, 52.

51. Philip Grover, *Henry James and the French Novel*, p. 129. "Her [Isabel's] responsiveness to paintings is not an isolated feature of her character."

52. Jean-Luc Godard, quoted by Toby Mussman, "Duality, Repetition, Chance, the Unknown, Infinity," in *Jean-Luc Godard*, p. 302.

53. Frank, "Spatial Form in Modern Literature," p. 21.

54. *What Maisie Knew* has received remarkably scant notice as one of James's most brilliantly wrought novels of perceptual relations. Those critics most useful are: Weinstein, *Requirements of the Imagination*, p. 73; Tony Tanner, *The Reign of Wonder*, pp. 278–98; Rowe, *Henry Adams and Henry James*, p. 41; Granville H. Jones, *Henry James's Psychology of Experience*, pp. 5–10; and J. A. Ward, *The Search for Form: Studies in the Structure of James's Fiction*, pp. 145–48, 152–63.

55. Jones, *Psychology of Experience*, pp. 6, 10.

56. William James, *Principles* 1:613.

57. Henry James, "Preface to *The Tragic Muse*," in *Art of the Novel*, p. 81.

58. Henry James, "The Tempest," in *Theory of Fiction*, p. 285.

6 * HESITATION AND ACHIEVEMENT

1. Jean Frantz Blackall, *Jamesian Ambiguity and "The Sacred Fount*," p. 144.

2. Krook, *Ordeal of Consciousness*, explores the "epistemological theme"; Tanner, *Reign of Wonder*, treats the problem of the subjective observer; Holland, *Expense of Vision*, discusses the "miracles of communication"; and Weinstein, *Requirements of the Imagination*, provocatively demonstrates how the Jamesian imagination manifests itself in the unreliable narrator/perceiver.

3. Henry James, *The Sacred Fount*, p. 37. Subsequent quotations will parenthetically incorporate within the text the page numbers from Leon Edel's 1953 edition of a reprint of the first American edition (1901).

4. François Truffaut, *Hitchcock*, pp. 98–99. Hitchcock says, "So the 'MacGuffin' is the term we use to cover all that sort of thing: to steal plans or documents, or discover a secret, it doesn't matter what

it is. And the logicians are wrong in trying to figure out the truth of a MacGuffin, since it's beside the point. The only thing that really matters is that in the picture the plans, documents, or secrets must seem to be of vital importance to the characters. To me, the narrator, they're of no importance whatever."

5. James, "The Art of Fiction," in *Theory of Fiction*, pp. 34–35.

6. See Leon Edel's introduction to Henry James, *The Sacred Fount*, p. xx.

7. See Weinstein, *Requirements of the Imagination*, p. 101n.

8. Henry James, *Partial Portraits*, p. 207.

9. Ian Watt, "The First Paragraph of *The Ambassadors:* an Explication," in *The Norton Critical Edition of Henry James's "The Ambassadors,"* pp. 472, 473.

10. Ibid., pp. 474–75.

11. See John L. Sweeney's introduction to Henry James, *The Painter's Eye*, pp. 28–29; Winner, *Henry James and the Visual Arts*, pp. 74–78.

7 ✳ JAMES THE IMPRESSIONIST

1. Krook, *The Ordeal of Consciousness*, pp. 234, 236.

2. Alan Rose, "The Spatial Form of *The Golden Bowl*," *Modern Fiction Studies* 12 (1966): 103–16.

3. Garrett, *George Eliot to James Joyce*, pp. 137–38. In general, this fine essay most closely approximates my approach; without conceptualizing impressionism, he focuses on the novel's ambiguity. See also Weinstein, *Requirements of the Imagination*, p. 173.

4. Krook, *The Ordeal of Consciousness*, pp. 176–77.

5. Henry James, "Preface to *The Golden Bowl*," in *The Art of the Novel*, p. 330.

6. Krook, *The Ordeal of Consciousness*, pp. 391–93. The symbol of the golden bowl "remains, to my mind, a clumsy, artificial graft . . . which is not organic to the poetic structure of the novel."

7. Wolfgang Köhler, *Gestalt Psychology*, p. 43.

8. Hocks, *Henry James and Pragmatistic Thought*, p. 68.

9. Garrett, *George Eliot to James Joyce*, p. 140.

10. Merleau-Ponty, *Signs*, p. 46.

11. Kumar, *Bergson and the Stream of Consciousness Novel*, p. 4.

12. Merleau-Ponty, *Signs*, p. 45.
13. Seymour Chatman, *The Later Style of Henry James*, pp. 2–5.
14. Bergson, *The Creative Mind*, p. 48.
15. Colin Murray Turbayne, *The Myth of Metaphor*, p. 20.
16. Jephcott, *Proust and Rilke*, p. 30.

* Bibliography

Abel, Darrel. "Frozen Movement in *Light in August.*" *Boston University Studies in English* 3 (1957): 32–44.

Adams, Henry. *The Education of Henry Adams.* Cambridge: Riverside Press, 1961.

Albérès, R. M. "Aux sources du nouveau roman: L'impressionnisme anglais." *Revue de Paris* 69 (1962): 74–86.

———. *Histoire du Roman Moderne.* Paris: Editions Albin Michel, 1962.

———. *Metamorphoses du Roman.* Paris: Editions Albin Michel, 1966.

Arnheim, Rudolf. *Visual Thinking.* Berkeley: University of California Press, 1969.

Auchincloss, Louis. *Reading Henry James.* Minneapolis: University of Minnesota Press, 1975.

Bahr, Hermann. *Zur Überwindung des Naturalismus.* Stuttgart: Kohlhammer Verlag, 1968.

Barthes, Roland. *Writing Degree Zero.* Translated by Annette Lavers and Colin Smith. New York: Hill and Wang, 1968.

Bazin, Germain. *French Impressionists in the Louvre.* New York: Harry N. Abrams, 1958.

Beach, Joseph Warren. *The Twentieth Century Novel: Studies in Technique.* New York: The Century Co., 1932.

Beckett, Samuel. *Proust.* New York: Grove Press, 1931.

Benamou, Michel. "Symposium in Literary Impressionism." In *Yearbook of Comparative and General Literature,* no. 17 (1968), pp. 91–94.

———. "Wallace Stevens: Some Relations between Poetry and Painting." *Comparative Literature* 2 (1959): 47–60.

Berger, Gaston. "Phenomenological Approach to the Problem of Time." In *Readings in Existential Phenomenology,* edited by Nathaniel Lawrence and Daniel O'Connor. Englewood Cliffs, New Jersey: Prentice-Hall, 1967.

Bergson, Henri. *The Creative Mind.* Translated by Mabelle L. Andison. Totowa, New Jersey: Littlefield, Adams and Co., 1975.

Bernard, Suzanne. "Rimbaud, Proust et les Impressionnistes." *Revue des Science Humaines* 78 (1955): 257–262.

Bicilli, Petr M. "Impressionismus." In *Anton P. Čechov: Das Werk un Sein Stil*. Munich: Wilhemfink Verlagmünchen, 1966.

Blackall, Jean Frantz. *Jamesian Ambiguity and "The Sacred Fount."* Ithaca: Cornell University Press, 1965.

Bluestone, George. *Novels Into Film*. Berkeley: University of California Press, 1961.

Booth, Wayne C. *The Rhetoric of Fiction*. Chicago: University of Chicago Press, 1961.

Bowie, Theodore Robert. *The Painter in French Fiction*. Chapel Hill: University of North Carolina Press, 1950.

Brown, Calvin S. "Symposium in Literary Impressionism." In *Yearbook of Comparative and General Literature*, no. 17 (1968), pp. 79–85.

Carrabino, Victor. *The Phenomenological Novel of Alain Robbe-Grillet*. Parma: C. E. M. Editrice, 1974.

Champigny, Robert. "Proust, Bergson and Other Philosophers." In *Proust: A Collection of Critical Essays*. Englewood Cliffs, New Jersey: Prentice-Hall, 1962.

Chatman, Seymour. *The Later Style of Henry James*. Oxford: Basil Blackwell, 1972.

Chekhov, Anton P. *Letters of Anton Chekhov*. Edited by Avrahm Yarmolinsky. New York: Viking, 1973.

―――. *Letters of Anton Chekhov*. Edited by Simon Karlinsky. New York: Holt, Rinehart and Winston, 1973.

―――. *Letters on the Short Story, the Drama, and Other Literary Topics*. Edited by Louis Friedland. New York: Benjamin Blom, 1965.

―――. *Polnoe sobranie sochinenii i pisem* [complete works and letters]. Edited by A. M. Egolin and N. S. Tikhonov. 20 vols. Moscow, 1944–51.

―――. *The Selected Letters of Anton Chekhov*. Edited and with an introduction by Lillian Hellman. Translated by Sidonie K. Lederer. New York: McGraw-Hill, 1955.

Chernowitz, Maurice E. *Proust and Painting*. New York: International University Press, 1945.

Chisholm, Roderick M. *Theory of Knowledge*. Englewood Cliffs, New Jersey: Prentice-Hall, 1966.

Chizhevsky, Dmitri. "Chekhov in the Development of Russian Literature." In *Chekhov: A Collection of Critical Essays,* edited by Robert Louis Jackson. Englewood Cliffs, New Jersey: Prentice-Hall, 1967.

Cluysenaar, Anne. *Aspects of Literary Stylistics.* New York: St. Martin's Press, 1975.

Conrad, Joseph L. "Unresolved Tension in Chekhov's Stories." *Slavic and East European Journal* 16 (1972): 55–64.

Davis, Harold E. "Conrad's Revision of the Secret Agent: A Study in Literary Impressionism." *Modern Language Quarterly* 19 (1958): 244–54.

Deleuze, Gilles. *Proust and Signs.* Translated by Richard Howard. New York: George Braziller, 1972.

Derrida, Jacques. *Speech and Phenomena.* Translated by David B. Allison. Evanston: Northwestern University Press, 1973.

Driver, Tom F. *Romantic Quest and Modern Query: A History of the Modern Theatre.* New York: Delacorte Press, 1970.

Durney, Ruth. "Impressionism and Naturalism in the Work of Stephen Crane." Ph.D. dissertation, University of Washington, 1936.

Earle, William. "Revolt Against Realism in the Films." In *Film Theory and Criticism,* edited by Gerald Mast and Marshall Cohen. New York: Oxford University Press, 1974.

Edel, Leon. *The Modern Psychological Novel.* New York: Grosset and Dunlap, 1961.

Eisenstein, Sergei. *Film Form.* New York: Harcourt, Brace and World, 1949.

Erickson, John P. "The Proust-Einstein Relation: A Study of Relative Point of View." In *Marcel Proust: A Critical Panorama,* edited by Larkin B. Price. Urbana: University of Illinois Press, 1973.

Esslin, Martin. *Brief Chronicles: Essays on Modern Theatre.* London: Temple Smith, 1970.

———. *The Theater of the Absurd.* Garden City, New York: Anchor Books, 1961.

Fasel, Ida. "Spatial Form and Spatial Time." *Western Humanities Review* 16 (1962): 223–34.

Firebaugh, Joseph J. "The Pragmatism of Henry James." *Virginia Quarterly Review* 27 (1951): 650–60.

Ford, Ford Madox. *Henry James, A Critical Study.* New York: Octagon Books, 1964.

———. "Techniques." *Southern Review* 1 (July, 1935): 20–35.

Francastel, Pierre. "La Fin de l'Impressionnisme: Esthétique et Causalité." In *Problems of 19th and 20th Century Studies in Western Art*, vol. 4. Princeton: Princeton University Press, 1963.

Frank, Joseph. "Spatial Form in Modern Literature." In *The Widening Gyre*. New Brunswick, New Jersey: Rutgers University Press, 1963.

Fraser, J. T., ed. *The Voices of Time*. New York: George Braziller, 1966.

Freeman, Ralph. *The Lyrical Novel*. Princeton: Princeton University Press, 1963.

Frierson, W. W. "Postwar Novel, 1919–29: Impressionists and Freudians." In *English Novel in Transition, 1885–1940*. Norman: University of Oklahoma Press, 1942.

Garland, Hamlin. *Crumbling Idols*. Cambridge: Belknap Press, 1960.

Garrett, Peter K. *Scene and Symbol from George Eliot to James Joyce*. New Haven: Yale University Press, 1969.

Gibbs, Beverly Jean. "Impressionism as a Literary Movement." *Modern Language Journal* 36 (1952): 175–83.

Gray, Camilla. *The Russian Experiment in Art, 1863–1922*. New York: Harry N. Abrams, 1970.

Grossvogel, David I. *Limits of the Novel*. Ithaca: Cornell University Press, 1968.

Grover, Philip. *Henry James and the French Novel*. London: Paul Elek, 1973.

Hagan, John. "Chekhov's Fiction and the Ideal of Objectivity." *PMLA* 81 (1966): 409–18.

Hale, Edward E. "The Impressionism of Henry James." *Union College Faculty Papers* 2 (1931): 3–17.

Hamlyn, D. W. *The Psychology of Perception*. London: Routledge and Kegan Paul, 1957.

Harvey, W. J. *Character and the Novel*. Ithaca: Cornell University Press, 1965.

Hassan, Ihab. *The Literature of Silence*. New York: Knopf, 1967.

Hatzfeld, Helmut. *Literature through Art*. New York: Oxford University Press, 1952.

Hauser, Arnold. *The Social History of Art*. Vol. 4. New York: Vintage Books, 1958.

Haynes, Walter. "The Middle Way of Miss Farange: A Study of James' Maisie." *Journal of English Language History* 52 (1965): 528–52.

Hemmings, F. W. J. "Zola, Manet, and the Impressionists." *PMLA* 73 (1958): 407–17.

Hingley, Ronald. *Chekhov: A Biographical and Critical Study*. London: Allen and Unwin, 1950.

———. *A New Life of Chekhov*. New York: Knopf, 1976.

Hocks, Richard A. *Henry James and Pragmatistic Thought*. Chapel Hill: University of North Carolina Press, 1974.

Holland, Laurence Bedwell. *The Expense of Vision*. Princeton: Princeton University Press, 1964.

Hourtique, L. "Realisme et Impressionnisme." In *L'Art et la Litterature*. Paris: Flammarion, 1946.

Howarth, Herbert. "Symposium in Literary Impressionism." In *Yearbook of Comparative and General Literature*, no. 17 (1968), pp. 66–71.

Humphrey, Robert. *Stream of Consciousness and the Modern Novel*. Berkeley: University of California Press, 1959.

Huyghe, René. "L'impressionnisme et la pensée de son temps." *Promethée* 1 (1939): 7–16.

———. "Shifts in Thought During the Impressionist Era: Painting, Science, Literature, History, and Philosophy." In *Impressionism: A Centenary Exhibition*. New York: The Metropolitan Museum of Art, 1974.

Ilie, Paul. "Symposium in Literary Impressionism." In *Yearbook of Comparative and General Literature*, no. 17 (1968), pp. 72–79.

Impressionism: A Centenary Exhibition. New York: The Metropolitan Museum of Art, 1974.

Jakobson, Roman. "Two Aspects of Language: Metaphor and Metonymy." In *European Literary Theory and Practice*, edited by Vernon W. Gras. New York: Dell, 1973.

James, Henry. *The American Scene*. New York: Charles Scribner's Sons, 1946.

———. *The Art of the Novel: Critical Prefaces*. Edited by R. P. Blackmur. New York: Charles Scribner's Sons, 1934.

———. *French Poets and Novelists*. New York: Grosset and Dunlap, 1964.

———. *The Notebooks of Henry James*. Edited by F. O. Matthiessen and Kenneth B. Murdock. New York: Oxford University Press, 1961.

———. *Notes on Novelists with Some Other Notes*. New York: Charles Scribner's Sons, 1914.

————. *The Novels and Tales of Henry James.* The New York Edition. 26 vols. New York: Charles Scribner's Sons, 1907–17.
The Portrait of a Lady, vols. 3, 4. 1908.
What Maisie Knew, vol. 11. 1908.
The Ambassadors, vols. 21, 22. 1909.
The Golden Bowl, vols. 23, 24. 1909.
————. *The Painter's Eye: Notes and Essays on the Pictorial Arts.* London: Rupert Hart-Davis, 1956.
————. *Partial Portraits.* London: Macmillan and Co., 1888.
————. *The Sacred Fount.* New York: Charles Scribner's Sons, 1901.
————. *Theory of Fiction: Henry James.* Edited by James E. Miller, Jr. Lincoln, Nebraska: University of Nebraska Press, 1972.
James, William. *The Principles of Psychology.* 2 vols. New York: Dover, 1950.
————. *The Will to Believe and Other Essays in Popular Philosophy.* New York: Dover, 1956.
Jephcott, E. F. N. *Proust and Rilke.* London: Chatto and Windus, 1972.
Jones, Granville H. *Henry James's Psychology of Experience.* The Hague: Mouton, 1975.
Jones, W. Gareth. "Chekhov's Undercurrent of Time." *Modern Language Review* 64 (1969): 111–21.
Kaelin, Eugene F. *Art and Existence: A Phenomenological Aesthetics.* Lewisburg, Pa.: Bucknell University Press, 1970.
————. *An Existentialist Aesthetic.* Madison: University of Wisconsin Press, 1966.
Karlinsky, Simon. *Letters of Anton Chekhov.* New York: Harper and Row, 1973.
Kockelmans, Joseph J., ed. *Phenomenology.* Garden City, New York: Anchor Books, 1967.
Köhler, Wolfgang. *Gestalt Psychology.* New York: The New American Library, 1947.
————. *The Task of Gestalt Psychology.* Princeton: Princeton University Press, 1969.
Kramer, Karl D. *The Chameleon and the Dream: The Image of Reality in Čexov's Stories.* The Hague: Mouton, 1970.
Kronegger, Maria Elizabeth. "Impressionist Tendencies in Lyrical Prose." *Revue de Littérature Comparée* 172 (1969): 528–44.
————. *Literary Impressionism.* New Haven: College and University Press, 1973.

Krook, Dorthea. *The Ordeal of Consciousness in Henry James.* Cambridge: Cambridge University Press, 1962.

Kumar, Shiv. *Bergson and the Stream of Consciousness Novel.* New York: New York University Press, 1963.

Kümmel, Friedrich. "Time as Succession and the Problem of Duration." In *The Voices of Time,* edited by J. T. Fraser. New York: George Braziller, 1966.

Kwant, Remy C. *The Phenomenological Philosophy of Merleau-Ponty.* Pittsburgh: Duquesne University Press, 1963.

Laforgue, Jules. "Impressionism." In *Impressionism and Post-Impressionism 1874–1904: Sources and Documents,* edited by Linda Nochlin. Englewood Cliffs, New Jersey: Prentice-Hall, 1966.

Lawrence, Nathaniel and O'Connor, Daniel, eds. *Readings in Existential Phenomenology.* Englewood Cliffs, New Jersey: Prentice-Hall, 1967.

LeSage, Laurent. *The French New Novel.* University Park: Penn State University Press, 1962.

Leymarie, Jean. *Impressionism.* 2 vols. Translated by James Emmons. Geneva: Skira, 1955.

Lowery, Bruce. *Marcel Proust et Henry James.* Paris: Plon, 1964.

Lubbock, Percy. *The Craft of Fiction.* New York: Charles Scribner's Sons, 1921.

Lytle, A. N. "Impressionism, the Ego, and the First Person." *Daedalus* 92 (1963): 281–96.

Mach, Ernst. *Contributions to the Analysis of Sensations.* Chicago: The Open Court Publishing Co., 1897.

Matson, Floyd W. *The Broken Image.* New York: George Braziller, 1964.

Matthiessen, F. O. *Henry James: The Major Phase.* New York: Oxford University Press, 1963.

―――. "James and the Plastic Arts." In *Discussions of Henry James,* edited by Naomi Lebowitz. Boston: D. C. Heath, 1962.

Mendilow, A. A. *Time and the Novel.* London: Peter Nevill, 1952.

Merleau-Ponty, Maurice. "Le Langage indirect et le voix du silence." *Les Temps Modernes* 7 (June, 1952): 213–44; 7 (July, 1952): 70–94.

―――. *Phenomenology of Perception.* Translated by Colin Smith. New York: The Humanities Press, 1962.

―――. "The Primacy of Perception and its Philosophical Consequences." In *Readings in Existential Phenomenology,* edited by

Nathaniel Lawrence and Daniel O'Connor. Englewood Cliffs, New Jersey: Prentice-Hall, 1967.

———. *Sense and Non-Sense.* Translated by Hubert L. and Patricia Allen Dreyfus. Evanston: Northwestern University Press, 1964.

———. *Signs.* Translated by Richard C. McCleary. Evanston: Northwestern University Press, 1964.

———. *Themes from the Lectures at the Collège de France 1952–1960.* Translated by John O'Neill. Evanston: Northwestern University Press, 1970.

Meyerhoff, Hans. *Time in Literature.* Berkeley: University of California Press, 1960.

Miller, James E., Jr. *Theory of Fiction: Henry James.* Lincoln: University of Nebraska Press, 1972.

Monnin-Hornung, Juliette. *Proust et la Peinture.* Geneva: Librairie E. Droz, 1951.

Moss, Howard. "A New Life of Anton Chekhov." *The New York Times Book Review,* June 20, 1976, Sec. 7, pp. 1, 25–29.

Mouton, Jean. "L'Optique de Proust, du regard à la vision." In *Entretiens sur Marcel Proust,* edited by George Cattaui and Philip Kolb. The Hague: Mouton, 1966.

Muller, Herbert J. "Impressionism in Fiction: Prism vs. Mirror." *The American Scholar* 7 (1938): 355–67.

———. *Modern Fiction: A Study of Values.* New York: Funk and Wagnalls, 1937.

Mussman, Toby. "Duality, Repetition, Chance, the Unknown, Infinity." In *Jean-Luc Godard,* edited by Toby Mussman. New York: Dutton, 1968.

Nilsson, Nils Åke. "Intonation and Rhythm in Chekhov's Plays." In *Chekhov: A Collection of Critical Essays,* edited by Robert Louis Jackson. Englewood Cliffs, New Jersey: Prentice-Hall, 1967.

———. *Studies in Čechov's Narrative Technique: "The Steppe" and "The Bishop."* Stockholm: Amquist and Wiksell, 1968.

Nochlin, Linda, ed. *Impressionism and Post-Impressionism 1874–1904: Sources and Documents.* Englewood Cliffs, New Jersey: Prentice-Hall, 1966.

O'Conner, W. V. "Wallace Stevens: Impressionism in America." *Revue des Langues Vivantes* 32 (1966): 66–77.

Øverland, Orm. "The Impressionism of Stephen Crane: A Study in Style and Technique." In *Americana-Norvengica,* edited by Sig-

mund Skard and Henry Wasser. Philadelphia: University of Penn-
sylvania, 1966.

Peckham, Morse. *Man's Rage for Chaos*. New York: Schocken, 1967.

Perosa, Sergio. "Naturalism and Impressionism in Stephen Crane's
Fiction." In *Stephen Crane: A Collection of Critical Essays*, edited
by Maurice Bassan. Englewood Cliffs, New Jersey: Prentice-Hall,
1967.

Pool, Phoebe. *Impressionism*. New York: Praeger, 1967.

Poulet, George. *Studies in Human Time*. Translated by Elliott Cole-
man. Baltimore: Johns Hopkins Press, 1956.

Powers, Lyall H. *Henry James and the Naturalist Movement*. Lan-
sing: Michigan State University Press, 1971.

Preminger, Alex, ed. *Princeton Encyclopedia of Poetry and Poetics*.
Princeton: Princeton University Press, 1965.

Proust, Marcel. *The Past Recaptured*. Translated by Andreas Mayor.
New York: Random House, 1971.

Raleigh, John Henry. "Henry James: The Poetics of Empiricism."
PMLA 66 (1951): 107–23.

Rayfield, Donald. *Chekhov: The Evolution of His Art*. New York:
Barnes and Noble, 1975.

Rewald, John. *The History of Impressionism*. New York: The Museum of Modern Art, 1946.

———. *The Impressionist Brush*. New York: The Metropolitan Museum of Art, 1974.

Reviakin, A. I. *"Vishnevii Sad" A. P. Chekhova* ["The Cherry Orchard," by A. P. Chekhov]. Moscow, 1960.

Robbe-Grillet, Alain. *For a New Novel*. Translated by Richard Howard. New York: Grove Press, 1965.

Rogers, Rodney O. "Stephen Crane and Impressionism." *Nineteenth
Century Fiction* 24 (1969): 292–304.

Rose, Alan. "The Spatial Form of *The Golden Bowl*." *Modern Fiction
Studies* 12 (1966): 103–16.

Rosen, Nathan. "The Unconscious in 'Vanka.' " *Slavic and East European Journal* 15 (1971): 441–54.

Rowe, John Carlos. *Henry Adams and Henry James: The Emergence
of a Modern Consciousness*. Ithaca: Cornell University Press, 1976.

Roy, Claude. "Anton Tchékhov et Henry James," *La Nouvelle Revue
Française*, XX (juillet-décembre, 1962), 876–87.

Saisselin, Rémy. "Symposium in Literary Impressionism," in *Year-*

book of Comparative and General Literature, No. 17 (1968), pp. 85–90.

Samuels, Charles Thomas. *The Ambiguity of Henry James*. Urbana, Illinois: University of Illinois Press, 1971.

Sarraute, Nathalie. *The Age of Suspicion*. Translated by Maria Jolas. New York: George Braziller, 1963.

Sartre, Jean-Paul. *Situation II*. Paris: Gallimard, 1948.

Schoeck, Helmut and Wiggins, James W., eds. *Relativism and the Study of Man*. Princeton: D. Van Nostrand, 1961.

Sears, Sallie. *The Negative Imagination: Form and Perspective in the Novels of Henry James*. Ithaca: Cornell University Press, 1968.

Sellars, Roy Wood. *Principles of Emergent Realism*. Edited by W. Preston Warren. St. Louis: Warren H. Green, 1970.

Seltzer, Alvin J. *Chaos in the Novel/The Novel in Chaos*. New York: Schocken Books, 1974.

Senanu, K. E. "Anton Chekhov and Henry James." *Ibadan Studies in English* 2 (1970): 182–97.

Serulloz, Maurice. *French Painting: The Impressionist Painters*. New York: Universe Books, 1960.

Shattuck, Roger. *Marcel Proust*. New York: Viking Press, 1974.

——. *Proust's Binoculars*. New York: Vintage Books, 1967.

Simmons, Ernest J. *Chekhov: A Biography*. Boston: Little, Brown, 1962.

Smith, Virginia Llewellyn. *Anton Chekhov and the Lady with the Dog*. London: Oxford University Press, 1973.

Solomon, Eric. *Stephen Crane in England*. Columbus, Ohio: Ohio State University Press, 1964.

Sommerhalder, Hugo. *Zum Begriff des literischen Impressionismus*. Zürich: Poligraphischer Verlag, 1961.

Spencer, Sharon. *Space, Time and Structure*. New York: New York University Press, 1971.

Stevens, Wallace. *The Necessary Angel: Essays on Reality and the Imagination*. New York: Vintage Books, 1951.

——. *Opus Posthumous*. Edited by Samuel French Morse. New York: Knopf, 1957.

Stronkes, James. "A Realist Experiments with Impressionism: Garland's Impressionism." *American Literature* (March, 1964), pp. 38–52.

Struve, Gleb. "On Chekhov's Craftsmanship: The Anatomy of a Story." *The Slavic Review* 20 (1961): 467–77.

Styan, J. L. *Chekhov in Performance*. Cambridge: Cambridge University Press, 1971.

―――. *The Dark Comedy: The Development of Modern Comic Tragedy*. Cambridge: Cambridge University Press, 1968.

Szanto, George H. *Narrative Consciousness*. Austin: University of Texas Press, 1972.

Tanner, Tony. "The Fearful Self." In *Twentieth Century Interpretations of The Portrait of a Lady*, edited by Peter Buitenhuis. Englewood Cliffs, New Jersey: Prentice-Hall, 1968.

―――. *The Reign of Wonder*. Cambridge: Cambridge University Press, 1965.

Terras, Victor. *Belinskij and Russian Literary Criticism*. Madison: University of Wisconsin Press, 1974.

Timmer, Charles B. "The Bizarre Element in Čechov's Art." In *Anton Čechov 1860–1960: Some Essays*, edited by T. Eekman. Leiden: E. J. Brill, 1960.

Truffaut, François. *Hitchcock*. New York: Simon and Schuster, 1966.

Turbayne, Colin Murray. *The Myth of Metaphor*. New Haven: Yale University Press, 1962.

Tytell, John. "The Jamesian Legacy in *The Good Soldier*." *Studies in the Novel* 3 (1971): 365–73.

Valency, Maurice. *The Flower and the Castle: An Introduction to Modern Drama*. New York: Macmillan, 1963.

―――. *The Breaking String*. New York: Oxford University Press, 1966.

van Peursen, Cornelis A. *Phenomenology and Reality*. Translated by Henry J. Korn. Pittsburgh: Duquesne University Press, 1972.

Venturi, Lionello. "The Aesthetic Idea of Impressionism." *Journal of Aesthetics and Art Criticism* no. 1 (Spring, 1941), pp. 34–45.

Vinogradova, K. M. "Stranitsa iz chernovoi rukopisi rasskaza 'Dama s sobachkoi' " [a page from the rough drafts of "Lady with the Dog"], *Literaturnoe nasledstvo: Chekhov* [literary heritage: Chekhov]. Vol. 68. Moscow, 1960.

Vivas, Eliseo. "Henry and William: (Two Notes)." *Kenyon Review* 5 (1943): 580–94.

Wallach, Hans. *On Perception*. New York: The New York Times Book Co., 1976.

Ward, J. A. *The Search for Form: Studies in the Structure of James's Fiction*. Chapel Hill: University of North Carolina Press, 1967.

Wasiolek, Edward. "Maisie: Pure or Corrupt?" *College English* 22 (1960): 167–72.

Watt, Ian. "The First Paragraph of *The Ambassadors:* An Explication." In *The Norton Critical Edition of Henry James' "The Ambassadors,"* edited by S. P. Rosenbaum. New York: W. W. Norton, 1964.

Weingart, S. L. "The Form and Meaning of the Impressionist Novel." Ph.D. dissertation, University of California at Davis, 1964.

Weinstein, Philip M. *Henry James and the Requirements of the Imagination.* Cambridge: Harvard University Press, 1971.

Wertheim, Stanley. "Crane and Garland: The Education of an Impressionist." *North Dakota Quarterly* (Winter, 1967), pp. 23–38.

Wild, John. *The Radical Empiricism of William James.* New York: Anchor Books, 1970.

Wilson, Edmund. "The Ambiguity of Henry James." *Hound and Horn* 7 (April–June, 1934): 385–406.

Winner, Thomas G. "Čechov and Scientism; Observations on the Searching Stories." In *Anton Čechov, 1860–1960: Some Essays,* edited by T. Eekman. Leiden: E. J. Brill, 1960.

———. *Chekhov and his Prose.* New York: Holt, Rinehart and Winston, 1966.

Winner, Viola Hopkins. *Henry James and the Visual Arts.* Charlottesville: University Press of Virginia, 1970.

Wogan, C. C. "Crane's Use of Color in *The Red Badge of Courage.*" *Modern Fiction Studies* 6 (1960): 168–72.

Woolf, Virginia. *The Moment and Other Essays.* New York: Harcourt, Brace, 1948.

Yermilov, Vladimir. *Anton Pavlovich Chekhov.* Moscow: Foreign Languages Publishing House, n.d.

Index

Index